C0-AMX-063

Reason and Controversy in the Arts

Reason and Controversy in the Arts

Mortimer R. Kadish

THE PRESS OF CASE WESTERN RESERVE UNIVERSITY
Cleveland 1968

Printed in the United States of America.
Library of Congress Catalogue Card Number 67–27796.

To the memory of

SAMUEL J. KADISH

Preface

This is in some ways a narrow book, although not, I fear, therefore an unambitious one. I have tried to see what has made it possible for men to reason with one another and, so far as they may, to reach justifiable decisions in matters of art. None of the questions of that great grab bag of questions, esthetics, have been treated independently of that end. Only those have been treated which have a bearing upon it, and only to the extent they have such a bearing.

What I have written is intended as a preparation. It is intended as a preparation for critics of the arts, whom perhaps it may assist to avoid some misapprehensions of their own enterprise. I grant that it might introduce them to new ones. It is intended as a preparation for philosophers who wish to consider the logic through which in art reasons may be given and differences resolved, even though there is no attempt made to fix in any systematic way the numerous and delicate networks of artistically relevant reasonings. There is nothing here for artists as such, who have their own, and better, problems. In general, I hope that the book may help dispel the widespread notion that while there is plenty of controversy in the arts, all or most of it is inappropriate and none of it is reasoning.

The specific views presented in this essay had their point of origin in an article I published in the *Journal of Philosophy,* "The Importance of a Choice of Context." [1] In the long history between that first publication and this book I am indebted to the encouragement and tolerance of many friends and colleagues. Robert Graves has written,

> He becomes dull, trusting his clear images,
> I become sharp, mistrusting my broken images.[2]

[1] Symposium, "The Evidence for Esthetic Judgment," *Journal of Philosophy,* LIV, 22 (Dec. 1957), pp. 670–79.

[2] Robert Graves, "In Broken Images," in *Collected Poems* (Garden City, N. Y.: Doubleday, 1961), p. 104.

Professors Abraham Edel, Isaac Levi, and Raymond Nelson have all read portions of this book and sought to induce in me a greater mistrust of my broken images than I might otherwise have achieved. Professor Ernest Nagel, my first teacher in philosophy, has been a constant and quiet source of encouragement. There are too many persons with whom from time to time I have discussed the elements of my view to enumerate. Though they may have forgotten those encounters, I have not.

Without the leisure provided at an early and crucial stage in my speculation by a fellowship which the John Simon Guggenheim Foundation was generous enough to award for 1954–55, this book would probably never have appeared.

The least I can do is to thank my wife, Ruth, and my daughter, Joey, for the warmth and patience with which they supported my endeavors.

Contents

Reason and Controversy in the Arts

Chapter 1

Introductory: The Gist of the Proposal

These pages are about criticism and what criticism entails. They aim to move a distance toward establishing that sense and force of artistically relevant controversy which the controversy manifestly possesses. Just what are we doing when we differ in the arts and seek to compose those differences? Let it be agreed that there are things in the arts that concern people other than arguing about them. I join in thankfulness for this state of affairs and propose to examine the rationale of artistically relevant controversy among people who don't dispute for the fun of it but who do so because they need to, given their concern with the arts. I will examine that rationale, be it emphasized, not legislate to it. Certainly, I will not tell the critic what he ought to think.

By a "critic" of a subject matter I mean a participant, whoever he may be, in a controversy concerning that subject matter. No one, therefore, becomes a critic just because he holds opinions. Anyone can hold an opinion. Holding an opinion is merely a fact. Similarly, people do not become critics simply because they express opinions. Most people can, and do, express opinions. But a critic criticizes that of which he is a critic—he joins issue. Being the critical fellow he is—not merely the dissenter, who may, of course, utterly lack criticality—he advances positions in anticipation of dissent and in the hope of making good his point in the competition.

So with a critic of the arts. A critic of the arts is a man who takes exception in a controversy about the arts in which it makes sense to take exception. *C'est son métier.* And he can take exception because in the artistically relevant controversy he differs in virtue of reasons, whatever the final import of those reasons. In short, his loyalty is to a "logical" argument. If people fail to recognize Canossa when they come to it, that's unfortunate but not crucial. If he himself fails to, that indeed is crucial.

Moreover, by a "good critic" I mean a man who feels called upon to put forward his reasoned exceptions in virtue of his interest or devotion to that of which he is said to be a critic rather than, for example, in virtue of a commitment to cultural one-upmanship. What concerns us is the logic of the good critic. Good critics of the arts are "responsible." They know that their business is not like Fortinbras', greatly to find quarrel in a straw, but to make sure it's no straw they argue and no mere whim guiding the argument.[1] So T. S. Eliot has written in a famous essay,

> The [good] critic, . . . if he is to justify his existence, should endeavor to discipline his personal prejudices and cranks . . . and compose his differences with as many of his fellows as possible, in the common pursuit of true judgment. When we find that quite the contrary prevails, we begin to suspect that the critic owes his livelihood to the violence and extremity of his opposition to other critics, or else to some trifling oddities of his own with which he contrives to season the opinions which men already hold, and which out of vanity or sloth they prefer to maintain.[2]

Never mind the nature of the "true judgment" commonly pursued. It is still not unfair to find in Eliot's words a commitment of the "justified" critic to the hope of rationality, a hope which has as its classic object the distinction between "disciplining personal prejudices and cranks" and not doing so, between "composing differences" and exploiting them, between good judgment and bad. Reason defines the role of the critic—of Eliot's justified critic, of the "good," the "responsible" critic—reason in a very ordinary sense of the word, and the love of art.

"Still," says the reader, "someone might claim that there is no critic in Eliot's noble sense and yours." But that is most probably cynicism. Even if the cynic should happen to be right, he would merely *happen* to be right; and even he must admit, unless, perhaps, he is a theologian, that no one has a right to call people "poor" or "irresponsible" at anything if they have no conceivable alternative.[3]

Of course the objection that there are no justified critics might aim at an apparently deeper point: that there can *be* no justification, no rationality in the arts. But this is a very confusing line, which probably few philosophers would care to take today. For, obviously, whatever the low opinion you have of reasons in criticism and however unfavorably you compare them with evidence in the sciences, the distinctions between responsibility and irresponsibility, good criticism and bad criticism, reason

[1] There are also, of course, "informed" critics and "uninformed" ones, amateurs and professionals, but those distinctions in no way determine what it *means* to be a "critic" and concern us only incidentally. One would hope that professionals and "informed" critics do a better job than the amateurs and the less informed, but everyone knows that they do not always.

[2] "The Function of Criticism," *Selected Essays* (New York: Harcourt, Brace, 1950), p. 14.

[3] To the best of my knowledge, no one has yet proposed an esthetic original sin.

and unreason remain in practice precisely what they were to begin with. Hence the chief value of cynicism would seem to be some good advice: "Make your case no stronger than it is. Don't confuse it with the case for science, even though science does have more prestige."

That advice is hereby accepted in general and for the question that promotes this book, now named, in current fashion, the "metacritical question." The metacritical question inquires after reasons and issues when artistically relevant positions come into genuine opposition, in some appropriate sense of "genuine," and it asks for the conditions under which they do so. In brief, and as already stated, "What are we doing when we differ in the arts and seek to compose those differences?" The trick is to be governed by no expectations that do not seem proper to the controversy, and, in general, to learn to expect the right thing of criticism in the arts, neither too much nor too little.

Therefore, in a manner neutral (as far as possible) to both the contested claims of critics in behalf of one critical strategy or another and the rival claims of philosophical interpretations, I must at the outset try to say how in practice one tells an artistically relevant discussion from an irrelevant one and what are the working differences between genuine and spurious argument of the artistically relevant sort. Then I may indicate the kind of answer sought here as an "answer" to the metacritical question.

Obviously, someone might have been talking about something else with something very different in mind, in referring to "artistically relevant controversy."

I. Controversy as "Artistically Relevant"

In order to say which controversies are "artistically relevant" there is no need to levy still another set of conditions fixing which things are works of art and which are not, which things form the proper subject matter of artistically relevant controversy and which do not. Indeed, that very controversy often has for its issue whether a particular object constitutes "art" or what sort of thing in general "art" may be. How presume even to attempt to define "art"? I prefer to let the question of definition alone and distinguish artistically relevant controversy from other kinds of recalling (1) the kinds of issues such controversy seems to involve, (2) its peculiar discourse, and (3) the historically given practice or set of practices in which it happens.

1. The immediate issues of the controversy are themselves hardly esoteric, whatever the interpretive difficulties. Critics, obviously, take issue

over the "proper" analysis, interpretation, evaluation, and appreciation of those objects they think of as works of art. They do not take exception to one another's views of the chemical composition, weight, location, or market value of those objects, except incidentally and as ventures into alien fields; and, while the appropriate critical functions surely lack gem-like precision, it is by no means clear either that they are supposed to have such precision or that the absence makes it impossible to determine what is going on.

Judgments offering specific analyses, interpretations, evaluations, and appreciations of alleged works of art constitute, then, the first of the immediate issues of artistically relevant controversy. Proposals for the general conduct of analysis, interpretation, evaluation, and appreciation constitute the second. To these, ordinary understanding now adds as artistically relevant those issues bearing on the resolution of immediate issues, to the extent of that bearing. Relevance is transitive. A process exists, therefore, for determining the artistic relevance of all sorts of arguments, including the argument over whether a specific controversy is artistically relevant.

2. Furthermore, everyone seems to speak a particular kind of language in describing the object of appreciation, saying how to react, evaluate, dissect, compare it, and so on. Because of the centrality of qualitative and valuative expressions at such times, it seems appropriate to refer to an "esthetic discourse." Artistically relevant controversy uses esthetic discourse; no other controversy does in quite the same way.

For one, artistically relevant controversy uses esthetic discourse to affect the perception of those who get the drift and, hence, to change minds. Moreover, the effect occurs not accidentally, as a by-product, but essentially, as part of the critic's contribution to the development of art and taste. For, in fact, the "responsible" critic, unlike most reviewers, really does try to influence the development of art and taste. He reaches his judgments with such an end in mind.

Again, artistically relevant controversy employs esthetic discourse in ascribing and denying "artistic merit." Argument wages over the appropriateness of a specific "merit" class of predicates: "good," "splendid," "perceptive," "beautiful," etc. Discourse lacking anything to do with artistic merit, either directly or by implication, would automatically be regarded as artistically irrelevant and any discourse asserting or denying artistic merit would be seen as artistically relevant. In consequence, anyone who has even a little to do with critics, artists, and the things called works of art recognizes the controversy that possesses "artistic relevance" without presupposing any conclusions about the special marks of works of art.

3. Finally, one decides that people have been arguing about an object in an artistically relevant sense by noting whether they have located it in certain denotable practices or subpractices. It is no discovery, though often enough scant use is made of the knowledge, that artistically relevant controversy deals with its objects as music, painting, sculpture, poetry, or the like: either, that is, as objects conforming to certain more or less institutionalized expectations and habits of work and criticism, or as departures from such affairs. Hence, in fact, knowledge of music, poetry, painting, and the other arts establishes the criteria by means of which people judge what sounds like esthetic discourse to be the real thing and not parody. As Plato systematically warned, against imitations only knowledge avails. In this instance the knowledge is of the business or doings of the arts, of the body of practices from which all artistically relevant argument takes off and finally refers.

On the present level of discussion, then, philosophical puzzlement about what turns an object into an object of art or even, for that matter, what makes an art "artistic," has no place. It suffices that a well-recognized group of undisputed "arts" exists, and that the introduction of new arts along with the modification of old ones becomes controversial in an artistically relevant sense only when considered in relation to that group, to its materials, methods, standards. That relation, and that relation alone, finally determines how seriously as artistically relevant controversy one takes a given argument.

In consequence, neither the "Mona Lisa" as such nor what it exacts of us makes a controversy over the "Mona Lisa" artistically relevant. Rather, the "Mona Lisa" functions in discussion as a work of art and exacts what it does only because it is placed in an historically given practice of painting. Whether that practice has to be Leonardo's is an entirely different question.

Let the following, then, serve for an account of artistic relevance. Unless a controversy exhibits certain concerns, a certain kind and use of discourse, and an orientation in a certain kind of human history, it is not artistically relevant. If it does—all of these things—it is. The extent to which one implies the other need not here concern us.

II. Artistically Relevant Controversy as "Controversy"

Rightly or not, it is a fact of history that in matters of art the possibility of controversy as reasoned exception-taking puzzles most people. Does artistically relevant controversy constitute—can it constitute—genuine instead of pseudo-argument, reason instead of influence, logic instead of salesmanship? Is there even a subject matter to examine? Some further comment seems in order to indicate the kind of subject matter that actually exists for metacritical inquiry before philosophical sides are taken.

1. To begin with, those who think they think that artistically relevant controversy amounts to a mere quarrel, to an effort of one critic to climb upon another's back, ought to recall that they probably distinguish between good critics and bad on just that basis—that the critics they admire are the ones most likely to leave the battle when it seems that imposing on the other fellow is all that is left to do. Very likely, anyone who cares for the arts prefers to pass through the galleries making his judgments without endlessly defending himself—a gentleman, he, knowing the true prince "upon instinct." Are there, therefore, *no* occasions on which reasonably self-contained people who care about the arts feel compelled to take exception? To go that far seems hard. *When,* in that case, do they find it necessary and fitting to compose their differences with others?

The answer provides the first rough, but practical, distinction between genuine controversy in the arts and controversy of the spurious sort. Genuine controversy in the arts stems from the fact that one's own withers are wrung, from the fact that in the grip of a "real and living doubt" one cannot with the best will in the world play the gentleman. The trouble is not finding that others in some sense disagree or even that one has changed one's own mind. The source of controversy for lovers of art lies in *present distraction,* conflict, and uncertainty in one's own mind, here and now, as the voice of the other becomes one's own, or seems on the verge of becoming one's own, and one hears one's own dissent nagging at the edges of one's mind.

The cause of such discomfort is, of course, no more secret than is the discomfort itself: the changing ways of art and taste, the collapse of the delightful equilibrium between the arts, the times, and the critic's desires. It has become a problem what precisely is (to be) relevant in the object that only just now repelled or delighted, what is (to be) significant, what is (to be) found of value. In sum, genuine controversy has been born of embarrassment; embarrassment constitutes its occasion. But we not only *feel* embarrassed: ridding ourselves of a feeling of embarrassment often requires merely a psychological contortion. We *are* embarrassed. Our withers, in fact, *have* been wrung. What are we to do?

Hence the shrill note so often heard in critical discussions may derive not merely from a perverse love of argument, but from the prodding of a spur: the need to "make up one's mind." That is why there exists a "genuine" artistically relevant controversy, and not simply another case of the engineering of consent. A "real and living" doubt exists about what to consent *to,* and the question of persuading the other fellow must wait until it has been decided what to persuade him to. Where such a doubt does not exist, the controversy is spurious.

2. Consequently, an argument becomes genuine only if conducted in terms of a consideration of alternatives. If, as has been said, the occasion for genuine argument is indecision, then the fashion that has the critic analyzing, pointing at, interpreting, or judging what is there as he sees it, treating his own responses as datum and oracle, cannot be correct. Quite naturally, the habit of conceiving artistically relevant controversy as the business of justifying decisions already made, of confronting one man's "can't helps" with another's in a war of esthetic nerves, will lead to the belief that controversy in the arts is dispensable. Instead of following the fashion that makes reasoned argument pointless at the start, therefore, the better part of wisdom suggests describing the true critic as the man who, when he analyzes, does so in the thought of another possible analysis; pointing, perceives he might have pointed elsewhere; interpreting, knows he has rejected some interpretation or other; and so on.

Therefore the critic's job is not to apply himself like litmus paper to the object of discussion, though apply himself he must. He is a dealer in alternatives. Litmus paper has no choice.

3. But what sort of alternatives? Controversy, in art as elsewhere, is genuine only when it involves alternatives that can advance some sort of claim to be accepted. Genuine controversy is "serious," as common sense would put it. Not all people who advance alternatives are serious. Some alternatives are felt to be wild, rooted in no publicly available body of action and institution, referring to none. They come from a logical Mars; they are dismissed as fanciful. The necessary seriousness exists only on the ground of some set of shared commitments, the depth and extent of which those engaged in the argument may not fully realize. Such commitments establish as "claims" the alternatives advanced.

Obviously, it is sometimes hard to say which alternatives may claim to be taken seriously and which not. Nevertheless, your true judge of the arts, your authoritative, if sometimes mistaken, critic is just the man who knows how to recognize the artistically relevant claims among which he must adjudicate. He knows the history and presence of art. Nor are the claims he recognizes merely certain preferences in their status as facts, for there would then be no possibility of *yielding* a claim. How could one yield a fact, though it be only the fact of seeing a thing in a certain way or finding a certain thing important? One yields a *claim.*

4. Lastly, let it be emphasized again that the artistically relevant controversy, if it is a genuine controversy and not a pitched battle among manipulators, is genuine in the culminating sense that it makes its appeal to good reason. The similarity or dissimilarity of the reasons proffered by the empirical scientist for accepting one explanation or another has no bearing. However that issue goes, there can be no possibility of advancing a claim rather than merely a demand—no possibility, certainly, of "evaluating" or "deciding" among claims advanced—unless a reference exists to some set of rules and considerations, however vague and shifting, which at least for the duration of the controversy legitimatizes the claim and backs up the decision. The ideal of artistically relevant controversy *must* be good reason; where good reason ceases to be possible (not merely unavailable) controversy loses its sense.

To be sure, many people, perhaps most, often argue about the arts in a manner that makes good reason irrelevant, and even the best discussions turn sour. For that very reason requiring good reasons for artistically relevant controversy has a great advantage: it forces raising the question when a reasonable man could care to dispute about the arts.

Such, then, are the characteristics of artistically relevant controversy as controversy which any account of the metacritical question must take into consideration, and which esthetic theory sometimes disregards. Artistically relevant controversy, arising in doubt, confronts open, not closed, issues, so far as they are open; differences of opinion always exist for alternatives conceived as having a *claim* to be heard; and carrying the day or not carrying it occurs in virtue of reasons advanced. It is beyond controversy that from time to time such arguments about the arts do happen.

III. What One Has in Mind: Putting the Questions

Having reduced the danger of confusing the artistically relevant controversy with something that resembles it and perhaps even goes by the same name but lacks its differentiating characteristics, it is time to say *in what sense* the controversy interests us. It is fair enough to ask, "How do people differ in the arts and seek to compose their differences?" But just what does that "How?" mean?

For an answer I shall (1) replace the metacritical question with three fairly obvious and more manageable part questions, and then (2) sketch a procedure and set of expectations for dealing with them.

1. Knowing how people differ in the arts and seek to compose their differences requires answering questions about (A) the kind of object over which they differ, (B) the matter at issue in their dispute, and (C) the rationale of the reasonings offered.

A. The Reference Question: Artistically relevant controversy comes down to considering some spatial and/or temporal object or class of such objects within some particular human practice. Yet to ask what sort of things they are as things, or how their physical characteristics determine the character of criticism, while perfectly legitimate, does not quite raise the reference question. That question asks how to interpret such an object *if* there is to exist an artistically relevant controversy about it. Moreover, it places a special emphasis upon the antecedent—since, though the "same" object may constitute the reference of different discussions, different discussions will not all construe the referred object according to the same principle.

What requirements, then, holding for the reference of artistically relevant controversy, make that controversy at once artistically relevant and genuine? That is our question; nor is it the same as that more famous question, "What is a work of art?" The more famous question never proposed, as does the reference question, to specify the particular artistically relevant respect in which to press a question about objects of art, but sought instead some entity, some "work of art," that would in itself determine what ought to be asked.

The following usages will help in the discussion of the reference of artistically relevant controversy:

"Work of art" will designate any sculpture, painting, novel, etc., which some or most good critics call by the name "work of art," whatever the interpretation given to the expression or whether the object is "really" entitled to that name or not. That use of the term will help avoid the clumsiness of long listings followed by the inevitable "etc." When, as will often happen, it becomes pertinent to deal with the expression other than as a class name of indefinite extension, quotes will be placed about it.

Any object conceived as the reference of artistically relevant controversy will be called a "critical object." Critical objects are the objects over which critics have come or will come to argue, as such. What are they like for the purposes of artistically relevant controversy? That is the reference question.

By an analogous mode of speech, works of art or other objects constitute objects of appreciation, objects of analysis, objects of evaluation, and so on. Given what has been said about artistically relevant controversy, their connection with critical objects is plain: Critical objects *are* objects of analysis, objects of appreciation, objects of evaluation, and so on, when and if a genuine doubt occurs over the question of the proper analysis, the proper appreciation, the proper evaluation, and so on, to be accorded the object. When no such doubt occurs there is no critical object. Clearly, critical objects do not constitute another class of special entities to be placed beside "works of art," any more than do appreciation objects, analysis objects, or evaluation objects. Since "work of art" has frequently included in one package works of art as objects of any conceivable artistically relevant interest, distinguishing the critical object may forestall confusing what is required by such various interests in so far as their requirements differ.

At any rate, not all works of art are critical objects—happily, nothing prevents us from often being at peace about them. Nor are all things called "critical objects" works of art, since people are not content to award the title "work of art" until a certain stage and type of agreement in artistically relevant controversy had been reached.

B. The Claims Question: In one sense the "matter at issue" in artistically relevant controversy is hardly in doubt. Claims are at issue. For the purposes of artistically relevant controversy, what are those claims advanced by critics over critical objects? Precisely what do critics of the arts, as critics of the arts, want one another to accede to? That is the "claims question." Critics, it would ordinarily be said, want one another to accede to their artistically relevant judgments. Hence the claims question means finding an interpretation of artistically relevant judgment that will not preclude in advance the possibility of reason in controversy—of both judgments that settle the nature of the object judged in an artistically relevant manner and of judgments that ascribe or deny artistic merit in any of its forms.

C. The Reasons Question: How does one interpret the reasons proffered in artistically relevant controversy to support the claims advanced within it and to adjudicate among those claims when they conflict?

A systematic analysis of the patterns of argument in which "good reasons" occur and of the manner in which they do occur would of course comprise a very central part of any adequate treatment of the reasons question. But since the end is primarily to see how good reasons are possible, I shall attempt only to indicate different sorts of artistically relevant arguments as they become relevant and deal directly with the reasons question primarily as it bears upon the reference and claims questions and as those questions bear upon it.

There are, of course, other general questions one could ask about artistically relevant controversy but these three interlocked ones would seem to be basic: when critics differ significantly, so that an obligation exists among them, in Eliot's phrase, to "compose their differences," what do they differ about, what sort of claims do they advance, and how do they make their peace? No one question is intelligible without the other. Dealing with each, we shall still be turning the same subject matter in our hands, making similar points over again in slightly different perspectives, formulating different points under different part questions—when different points are indeed formulated—more for purposes of exposition than because the subject matter forbids handling them otherwise.

2. In establishing the metacritical question, one last but basic step remains. It is not enough to describe the end as "clarification" or "understanding" of the part questions. Clarification and understanding, as philosophical ends, function too readily as screens to obscure the specific purposes of inquiry, or the lack of them. There is a logical obligation to state what is of interest in the part questions, to stipulate the context in which they are found puzzling, to say, in effect, what one has in mind regardless of the merit or demerit of other possibilities.

This, then, is the rather modest way through which the obligation will be assumed here: by studying that "normal version" (as I shall call it) of artistically relevant controversy in virtue of which philosophers and critics have directly or indirectly tended to answer the metacritical question. The "clarification" sought will come from the resolution of those perplexities about the arts and criticism that have been engendered by normal version answers to the part questions. The "understanding" of the arts and criticism secured will be the understanding to which the effort of clarification leads. The importance of the job to be done will follow from the persuasiveness of the normal version (which I think considerable, as the use of the adjective "normal" testifies) and to the depth of the mistakes that the normal version may engender.[4]

The following set of positions constitutes the substance of the normal version:

A. The reference of artistically relevant criticism is to an entity sometimes called the "work of art itself."

[4] It is to be understood that the "normal version" now to be presented constitutes a kind of abstract model, not a rendition of any particular view. Undoubtedly, there are few writers who would accept the normal version in every jot and tittle as set forth here, and fewer still who would find in it a *sufficient* account of artistically relevant controversy; nevertheless, as we shall see, in one way or another, in whole or part, the basic pattern keeps reappearing.

B. Objects are taken as "works of art" when taken as configurations of "esthetic quality," as "esthetic objects." As Kant puts it, "That which is purely subjective in the representation of an Object, i.e., what constitutes its reference to the Subject, not to the Object, is its aesthetic quality." [5] The "work of art itself" is the "esthetic object" itself.

C. The claims advanced in artistically relevant discourse are, therefore, expressed in "esthetic judgments." Esthetic judgments are the affairs at issue in artistically relevant controversy. They are the deliverances of "taste"; and there are no artistically relevant judgments as such that are not *deliverances* of taste. They advance claims to respond one way or another.

D. Having esthetic quality as its object, esthetic discourse is both nonpractical and nontheoretical—whatever the advantages of a *special* kind of "knowledge" labeled "esthetic knowledge." Whether one talks about "delight or aversion apart from any interest," "objectified pleasure," or even "three forms of primary discourse," the end of esthetic judgment becomes in all respects distinct from the end of judgment anywhere else.

E. Whether or not a "work of art" meets the demand of "good taste" determines its success as a "work of art"; and an act of inspection, a "tasting" essayed by some proper judge, tells whether that demand has been met. These principles are in effect maintained even when inspection of "great" "works of art" is held finally to reveal Ideal Beauty, Truth, or the Beautiful Good, for such transcendental properties still depend upon the perception of "esthetic quality" to certify their presence.

F. Finally, to the extent that esthetic judgment admits of justification, justification will be managed by resolving such judgments through a process of "analysis," into recognitions of "esthetic value." So, presumably, those who differ over whether Edgar Guest's poetry has "esthetic value," whatever that might be, will attempt to break down their overall responses into a series of component inspections upon which they can agree. Judgments of taste, in so far as they *can* be grounded, are grounded on judgments of taste.

In sum, artistically relevant controversy, according to the normal version, has as its point of issue whether a judgment of taste, made with respect to a critical object taken in itself and for no purpose but the tasting, is in "good" taste; and the reasons offered one way or another are

[5] *The Critique of Judgment,* trans. J. C. Meredith (Oxford: Clarendon, 1952), p. 29.

made dependent upon the perceptions of the one who possesses the qualifications of a proper judge, whatever those qualifications may be.

What follows will attempt to respond to the reference, claims, and reasons question by considering the normal version schema in the light of the "neutral" description of artistically relevant controversy this chapter has attempted. Are references, claims, and reasons in artistically relevant controversy *sui generis* in the sense that the normal version holds them to be, or are they not? *And what kind of thing must we say about them if they are not?* Such is the "metacritical" problem of this book.

We turn first to the reference question.

Chapter 2

The Doctrine of the Work of Art Itself

Just what do critics examine when, as critics of the arts, they examine the object of their criticism? To what do they refer when they take exceptions to works of art, or to remarks about such works, and seek to ground their opinions? Chorused by critics and philosophers alike, the answer can hardly be missed: "Why, the work of art itself! What else?" The answer comes in so many words or with a substitution of the particular critic's object of interest—"the painting itself," "the music itself," or "the poem itself." Critics, unlike some other people, consider "the work of art itself." How can one deny it?

One cannot, of course, not in the sense in which it is patently true. Yet there is, I shall suggest, another sense in which the notion of considering only "the work of art itself" stretches beyond the obviously true enough to the far from clear and the conceivably false. That is the sense in which this familiar idea works as a sufficient answer to the reference question, to create "the doctrine of the work of art itself." Far from logically trivial, the doctrine is fundamental in the normal version of critical controversy and even in some accounts that refuse other normal version positions; it is as deep as it is apparently innocent, and it provokes this inquiry.

The doctrine states that the critical object is the work of art itself, nothing more, nothing less. It maintains that the work of art qua work of art—the proper critical object—comes complete and finished prior to the criticism that receives and examines it. It denies the relevance of any conditions in any way "external" to the object and requires settling controversies by a heedful description of what is there to be found.

Just how the doctrine can say all this, what it means to say it, and, being said, what it imports, belongs to the course of discussion, not to the start. For I shall want to say that the doctrine is not as it may seem—a report of what happens in artistically relevant controversy and hence, in some interpretation, unarguable; rather, the doctrine's force and point inhere in complex commitments that do not appear in statements of that doctrine and rarely are specifically recognized.

A procedural word: because the doctrine asserts for each and every art form what a "doctrine of the poem itself" would assert for a poem, I shall feel free to substitute "the poem itself," "the painting itself," or some similar expression for "the work of art itself." The end is to sail somewhat closer to the winds of actual criticism and to keep open the option *not* to talk about "works of art" as such when it is inconvenient to do so.

"The poem itself" will perform as principal surrogate. "Poem" will continue to refer here as ordinarily to any verbal artifact of the sort often called by that name but also, more broadly, to plays, novels, and stories. Poems are chosen rather than, say, musical compositions, because they show to clearer advantage the first discomfort of asserting the doctrine of the work of art itself: that while it is pointless to warn anyone who listens to music without daydreaming to listen to "the music itself," the competing readings of poems offered by perfectly good critics suggest that one may concentrate upon the poem and, inexplicably, miss "the poem itself."

What can "the poem itself" mean?

I. "The Poem Itself" in Criticism

"We must return to," says Allen Tate, "we must never leave, the poem itself." [1] "The poem itself" as employed here and elsewhere may mean a number of things, which in an account of the doctrine of the work of art itself need distinguishing.

1. Most obviously, the call to the poem itself conveys a call to poetic relevance, whatever that might be. Poetry is sometimes read as though it were something else. There is no possible quarrel; neither is it necessary to embrace the doctrine of the poem itself to heed the call. Even if Tate's dictum enjoins a more or less specific set of relevance criteria, the doctrine of the poem itself is not to that extent involved. The chief target of the new criticism was the old criticism, and the force of the call to the poem itself probably did run something like this: "To criticize poetry in an artistically relevant way do not introduce the considerations that some of the old critics do. Remember that you are neither historian, sociologist, psychologist, nor lover, but a critic of poetry, and explicate." There can be no logical objection to shorthand. As for the rights and wrongs of that faded debate over the "new criticism," they lie beyond our interest.

2. Much closer to that interest is the possibility that in exhorting a return to the poem itself Tate may be offering *ground* for some good advice along with the advice. There *is* a poem itself, he seems to be

[1] Allen Tate, *On the Limits of Poetry* (New York: Swallow, 1948), p. 48.

saying, to return to, and here is the trouble. Imagine a friend explaining how to visit him at his new place: "If you want to visit me bear in mind as you travel where you're going. Avoid alternative destinations. Remember you are not an explorer, geologist, or tourist, but a visitor. My home itself is your destination." Where *is* "the poem itself"?

3. More than likely, part of the intent of the use of the expression is to point to the page or manuscript. "The poem itself is the poem: 'Mary Had a Little Lamb,' *Paradise Lost,* that significant arrangement of phonemes in a language." I have already indicated the oddity that people may read the poem and miss the poem itself, which suggests that while it may be necessary to read the poem to get the poem itself it is hardly sufficient. Further, however, the newest of new critics did not suppose, or ought not to have supposed, that only *he*—not the historian, psychologist, sociologist, or lover—dealt with this particular poem as this poem in particular. So not even the poem in all its particularity, if that is what is meant, can be the poem itself. What else would the historian deal with except the particular history of this particular poem, if indeed the history of this particular poem interests him? It still follows that, if "the poem itself" means only the poem, anyone who keeps in mind what he is talking about when he talks about the poem will deal with "the poem itself." If the critic deals with unique objects, so do many people. What is ontological for the goose is ontological for the gander.

4. Granted, then, that the poem itself must be the poem, there is danger in thinking that the poem is the poem itself. A new and far from innocent sense of "the poem itself" now emerges: the entity that fuses, or confuses, the poem as the particular poem with the artistically relevant rules for describing poems. (Whether Tate had such an entity in mind does not particularly matter.) So "the poem itself" comes to mean more than "the poem" while still signifying the poem, and the rules for describing poems receive a highly privileged status. The poem itself becomes the intrinsically intelligible object; an object intelligible as such is presupposed by the doctrine of the work of art itself. Probably, some critics intend by the injunction to return to the poem itself, "Return to the intelligible object."

I should like to name the rules for artistically (poetically, painterly, etc.) relevant descriptions, "formative rules." That they exist is of the highest importance to any account of criticism, whatever the ultimate analysis of the concept of a "rule"; and they exist on all levels of critical activity. They tell us, for example, how to describe certain classes of critical objects: "Forget (or mind) the truth values of the assertions in the poem." (For otherwise, it is said, one misses the poem itself, the poem qua poem.) They say how to group in significant ways different kinds of poems, paintings, etc.: "Read poems of the kind called 'tragedies' with expectations of such and such a sort." (The *Poetics* is a mine of illustrations.) Formative rules even organize descriptions of the most specific texture of specific works of art: "Grasp the pervading importance of Othello's color, if you want to understand Othello and the play itself." I do not of course mean that formative rules are necessarily announced, merely that they are observable to the observer of artistically relevant controversies. But we shall return to the subject of formative rules.

5. Observe now, that even when critics confess themselves to mean "intelligible object" by "the work of art itself" the difficulty may remain purely abstract. Critics in implicit agreement on the proper terms of criticism lose nothing by packing into a work of art an entire complex of rules for dealing with works of art. The danger in thinking of the poem as the poem itself becomes practical one step ahead, in view of the fact that not all critics agree on the proper terms of criticism. For if it is the critic's business to evaluate the terms of criticism, then to pretend that those terms await for all men of good sense to see blocks the road of critical inquiry. The insistence on never leaving "the poem itself" becomes a means for denying the very right to a hearing to someone who seeks to change the rules in order to read a poem in his own way. He is neither wrong nor ill advised; his remarks are irrelevant to the "nature" of the poem. He is like the man who uses a fine knife to pry open tin cans, or a can opener as though it were a knife. Quite properly such a critic is read out of the society of critics, as a matter of principle, no defense possible. Such an end "Consider the poem!" would never accomplish.

It ought to be clear, then, that not all uses of "the poem itself" in the discourse of critics are equally innocent, and that when the vital measurements of the object of artistically relevant controversy as such are asked for, the answer "the work of art itself" is not nearly as self-evident as it may first appear. For the doctrine of the work of art itself finds support only in the most discomforting critical usage—the "dogmatic usage," if, for obvious reasons, I may so call it—in which the poem becomes the poem itself by absorbing the rules for its description and declaring out of bounds adverse comment on, or addition to, those rules. And, of course, the doctrine can find support there because it provides the kind of abstract formulation and justification of the usage that, according to some, Cartesian metaphysics gives to certain ways of talking about "mind."[2] For if

[2] Which came first, the usage or the metaphysics, and how good an analysis of either people like Gilbert Ryle present, is not to the point here.

indeed the critical object is the work of art itself, nothing less, nothing more, if the critical object awaits full-blown the explorations of criticism and requires to settle differences by a heedful description of what is there, then to use the poem itself to absorb the rules for describing poems becomes utterly fair and reasonable.

The great question, of course, if the above account be correct, is how indeed reflective persons in no way interested in justifying dogmatism as such can, after all, in the face of controversy, justify it in the arts. Yet there it is, the work of art itself, the intelligible object we need merely examine:

a. Witness an artist: "The work of art is the created image and symbol of a specific value; it was made to contain permanently something that was felt and thought and believed. It contains that feeling and nothing else. All other things have been excluded" . . . and, "The viewer may comprehend or may not comprehend but the value remains crystallized in an image available to those who are able to see." [3]

b. A philosopher: A poem is "self sufficient," it "contains within itself all required to make it intelligible," presents a "full bodied, ordered, self-sufficient world," while "the esthetic object appears in esthetic transactions as involving uniqueness and self-sufficiency." [4]

c. A poet:

"A poem should be palpable and mute
As a globed fruit."

"A poem should be equal to:
Not true."

"A poem should not mean
But be." [5]

II. The Normal Version of the Doctrine

Having considered the doctrine of the work of art itself as it faced toward the uses of criticism, it is necessary to consider now what can be made of the doctrine as it looks toward theory and justification. On the hypothesis that that doctrine receives its primary rationale from a formulation here called "the normal version," let us see the process occurring

[3] Ben Shahn, *The Shape of Content* (Cambridge, Mass.: Harvard University Press, 1957), pp. 107–08. Presumably the last sentence is not analytic.

[4] Eliseo Vivas, *Creation and Discovery* (New York: Noonday Press, 1955), pp. 76, 87, 116.

[5] From Archibald MacLeish's "Ars Poetica."

in a clear and specific case. Wimsatt and Beardsley wrote some years ago:

> Judging a poem is like judging a pudding or a machine. One demands that it work. It is only because an artifact works that we infer the intention of an artificer. "A poem should not mean but be." A poem can *be* only through its *meaning*—since its medium is words—yet it *is,* simply *is,* in the sense, that we have no excuse for inquiring what part is intended or meant. Poetry is a feat of style by which a complex of meaning is handled all at once. Poetry succeeds because all or most of what is said or implied is relevant; what is irrelevant has been excluded, like lumps from pudding and "bugs" from machinery. In this respect poetry differs from practical messages, which are successful if and only if we correctly infer the intention. They are more abstract than poetry.[6]

Note that the passage presents a rationale within which the doctrine of the work of art itself ceases to be gratuitous. It does not make the merely truistic observation that people usually want to appreciate poems, while for the most part they want only to understand messages. Of far greater moment, it describes what the poem, as a poem to be appreciated and to be judged, is like. The poem—the poem itself—is like a pudding or machine, which begins to explain how the nature of a poem may incorporate the rules with respect to which we construe it. If poems are like puddings or machines, ways that involve other considerations than the immediate business of the thing—of a pudding that it be eaten, of a machine that it work—become poetically irrelevant and errors in principle. A succession of "fallacies" now rims the artistically relevant controversy, or pierces it through and through.

To understand the position one must see what is wrong with it, see the important sense or senses in which poems are not like puddings nor machines, even though they be very like them at the moment of appreciation, when all controversies are settled or suspended. I shall say that, in consequence, some attempts to construe poems in terms of artists' intentions, whether well advised or ill, commit no "intentional fallacy." But "intentions" are being defended against fallacy-mongering only to illuminate the dogmatic consequence of the pudding (machine) analogy. It became clear enough long ago that the wholesale rejection of intentions from criticism will not really do.[7]

This, then, is the heart of the disanalogy between poems, puddings, and

[6] W. K. Wimsatt, Jr., and M. Beardsley, "The Intentional Fallacy," in W. K. Wimsatt, Jr., *The Verbal Icon* (New York: Noonday Press, 1958), p. 4.

[7] See, for example, Henry Aiken's "The Aesthetic Relevance of Artists' Intentions," *The Journal of Philosophy,* LII, 24 (Nov. 24, 1955).

machines when one tries to understand poems as critical objects: for puddings, as for machines, in the everyday context Wimsatt and Beardsley seem to have in mind, we know both the kind of thing to expect if something is a pudding or a machine *and* that a presented object *is* a pudding or a machine. Standards of puddinghood and machinehood come implicit in the use of language; nor is there usually much question whether an object is a pudding or a machine. Of what use would it be, therefore—of what possible relevance—to know the intentions of the cook or the manufacturer? Without confusion one can talk about the pudding itself or the machine itself. All relevant decisions have already been made.

But who on reflection would care to make like assertions about poems, unless he were set on doing so in the interest of some overriding prior commitment? Poems in the concrete, specific poems, are precisely the entities for which standards of poem-like subsistence are *not* built into the language, and the mode of application remains perpetually at issue not only at the periphery but also and pre-eminently at the vital center. The pudding analogy, the machine analogy, can hold only when poems are taken out of critical situations, exception-taking situations, and placed in situations where no issues are open and what remains is to explore for ourselves or for others what we have decided.

The need, not necessarily for the determination of relevant intentions, though possibly for that, but for some kind of reference outside "the poem itself"—the poem in the sense of the pudding, of the machine—follows directly. The intentionalist critic, whatever the dubious purposes he may sometimes entertain, seeks to meet that need. ("The" intentionalist critic is an obvious fiction for the invention of which I am indebted to others.) He proposes, or may propose, to make sense of the putative poem by locating the environment within which it was "intended" to function. He proposes to help prepare the poem for appreciation qua poem, and if his recommendations are not necessarily useful, neither are they necessarily useless. But whether they are useful or useless, it is itself a fallacy to suppose that intentional criticism must produce a variant of the genetic fallacy; that would be true only if "poem" were indeed a "pudding" or "machine" type of expression.

Nevertheless, of course, one is obliged to consider how the pudding likeness is spelled out and whether, contrary to present expectations, the spelling out might not work. (I shall leave off talking of "machines," since for the problems of criticism "pudding" seems the closer analogy and nothing is lost.)

First, it is noted that as with a pudding, so with a poem, "we have no excuse for inquiring what part is intended or meant." Yet, surely a great deal depends upon the sense of "part." No critic, whether Beardsley's and Wimsatt's or some other, would ever permit a poet to defend himself against a criticism by assuring his reader that he didn't mean to say what he clearly and patently did say. In art no more than in life do we wipe the slate clean by insisting that we didn't mean it. If, however, one considers the "parts" of a poem in the sense that it becomes a problem establishing just what those parts are—just what, for example, did happen in *Hamlet* to which we ought to have attended—then it is by no means self-evident that no excuse exists for asking what "part" was intended or meant. More, unless one binds oneself on principle to consider the parts of a poem like the parts of a pudding, it is evident that any part may fairly be read according to the way other parts are read, that there may exist a variety of contestant readings for the parts of a poem, and that how to read the parts may be a serious puzzle for which the intentionalist makes a proposal: "Read it in the author's way."

The "parts" of a poem, then, are not like nuts in pudding, to be tasted on their own, along with the lumps, not to the extent that those parts are problematic. To the extent they are not, they constitute no problem in criticism and the recommendation to take poems like puddings (or machines) is by the way.

Poems are also like puddings, we are also told, in a variant of the "parts" point, because in a successful poem as in a successful pudding, "all or most of what is said or implied is relevant," and "what is irrelevant has been excluded." Now, of course, it is very nice to have a fully successful poem. But the real question is whether the "success" is actually pudding-like success, with each mouthful itself successful on the clear mandate of a happy appetite. How does one know what is relevant and what is irrelevant? It is by no means clear that "relevance" or "irrelevance" is determined for poems as it is for puddings. The misleading spatial metaphor of what is "there" in the poem as a part and what is not only *seems* to make it clear. If they wish to take the pudding analogy seriously, then, Wimsatt and Beardsley must be contending that the poem itself is like the pudding because both come equipped with their own codes, however those codes may differ, for determining what is relevant and what is irrelevant.

As for the odd notion that the parts of a poem become relevant simply because they were intended to be relevant, or that a lack does not exist in a poem because the poet never intended the poem to exhibit the lack, it would be interesting to find an example of a critic, however wildly intentionalistic, who seriously advances such a claim.

One last justification for the pudding analogy among those stated above remains now to be considered: that practical messages are "more abstract" than poems, which in their lack of abstractness are more like puddings. I would suggest that abstractness has nothing to do with the case. It seems clear that there may be "abstract" poems, like MacLeish's "Ars Poetica," and very concrete messages. What differentiates poems from messages is what is done with them; and indeed the qualification "more" placed before the "abstract" suggests that those who put it there were themselves uneasy over introducing "abstraction" to differentiate between poems and messages.

Nevertheless, it does seem to follow that unless poems are abstract—as messages are—then the whole category of saying anything through poetry turns irrelevant, provided that saying anything always requires abstraction; and it is a downright error to ask intentions of the poem, which says nothing, which does not mean but simply is. On the other hand, if comparing poems and puddings on a scale of abstraction is itself an error, then it is at least *open* to the "intentionalist" to advise us, if we wish not to use the poem merely as a stimulus to daydreams, to consider the poem as a kind of communication from the poet to those who read him.

Undoubtedly, the pudding-poem analogy has not been exhausted either in the defense or the criticism. Nevertheless, two things follow from the principal objections I have pressed: the thrust to defend the dogmatic usage in terms of the pudding analogy cannot stop at a prima facie explication, but must produce some very special theory to make it good, and secondly, if poems are like puddings, their actual structure identical with their presented structure, reflective men can defend the dogmatic usage.

Indeed, they discover, they must defend it. They must defend it so far that after a while they are hard put to show how any argument in the arts is possible at all.

III. The Logical Ground of the Doctrine

Dropping considerations of the function of "the poem itself" in criticism and of the appropriateness of pudding analogies, consider now some of the logical commitments undertaken in posing the work of art itself as an answer to the reference question. I shall discuss five. They show the depth of the doctrine of the work of art itself, particularly in the normal version.

In that version, for a poem to exist qua poem means that it exists in a manner significantly analogous to the sense in which a pudding exists qua pudding. The doctrine of the work of art itself has been conjoined to the notion that artistically relevant judgment is always esthetic judgment. I will have considerably more to say on this point later, but now the reference question is the issue, not the claims question, and I return to the problem of the critical object.

1. First and most essential for understanding the normal version of the doctrine is the consideration that, in disputing whether poems are like puddings, and whether "poems themselves" are the sole objects of the critic's legitimate concern, much more than a linguistic issue is at stake, or even than a question of fact. Wimsatt and Beardsley, for example, do not only say that poems *are* like puddings; they are also saying, "Be smart, take poems like puddings!" (in the pertinent respects) or, "Would that everyone took poems as puddings!" Similarly, those who insist that "the proof of the pudding is in the eating" do not just give information of a kind otherwise lacking. They *want* the proof of the pudding to be in the eating rather than, say, in the cooking. They think that in matters of art it is only *right* that pleasures received determine values attributed. Why are the people who so disguise their choices unaware? What makes possible the transition from fact to choice that I have attributed to the normal version of the doctrine of the poem itself?

2. The answer constitutes the second point about that doctrine. There seems to occur what may be labeled a "contextual slide." One moves from a context defined by the requirement of appreciation and the appreciative functions of esthetic discourse, where the entire point lies in an intensity and restriction of focus, to a context defined by the requirements of controversy. One does so quite as though the move made no difference. Appreciative objects are taken for critical objects in a manner entirely appropriate for puddings, which fact implies considerably more than the truism that, to be artistically relevant, criticism must terminate in a difference for appreciation. The reader's intent as a liker of what he reads merges with the reader's intent as a man puzzled about poems and moved to construe them. So the relevance of scholarship and art history becomes a problem in principle. So, also, the doctrine of the work of art itself systematically assumes the familiarity of the objects under judgment: the less familiar, the more difficult to describe adequately the thing itself without making quite explicit the assumptions of the description.

3. I am brought to the doctrine's consequence for the distinction between "description" and "interpretation." When the work of art itself—the poem itself—is taken as the critical object, a chasm opens between interpretation and description, a chasm strange to artistically

relevant controversy, and hence one to be avoided. Either there is a sharp difference between interpreting a poem and describing a poem, interpreting a picture and describing a picture, or it is pointless to speak of a poem itself or a picture itself. If the critical object is familiar, to that extent there will be no great problem in distinguishing interpretation from description; the work of art itself will impose no difficulties in its status as critical object. But if the critical object be unfamiliar, the whole structure breaks down and one cannot distinguish description from interpretation. This is an old story, repeatedly told in the psychology of even the visual arts, where the possibilities of alternative "readings" are often—mistakenly, as it turns out—passed over. And the problem worsens when it is perceived how even the most familiar object can at some point be viewed in a new light capable of making background foreground, and foreground background, and in the process completing the disintegration of the work of art itself.[8]

For observe: unless I can say, "Here I see and here I imagine; here I read and here I interpret," and mean by it more than a greater or lesser degree of commitment to the point at which I draw this line, the doctrine of the work of art itself makes a merely conventional distinction between the poem and the poem itself. Immediately, therefore, the distinction between interpretation and description becomes a philosophical problem as, in the interests of doctrine, I seek to circumscribe at least some central area for the poem itself. The pudding analogy provided by the normal version constitutes one way of handling the problem. The poem, in the sense of the poem itself, will be an object possessing the characteristics it is *found* to have or which people can be caused, through the proper manipulations of their attention, to find in it. For a pudding, too, dealt with according to the nature of pudding objects, possesses the characteristics it is found to have or which people can be caused to find in it. Description then tells the reader or diner what, under certain conditions, he experiences or might hope to experience and establishes the critical object as an "esthetic object." For esthetic objects all nonlying reports are indubitable.

Interpretation on the other hand shifts the attention from the esthetic object to the relation of that object to other things. Hence it distracts. It was from this country of interpretation that Tate wanted us to return. He wanted us to stop interpreting sociologically, psychologically, symbolically, and to describe the presented object—the esthetic object.

What could be sharper than the distinction between what distracts and is dubious on one hand and what focuses and is indubitable on the other?

[8] See E. H. Gombrich, "Illusion and Visual Deadlock," *Meditations on a Hobby Horse* (London: Phaidon, 1963).

4. The fourth point, then, is that the logic of the doctrine leads to a break between description and interpretation, which cannot be sustained on an empirical level—and which the doctrine may therefore seek to sustain, at least in the normal version, through the idea of an esthetic object.

5. The last serious consequence of the doctrine of the work of art itself, which shows the doctrine's pervasiveness and power, is the so-called emotivist theory of esthetic discourse.

In "analytical criticism," C. L. Stevenson writes, the "analysis" of a work of art "leads us to scrutinize the work of art itself with a sensitivity to these or those details, in the hope that we shall come to discern or understand a certain feature of it that might otherwise escape us." [9] "The work of art itself" designates "a special kind of physical object or event," [10] available for "scrutiny," the object of our "synoptic" and "dissective" attentions.

Who can scrutinize that which is not "there," not given to scrutiny? The critical object of the critic's analyses ("the work of art itself") constitutes an "uninterpreted" object, a "datum," as surely as any "esthetic object." One analyzes not a construction but a presentation, not a proposal but a fact.

Now, the point is quite simple. Whoever accepts the doctrine of the work of art itself, if he hopes to avoid esthetic objects and keep his remarks artistically relevant, has no recourse in his criticism but to manipulate the opponent's attention with respect to that object. "See this! See that!" If the opponent does *not* see, that's all there is to it. There can be no *argument* about a proper description; and it seems to Mr. Stevenson, having examined the ways in which people learn to produce certain effects in the arts or to increase their "sensitivity" to poems, that "we now have as good an understanding of the term [analysis] as the purposes of criticism or aesthetics are likely to require." [11]

Yet the problem that bothers critics when they take exception in the analysis of poems consists neither in learning how to write poems nor, particularly, in increasing their sensitivity, though both ends may of course interest them. They are bothered by whether or not their own or somebody else's analysis of a poem is a "correct" one. Literally, as we might expect, Mr. Stevenson's analysis of "analysis" holds only for familiar poems in familiar perspectives. How then can he claim "as good an

[9] C. L. Stevenson, "On the 'Analysis' of a Work of Art," *The Philosophical Review,* LXVII, 1 (Jan. 1958), p. 33.

[10] *Ibid.,* pp. 41–42.

[11] *Ibid.,* p. 41.

understanding" of analysis as criticism or esthetics requires when critics, through their analyses, seek to work up poems for *subsequent* instruction and appreciation?

Though the problem does not concern Mr. Stevenson in his article on "analysis," the rest of the emotive theory constitutes the answer: providing a "correct" analysis adds nothing new in principle to the manipulative uses of esthetic discourse already mentioned. The logic of "the poem itself" must reduce to the attempt to absorb those features of discourse in which one assumes and attempts to defend a position into those features of discourse in virtue of which one expresses appreciations persuasively. For objects as data, as "things," as with puddings, at best there is only manipulation; and artistically relevant disagreements of the kind critics feel themselves especially competent to argue turn into clashes of "attitudes" as each party to the disagreement, seeking to persuade his opponent, offers for his "evidence" still another "persuasion."

All this, of course, does not "refute" the absorption of "normative" and "evidential" features of esthetic discourse into the "emotive" and "persuasive." But, in showing how the "emotivist" strategy for dealing with the critical argument follows from accepting the gambit of "the work of art itself," it does suggest a possible gratuitousness to that strategy. And it appears that if an alternative to an emotivist account of the critical argument can be found at all, it will be by interposing between the denoted object of criticism and the critical argument a "construction" in virtue of which the critical object will cease to function as a datum.

Why, then, given the confusion-making power of the doctrine of the work of art itself, and of the normal version of that doctrine in particular, continue the argument? What makes the doctrine seem right, anyway, and deserving of indefinite defense?

IV. The Choice of Consumption

An extra-logical decision sustains the normal version answer to the reference question, and, as will eventually be seen, the normal version answer to claims and reasons question as well: the choice of a "context of consumption" for dealing with works of art. That is what makes people assume the doctrine. *First* comes the substantive decision to deal with works of art as one deals with puddings, entertainments, and a vast variety of consumer goods; *then* comes the doctrine of the work of art itself as a kind of corollary whose truth seems self-evident and which in its own turn supports the decision. Now, given the perspective of the consumer on works of art, the contextual slide is no slide after all;

emotivist accounts of the reason-giving process seem quite natural; and works of art come indeed like "globed fruit" packaged in museums and effectively severed from any past, future, or hope of relationship.

So the poet finds (or loses) himself as an entrepreneur in the writing industry; the critic examines the possible market for the poet's products; and the market by natural right decides what a poem "is" and what it ought to have been. There can be no alternative to the work of art itself, short of somehow, absurdly, forgetting what it is to be a consumer.

It is now, I think, at once possible and useful to state in at least a rough and ready way the *regulative* principles that the normal version applies to the doing of criticism, and more particularly to the handling of those "formative" rules already mentioned for making something of critical objects. It is vital to note that such "regulative" principles can indeed be *chosen* and the choice can affect not only the interpretation of the controversy but its fruits. It is in virtue of three such principles—higher order "rules"—that critical objects taken in the sense of the normal version may fairly be said to presume a "context of consumption."

1. If to refer a man in normal version fashion to "the poem itself" for his critical object means referring him to a "given" of some sort—a completeness, a globed fruit—then to that extent it means enjoining him to construe poems as one who has achieved the rights of purchase to an article: he *may* deal with it as he chooses, or as circumstances may induce him to deal with it. This perhaps most generic of the rules of consumption we may call the "rule of right." It is of course by no means *sufficient* to describe the normal version proposals for construing critical objects. Its essence is to deny the legitimacy of any *claims* for the use of the object that the producer, his spokesmen, or, indeed, anyone else may seek to press upon the consumer. They can merely toss inducements into the hopper.[11] Pointing out that an object will do better for certain purposes than others amounts to trying to influence a man in the employment of his right. The rule exempts him from having to take that pointing out as a reason.

2. Constrained to judge poems "like puddings" and never to forget that the proof of the pudding is in the eating, the effect is to cut off poems from all consumer interests but those of a specific sort, which involve "immediate fulfillments" or "intrinsic values." Puddings are natural examples; so are holidays, automobiles (where more than utilitarian values

[11] The connection of the "rule of right" with emotivist analysis of the logic of artistically relevant controversy is particularly strong. It will be more convenient to leave it for the next chapter and the critique of the choice of consumption.

are involved), love affairs, and paintings or driftwood for the mantel. The logic of "the poem itself" instructs: "Construe the poems you read as objects of taste." That is the next regulative principle, for goods taken in the context of consumption as works of art are taken in that context: "the rule of taste."

Accepting the rules of right and of taste, then, the artistically relevant poem, "the poem itself," becomes precisely like a globed fruit or thumbed medallion, "mute" and "there" *to the touch* or not there at all. The consumer, on the basis of his "esthetic" responses, does the talking. Hence the contextual slide is positively required—"the poem itself" is a "consumer does the talking" type of object.

From these two rules follow such delicate problems as that of the relationship between enjoying and judging, of how one taste can be "better" than another, or that other perennial problem of esthetics: how to explain the peculiar significance of the "esthetic object" freed from the artist's or anyone else's intentions, times, or directions, from truth or falsity, social utility, or any ends beyond the consumer's vision. For, after all, everyone, including the dogmatists of the work of art itself, knows quite well that works of art have "significance," that a poem is *not* entirely like a pudding, and that somehow or other the line must be drawn.

3. A third rule, incorporated within the doctrine of the work of art itself, differentiates the class of consumer goods to which works of art belong from other classes of consumer goods that are meant to be enjoyed. Despite commitment to the rules of right and taste, most people who buy the normal version still seek to save the critical argument by pushing one step further the resources of a context of consumption. The central fact about certain sorts of consumer goods is that by one's taste in them one will be known. Turning that social fact into a principle worth following in certain restricted forms of consumption, one applies it pre-eminently to the criticism of works of art and distinguishes a "refined" context of consumption.

We are all familiar with the phenomenon. Normally, neither disgrace nor distinction attaches to disliking puddings or preferring one pudding to another. "*De gustibus non disputandum*" means "Taste in puddings is not to be used for judging people." Otherwise, people talk about connoisseurs of puddings and refer to pudding-making as an art. Similarly, many are given to speaking of hair-dressing and the like as arts because they think making invidious distinctions among tastes establishes an art. Certainly they believe the converse, and a kind of disgrace does indeed seem to attach to preferring, say, Edgar Guest to T. S. Eliot. So poems are not like puddings all the way. Works of art are objects constructed to show what you are, in a very special way, in certain rather vague, but elevated respects.

Accordingly, it is clear what poems are like in the context of consumption. They are like Rorschachs: people appear to judge what the blob is like, and, of course, in a sense they do, but actually, behind the scenes, the blob because it is *only* a blob ("the blob itself") says what the person who does the judging is like. So with poems, as a "refined" kind of consumer good. The poem, because it is "the poem itself," completed and entirely given, announces through your response what you are like. Precisely, and only, *your* "interpretation" signifies now about the Rorschach poem. Therefore "the poem itself" must remain the poem uninterpreted, a "datum," by specific instruction, in order to remain open to all interpretations and satisfy the Rorschach function.

Hence the third regulative rule imposed by "the poem itself" for the sake of explaining arguments in the context of consumption: "Remember that, as an object of taste, a poem is like a Rorschach. The poem you are about to read is being ministered to you." In all deference, I call this "Rorschach's rule." Rorschach's rule generates obscure but logically significant arguments, for it can now be meaningfully questioned just what taste in poems says about a man's own style and sensitivity and even whether in any instance it says the truth.

One ought never underestimate the importance of Rorschach's rule in establishing the classifications of refinement. The very feelings themselves become socialized and subjected to control. Who does not want to be known as the sort who really and truly enjoys himself the way only a noble, informed, sensitive sort of fellow could? After a while it becomes hard to know what one likes. After a while it becomes a boon to be able to say that regardless of what one "ought" to like, this, and only this, is what one feels.

V. Non-Normal Versions

Mr. Northrop Frye's program for criticism as "an impersonal body of consolidating knowledge"[12] offers the almost ideal case of a non-normal version of the doctrine of the work of art itself. A non-normal version

[12] Northrop Frye, *Anatomy of Criticism* (Princeton, N.J.: Princeton University Press, 1957), p. 8. I do not, of course, propose to give anything like a complete account of Mr. Frye's theory of criticism, but only of a special aspect of that theory probably of less than immediate concern to Mr. Frye himself.

formulates the doctrine independently of the requirements of a context of consumption. To avoid critical programs in any way animated by the rules of right, of taste, or of Dr. Rorschach, and to develop the impersonal and objective criticism espoused a generation earlier by T. S. Eliot, Frye has proposed for literary criticism a rendition of the ideal of empirical science:

> If criticism exists, it must be an examination of literature in terms of a conceptual framework derivable from an inductive survey of the literary field . . . if there are any readers for whom the word "scientific" conveys emotional overtones of unimaginative barbarism they may substitute "systematic" or "progressive" instead . . . scholars and public critics are directly related by an intermediate form of criticism, a coherent and comprehensive theory of literature, logically and scientifically organized, some of which the student (unconsciously) learns as he goes on, but the main principles of which are as yet unknown to us. The development of such a criticism would fulfill the systematic and progressive element in research by assimilating its work into a unified structure of knowledge, as other sciences do.[13]

There is no question but that if criticism is the kind of thing Frye takes it to be, literary objects as objects of criticism are removed from a context of consumption. Yet is criticism that kind of thing? Can it be that kind of thing? The argument that it is depends, as Frye himself implicitly suggests, upon assuming the work of art itself —the literary object itself, the "poem itself" in the present convention—to be the object of an "inductive survey of the literary field":

> Aristotle seems to me to approach poetry as a biologist would approach a system of organisms, picking out its genera and species, formulating the broad laws of literary experience, and in short, writing as though he believed that there is a totally intelligible structure of knowledge attainable about poetry which is not poetry itself, or the experience of it, but poetics. One would imagine that, after two thousand years of post-Aristotelian literary activity, his views on poetics, like his views on the generation of animals, could be re-examined in the light of fresh evidence.[14]

Poems, then, if not objects of taste or devices for focusing useful lessons or insights, are like organisms; and as such they have natures to be described, classified, and, after literary criticism passes the present "state of naïve induction," explained "in terms of a conceptual framework." That is the key to Frye's "assumption" of the doctrine of the work of art

[13] *Ibid.*, pp. 7–11.
[14] *Ibid.*, p. 14.

itself. Literary objects are facts in the world: literary facts, poetic facts, novelistic facts, dramatic facts, which are not merely documentary facts, social facts, religious facts, or the like. Such special facts and such special objects comprise the materials of a unique discipline such that in Aristotelian style one pieces out genera and species; and "poetics" is the name for that discipline, theory, or "totally intelligible structure of knowledge attainable about poetry" which has "the poem itself," in present jargon, for its object. No poem itself, no poetics. The difference with Aristotle, perhaps, would be the conjoining of an ideal of a contemporary scientific method with the aspiration to a poetics. At any rate, the poem itself, not just the poem, exists as the object and justification of this special discipline—a discipline issuing in a set of statements simultaneously both true and artistically relevant.

Now there can be no serious quarrel with the need of both art history and criticism for a "conceptual framework" and a "theory of literature." The revealing characteristic of Frye's version of criticism is that he thinks he must satisfy that need by having critics qua critics fix the properties of poems as empirically-minded naturalists do those of fauna, flora, stars, or men; the notion has an immediate, ground-floor strangeness. Certainly, considering the lilies of the field, there is all the difference in the world between botany and fancy, fact and parable, whatever the final epistemology of descriptive science. But does the difference hold in the same way for poems and criticism, so that there is a "science" of poetics? Does the distinction between interpretation and description in biology and in criticism occur on the same axis and with the same kind of sharpness? Frye would have it so: "Value judgments are founded on the study of literature; the study of literature can never be founded on value judgments." [15] It is not merely that the study of literature depends upon avoiding the idiosyncratic and irresponsible judgments against which Eliot warned; it is that for that avoidance to be possible the study of literature must be, in a functional way, "value-free." Poems *are* like flowers, not only poetically.

Yet they cannot be, not from the point of view of the reference question. For a vision of literary criticism as progressive and scientific must give an account of two forms of progress for literary criticism, not of one. It must account not only for a continuous increase of knowledge in scope and in depth within some real or possible theory of literature, but

[15] *Ibid.*, p. 20. That there is a good deal wrong with such a statement is, of course, no novelty in contemporary discussion. Consider, for example, Charles Stevenson's well-known "normative conception of interpretation," in "On the Reasons That Can Be Given for the Interpretation of a Poem," in *Philosophy Looks at the Arts*, ed. Joseph Margolis (New York: Charles Scribner's Sons, 1962). A view similar in some respects, but not in all, to Stevenson's will be developed here.

also for progress among theories of literature. It must do so because the most exciting disagreements about poems or other works of art seem to have the habit of coming down at one or more points to disagreements about such theories. (Why and how this is so will have to be seen.) And a problem in principle arises because even though at any point a choice might be possible between one theory and another it does not follow that the succession of such choices must order into a "progress," given Frye's criteria for "progress." The truth is that if scientific theories in their coming and going come and go according to more or less determinate rules which fix their adequacy, it is by no means clear that so do literary theories, according to cross-theoretical criteria sufficient to discriminate among theories. Rather, the theories of critics seem to incorporate many, though probably not all, of their rules of adequacy within the theory itself, as an ineradicable and special prize; nor, in any event, do such theories seem to have for determining relative adequacy anything as strong as prediction, control, or even "simplicity," whatever the simplicity of scientific theories might come to mean.

To be sure, if a critical apparatus of formative rules were established and standardized, criticism could conceive its task as penetrating description while leaving mere "interpretation" to amateurs, edifiers, and people with all manner of extrinsic interests. Frye's vision would have secured direct authority. In fact, however, a critical apparatus tight enough to justify the ideals of botany would become a major obstacle to critics interested in the creative possibilities of the arts—"creative" in just the sense that they do not present variations within an accepted artistic framework. So the source of the strangeness of Frye's version of the doctrine is this: whatever their occasional pretensions, critics do not, and cannot, act as though they wanted a "progressive" and "systematic" criticism. They would be positively discomfited by any handbook of rules, "laws," or "concepts" which a doctrine of the work of art itself such as Frye's must aspire to press upon them. Only an art itself progressive as the sciences are could make it appropriate to accept the gift.

Such, then, are the normal and non-normal versions of the doctrine that there exists a distinction in principle essential to the artistically relevant controversy between the poem and the poem itself. Normal versions draw their picture of the poem itself in virtue of the requirements of the rules of consumption; non-normal versions prefer other entities to puddings in virtue of a preoccupation with some other set of rules (as, in Frye's case, the rules of empirical science). Both see criticism as the kind of thing in which one argues over objects that are in one way or another to be unfolded or discovered. Enough has perhaps been said to indicate generally why at least one non-normal version won't work for criticism; a more conclusive explanation depends upon that fuller understanding of the requirements of the artistically relevant controversy which is sought here through the study of the normal version.

Other non-normal versions which press for constructions of the work of art itself as, for example, a sort of Platonic entity or intuition, might of course account for the artistically relevant controversy, for all that has been proven to the contrary. Such versions are too numerous to be dealt with here. There is, however, a prima facie probability that the peculiarities of other non-normal versions than Frye's will not finally avoid the difficulties of taking the critical object as an object of refined consumption, as the normal version takes it, or as an object of description. Those are the difficulties involved in mistakes over the relation of interpretation and description, the performance of contextual slides, tendencies toward fruitless hypostatizations, and, in general, warpings of the business of criticism in the interest of preconceived conclusions.

I return now to the normal version.

Chapter 3

Toward the Poem in Proper Relation

It is, I have suggested, chiefly the choice of a context of consumption which makes the doctrine of the work of art itself plausible. Indeed, given sufficient determination to consider works of art as objects of consumption, the urge to reformulate the doctrine of the work of art itself to meet all possible difficulties may prevent seriously considering an alternative to that doctrine. As a first step toward an alternative, therefore, prudence suggests considering how the specific regulative principles of consumption themselves misrepresent the practice of artistically relevant controversy. Then it will be reasonable to ask what construction of the critical object does serve the purposes of that controversy.

I. The Trouble with Consumption

Now nobody denies that poems are consumed and that the consumption is important to the consumers. So, in one way or another, is everything else consumed that is neither ignored nor destroyed. Only it does not follow that therefore the principles of consumption are right for criticism any more than they are right for science, law, morals, or politics. Significantly, from time to time people have tried to apply the rules of right, taste, and Rorshach to those fields, to produce scepticisms of varying degrees of implausibility. Those rules are also wrong for the arguments of critics.

1. *Rorschach's Rule:* This is the rule that saves the controversy in "artistically relevant controversy" for those who have made the choice of consumption. What kind of objection can there be to seeing poems and other works of art as objects whose nature it is to place their judges on trial? They obviously do so. Since the argument against the Rorschach rule cannot be that it makes argument impossible, the argument against the rule must be that it makes *artistically relevant* argument impossible. We must show that while Rorschach's rule sets up a game, it does not set

up the right game, or else in some other way breaks with what is required of "good" critics.

Most obviously, then, critics who fix their positions by considering the group with which their judgment associates them break with the critical business. What critic worthy of the name, given a serious disagreement, would ask whether his judgment places him with the right people? He instead is supposed to play Luther: "No matter what the world thinks—no matter what my superiors think—here I stand. I can do no other." Honesty and courage are defined for critics *in virtue* of the capacity of critics to withstand the fear of Rorschachs, a fear suitable only to learners, not disputants. For, in general, with respect to the "appreciators" of poems, and other objects of art, the critic thinks *he* makes the standard by which they measure off, or should measure off, relative positions.

Next, imagine any two persons, formally "critics" or not, in the throes of argument over a poem, either how to read it or, for that matter, how to evaluate it. If either argues against the other's judgment that it won't do because only an insensitive, immature, and uninformed person would render it, an immediate and devastating reply does not even require mention of the poem under consideration: "You are right only on the assumption that my judgment is wrong—which, of course, is the point at issue."

The use of Rorschach's rule, moreover, will not serve the needs of actual controversy even if the charges of insensitivity, immaturity, and lack of information have been successfully sustained *independently* of the judgment at issue. A defendant before the critical bar may grant the limitations of his taste only to point out that the concession merely lends a probability that he has given a bad reading. His limitations incline him to *modesty,* not to a change of heart. He will urge that having defective taste does not itself suffice as an argument against his position, only against the likelihood of his position's being sustained. Further, the defects of his taste would enter the lists against his specific judgment only if a "wrong" choice in the critical argument *meant any choice* rendered by an uninformed, insensitive, etc., person. But it does not.

Someone may urge that of course the "wrongness" of the defendant's position is not that *one* insensitive and so on person made it, but that it was the kind of position the class of insensitive, etc. persons *would* take up. We have now encountered the full force of Rorschach's rule: what makes an opinion "wrong" or "inferior" is its being adopted by number of persons of a certain order confronted by the same object. This way of defining wrong judgments suffers, of course, from an incapacitating vagueness, and it makes all kinds of doubtful assumptions about how certain classes of people would behave. But there exists a more crucial difficulty: how in any instance does one discover the "sensitive," "truly informed," and "mature" in their artistically relevant choices, *when the accolade is disputed?*

Either we construct the "mature," "sensitive," and "informed" characteristics attributed to tastes from some class of specific and artistically relevant decisions (whatever the "ground" of those decisions), or else what appears to be artistically relevant argument amounts to an argument about certain interesting but artistically irrelevant considerations: historically, about social prestige and class. If critical objects function as indicators, they indicate what George Boas characterized quite a while back as "snobisme." To be more "refined" ("sensitive," "informed," and so on) *means,* under the rule, being a member of some group to which people aspire and which happens to prefer one sort of thing in the so-called arts to another. Argument about poems now constitutes a kind of ritual contest through which people try to show how "refined" they are. The more refined, the less they need to refer explicitly to class to show it; and the very indirectness of the ploy shows the deeper propriety of their membership in the class they aspire to join.

Either, therefore, arguments that use the Rorschach rule in criticism function in a secondary way, or they move out of the critical argument to something which passes for it—and which *can* pass for it, furthermore, just because of the habit of considering objects of art consumer goods of a "nonproductive" or "impractical" order, Rorschachs of the sensitive and uncertain soul.

2. *The Rule of Taste:* Consider now that application of the rule of taste to the critical object upon which all Rorschachs depend. Are poems in artistically relevant controversy taken as the kind of pudding-like things one judges in the tasting? That "are taken" needs a word of explanation. No one denies that there is a perfectly good sense of "judging" according to which one judges what is to one's taste, or "decides" what one "really" thinks; or that in the appreciation of the work of art one judges, or decides about, the thing in just that way; or even that in estimating logical relations this kind of judgment or decision plays a fundamental role. Only, it does not therefore follow that the consequent construction of the critical object as an object of taste meets the requirements of an artistically relevant controversy any more than the construction of a logical argument as an object of taste (insight) meets the requirement of the logical argument.

Poems, then are not like puddings or Martinis, even though poems also must be savored, because in dealing with poems as objects of artistically relevant controversy they are not "objects of taste" as one actually differentiates between things that are and things that are not. The point is an immediately available one, which a brief reflection on the cases of both the competent and incompetent judge brings home:

Consider first the incompetent who laughs aloud at the play's delicate moment. Among the many possible reasons, is not one of them that he has simply "missed" the play? He has seen the action the competent judges have seen, yet he fails to understand it. But no one would presume to tell a man who spat out pudding or Martini that he had "missed" the thing. He "got" it, all right; he merely doesn't like it.

To be sure, repeated experiences with puddings or Martinis might change the fellow's mind, and also repeated experiences with plays might lead to a more appropriate response. But consider what happens if not. Then, with things that really are taken as objects of taste, he goes his way immune to a certain kind of criticism. *"De gustibus,"* we say, while if he repeatedly fails to "get" the play we may call him "obtuse." For if no one *can* "misunderstand" an object of taste, one can "misunderstand"—whatever the final analysis of "understanding"—a poem or a painting or a piece of music; it makes sense to blame a failure in *mind.* Hence, it makes sense to give instructions to the man who misses the point as one cannot give instructions for construing puddings. A pudding is an object of taste. In practice, we do not treat a poem that way at all.

And consideration of the competent critic and the common judgment of him suggests the same. Precisely the most sophisticated critic most consistently considers the poem as a fact in the public domain of proper understanding and instruction. A purely personal [1] way of regarding a poem, no matter how delectable, would drop the holder outside criticism. Of course, someone may value a poem for a tang and force of which conceivably he may never convince others. Only, when that poem has such tang and force as an object lodged in an individual's own unique biography, how can he expect others to defer to his sentiment or consider its expression criticism? Quirks and prejudices are often the sources of the deepest pleasure—but they are causes, not reasons.

Poems, therefore, are disqualified as objects of taste in just the way in which objects of taste and sentiment are qualified—and to insist on handling poems as sentimental objects, as nothing prevents, misses the whole point of the art. "Poetry," says Wallace Stevens, "is not personal."

[1] The question whether anything "purely personal" exists is beside the point. There clearly is a common-sense way of talking about "purely personal" affairs, and that is the sense at issue here.

Hence the vital question about a poem is always whether the poet has presented the kind of structured affair regarding which one reading will *not* do as well as another. If he has not, if the poem fails to offer the possibility of coherent and desirable argument, competent critics will say the poet has "failed to communicate."

In general, then, precisely for the most sophisticated, the most complicated, the richest subjectivities, the work of art as critical object imposes an inevitable transition from object of taste to public object. But leaving further consideration of the rule of taste as such for the claims question, let us return now to the more general "rule of right" to which other objects, as well as "objects of taste," are exposed.

3. *The Rule of Right:* Of all the rules of consumption, the rule of right brings discussion most sharply against the trouble with critical objects in the context of consumption. For the rule (presented in the idea that "the poem itself" is the thing we interpret) renders the poem an object for which, concerning formative rules, there is no disputing: "It is hereby recommended to take the poem as datum; all (other) recommendations are out of order." Therefore the requirements of consumership and the requirements of artistically relevant controversy directly conflict.

Suppose I purchase a pair of shoes. If I decide to hammer nails with those shoes rather than wear them and somebody objects, I answer, "What do you mean? They're my shoes, aren't they? I have a *right* to do with them precisely as I choose." And so I do. They are *my* shoes; and a similar rejoinder is perfectly good for poems or any other objects taken as consumer goods. "You read your poem as you like and I'll do what I like with mine." The "rule of right" has dropped both shoe and poem in the same proprietary pocket, the pocket of "my," "your," and "his" type of objects. Under such circumstances it is no more surprising that works of art turn into problems in principle than that property does when abstracted from the network of social choices that create it.

It is now immediately perceivable why considering objects of art according to the rule of right, however appropriate for consumer goods in general and for poems approached simply as objects of enjoyment, hopelessly dislocates the critical argument. For where the rule applies it positively denies the possibility of argument, and as a matter of principle it insists that all worry cease about criticism. "It's mine, isn't it?" Where one decision will do as well as another—must do as well as another—the very occasion for the critical argument has disappeared.

To put the matter a trifle differently: the rule denies any exception proposed to the construing of a poem, *binding* force. Against the hammerer with shoes or the fantast of poems no objection can lay *claim* to consideration under the rule of right, even though either hammerer or fantast may attend to what you tell him and allow it to influence his activities. In a game determined by the rule of right, however, which is the game our "consumer" has entered, no legitimate claim can exist to impose relevance on one remark, and impertinence upon another. In short, exception-taking in the matter of appreciations and "genuine" arguments in the arts generally has become impossible not in virtue of the "logic" of art and criticism, but in virtue of a maxim every salesman someday learns: "Never argue with the customer!"

The point is not without its relevance for current controversy, and most particularly, of course, for the attempt to analyze critical discourse by denying the distinction between "reason" and "cause." So Mr. Stevenson writes that "when his [a critic's] knowledge acts as a psychological *cause* of his decision—when it is *one* of the factors, that is, that determines him to make this decision rather than that—then it may also be said to 'guide' his decision." [2]

Whatever a "reason" does to a critic, provided it does *something,* it "guides" him; and indeed so it is, so it, logically, "must" be, under the rule of right. The mistake consists in the confusion of two types of enterprise and the decision to consider both according to the requirements of one. The first enterprise is the enterprise of consumption, for which the rule of right *requires* a "persuasive" or "salesman-like" theory of reasons; the second, of artistically relevant decision in which it is essential to be able to claim some decision better than another against an opponent.

II. What Is a Poem Like?

If, then, the guiding principles of a context of consumption will not in fact serve to provide answers for the reference question—in brief, if poems are not like puddings—what must they be like? What would constitute an acceptable alternative to the doctrine of the work of art itself?

The central contention is this: "poem," as it occurs within artistically relevant controversy, constitutes a relation-type noun like "home" or "mother" rather than a thing-type noun like "pudding"; and construing the critical object as "the poem itself" mistakes the kind of noun it is. We do not forget Mother as Mother Herself when we consider her in relation to her children; nor have we forgotten the meaning of the term "home"

[2] C. L. Stevenson, in *Philosophical Analysis,* ed. Max Black (Ithaca, N.Y.: Cornell University Press, 1950), p. 359.

in wondering *whose* home is mentioned. We turn now to more specifically relevant analogies.

1. If for the purposes of critical debate poems are not very much like Beardsley's pudding, they are like Ryle's Queen of Hearts, where to be the Queen of Hearts—the card itself—depends upon the other cards in the deck and the games played. That I may do anything I choose with the Queen of Hearts, on the ground that it is *"my"* card—for example, build card castles with the children rather than play cards—in no way affects the fact that it "is" the Queen of Hearts in the class of card games. Like the Queen of Hearts in *its* games, then, the poem is the poem it is—"the poem itself"—in virtue of the critical and artistic context in which the poem occurs.

What it means to be "the poem" as a critical object depends, therefore, not merely on the photostat thereof, but (a) upon the other poems in the deck and (b) the critical context in which it is read.

A. There is actually formidable testimony for the notion that the critic considers poems "as poems" within their place in a deck of poems. Something of the sort seems to have been part of the point of Eliot's famous essay, "Tradition and the Individual Talent":

> No poet, no artist of any art, has his complete meaning alone. His significance, his appreciation is the appreciation of his relation to the dead poets and artists. You cannot value him alone; you must set him, for contrast and comparison, among the dead. I mean this as a principle of aesthetic, not merely historical, criticism. The necessity that he shall conform, that he shall cohere, is not onesided; what happens when a new work of art is created is something that happens simultaneously to all the works of art which preceded it. The existing monuments form an ideal order among themselves, which is modified by the introduction of the new (the really new) work of art among them. The existing order is complete before the new work arrives; for order to persist after the supervention of novelty, the *whole* existing order must be, if ever so slightly, altered.[3]

Suppose one changes the valuation of a card—then one changes the valuation of at least some of the other cards in the deck. Similarly, if one

[3] *Selected Essays* (New York: Harcourt, Brace, 1950), pp. 4–5. Northrop Frye, also, of course, asserts, giving due credit to Eliot for the idea if not for the language, that "the existing monuments of literature form an ideal order among themselves" (Frye, *Anatomy of Criticism* [Princeton, N.J.: Princeton University Press, 1957], p. 18). But where Eliot has that "ideal order" reconstituting itself and reconstituting as well with the advent of new poetry the very natures of existing poems, Frye seeks an "ideal order" roughly parallel to the one scientists seek in nature. It is Eliot's point which is the valuable one for this essay, not Frye's.

changes the sense in which one understands a poet, as Eliot, for example, himself did for Milton, one changes one's understanding, one prepares to render another "explication," if not of all the other poems in the language (though Eliot suggests as much and more) at least of some of the others (those which, with respect to the change, are "in the deck"). Hence the artistically relevant or "esthetic" force of "tradition." "Tradition" is Eliot's deck of cards qua deck.

A similar parallelism now defines his "individual talent." Such talent adds genuinely new poems to the deck rather than merely additional poems, which latter (such is the difference between a deck of poems and a deck of cards) do not affect the poetry deck. According to the depth of the talent, that effect is great or small; the greatness or smallness of the effect measures the depth of the talent.

B. Not only do other poems in the poetry deck determine the value of any particular poem; so, of course, does the critical game played. What makes the three of spades a wild card? What makes the novel a satire? How one chooses to take them, surely, as part of which particular gambling or literary game. To be sure, dealer's choice suffices to make the three a wild card while critic's choice—simply that it suits him to handle the novel that way—does not make the novel a satire. Still, in each case, the rules of the game construct the object of criticism by a sort of implicit definition.

Of course, poems are less like cards for criticism than like other affairs where the rules for definition are less clear than in games and less fixed. Also, of course, unlike the cards in a card game the pieces in the critical game have a reference *outside* the critical deck—for (except for extreme formalists) most people deny that poems are what they are *only* in relation to other poems and the rules of art.[4]

2. Considering poems, then, outside their strictly game-like or "formal" characteristics, I next suggest that poems are like jokes, which similarly demand a context other than other jokes and function through a by no means explicit or easily stateable set of rules.

Poems are like jokes in that the same ambiguity occurs for them that occurs for jokes when one asks, "What's the joke?" Suppose, for example, that on entering a room I overhear an apparently innocuous remark and then a burst of laughter. "What's the joke?" I ask. Unless given the circumstances of that remark I will never know "what the joke is," even

[4] The implication is, of course, that the *relational* position of poems enters fundamentally into their "formal" character—and so, later, I shall come to stress, and not only for poems.

though I have in one sense heard and understood the remark. We "make jokes" by putting remarks (or, of course, acts) in relation—by the decision to select these events or those in the construction of the joke.

But, if poems are like jokes, the same holds for poems. Unless I know what sorts of relation to look for in the remark called a poem, I observe "the poem" only through an ambiguity. The ambiguity need not invoke "esthetic objects." The expression "joke" and the expression "poem" each have a way in common usage of designating *both* the verbal expression as such, formed in terms of the rules of grammar in the language, and the verbal expression understood in that language and *then* taken as a "poem" or "joke." Given that distinction, the mistake of Wimsatt and Beardsley and of the other theorists of "the poem itself" becomes intelligible: they confuse the two senses—supposing that all one needs to understand a "poem" in the second sense (of the poem qua poem) is to understand the "rules of language" that apply to poems in the first (the poem qua bit of language).

At any rate, the double significance of "poems" need cause no more trouble than the double significance of "jokes," except that substantive considerations cause us systematically to ignore the relations and circumstances that apply in constructing "poems" or in "seeing" the poem. That the human affairs in virtue of which remarks become "poems" are subtle and varied, requiring often considerable insight for their perception, rather more than do many jokes, ought not induce us to forget the necessity of those affairs.

In sum, if the question "What's the joke!" is a good one, so is the question "What's the poem?"—and in the same way.

3. One last analogy: poems, like some jokes, are conceivable in relationships like those which define gestures. One defines the gesture by reference to the individual whose gesture it is; and this, far from introducing a note of subjectivity, makes the gesture what it is, with all the qualities it possesses.

No one, for example, imagines that tugging at the brim of a hat is a "gesture in itself," as people appear sometimes to consider a remark "the joke itself" or a poem "the poem itself." Everything depends upon who tips his hat, to whom, and when. Considerations such as this turn the neutral act into a gesture of gallantry, an insult, a formal act, or what not; and it won't do at all for the gesturer to insist that the act's *his* personal act and to deny anyone else the right to say what the act means. The constituting environment is a fact; and within that environment the gesture constitutes a kind of floating message. The grammar's hardly universal, but to those who know it, the import's plain.

If, therefore, poems are like gestures, it does not follow that to construe a poem means making it my poem, according to the rule of right. My will does not suffice, though the poem be linked to me, to make it one thing rather than another or to lift it beyond another's appraisal. And, in fact, we are most of us quite prepared to acknowledge ignorance both that we have performed a gesture and what an admitted gesture means.

Poems, then, are poems *of;* and this seems like a peculiar statement only because gestures are conceived as the gestures of individuals, and of the individuals who make them, while poems typically function as poems of *classes* of individuals, including the individual who makes them. That they do indeed possess such relationships, and that those relationships are significant in artistically relevant controversy, will be seen more clearly in the later discussion of nonformal properties of works of art.

The poem not-in-itself, then, the poem-in-proper-relation, which is the alternative to the poem itself, involves certain of the characteristics of the card, certain characteristics of the joke, and certain others of gestures. Critics, therefore, do nothing mysterious in appraising poems, for in the appraisal they no more take poems "in themselves" than anyone concerned with things other than the arts takes those things by and in themselves.

III. The Poem as Poem

If the alternative to "the poem itself" be "the poem in proper relation" and if "the poem itself" will not work for artistically relevant argument, then "the poem in proper relation" must. "The poem in proper relation" must be the critical object of poetically relevant controversy, "the work of art in proper relation" the critical object of artistically relevant controversy in general.

Suppose, then, that one wishes to explicate the verse of Mother Goose as poetry. How does one read her differently than if one did not read her as poetry? Where does the difference lie?

The difference must lie in a *choice* of relations. If Mother Goose has said a poem, you will not find the poem simply by reading the script itself, and if she has not said one you will not find that out by reading the script itself. Of course, I have been assuming that it is possible to read the same words as poetry and as something else. Since a child understands the written or recited verse of Mother Goose, and so does the man who knows poetry, any difference in their understandings cannot reside in the poem itself, in isolation. "The cow jumped over the moon. . . ." The very obviousness, the straight declarativeness of the language testifies that not even Mother Goose speaks, as a poet, for herself. The child takes the speech in one context, the judge of poetry in another, and that makes all the difference. If you consider the child already a poet and innocent judge of poetry, replace him by the parent reading the lines.

It follows that poems as poems are not messages, just as the doctrine of the poem itself declares. They are not even messages with sound effects, I would add, as though any message could be turned into a poem simply by making it rhyme or jog along in iambic pentameter. But the interesting thing is that the doctrine of the poem itself has it quite wrong why poems are not messages. "Messages," actually, are the sorts of entities properly taken "in themselves," not poems. Messages, because they exist in an established grammar, stand independently of the environment in which they are written or read and may be grasped for "what they *themselves* say." Yet because poems exist as such in a given language with a given grammar, normal version adherents may now assume as an immediately given fact, with which only perversity can quarrel, that which they have chosen to accept on other (consumer-like) grounds: that all good critics consider "the poem itself" the subject of their arguments. And so a further inspiration is lent to the metaphysical imagination, another way devised to lend credibility to the doctrine of the work of art itself in arts like music and painting, which are not done in a language. One argues, to save the doctrine of the work of art itself, that they *must* be done in a language, that musician, painter, and the like communicate in a strangely esoteric and untranslatable language each of his own—the "language" of painting, the "language" of music.

How, then, does one find the poem if poems as critical objects are not messages and not even Mother Goose speaks for herself? Cards, gestures, and jokes suggest how, provided one really makes an effort to distinguish the message from the poem. One doesn't "find" poems at all. One doesn't decode them. One *institutes* them, as critical objects, and the "language of art" must not be turned into a way of blaming the institution or "construction," as I shall call it, on the facts as they are discovered. One knows the poem Mother Goose has said by *deciding* on what she has said (by no means arbitrarily, as will be seen) and that means placing the poem in its "proper" relations.

As with jokes: recollecting that Mother Goose rhymes began as lampoons, satire, or social protest rather than nursery rhymes, one asks, "What's the poem?" not *necessarily* committed to history but in the way one asked, in an earlier example, "What's the joke?" By learning the "facts" one may see a deeper joke, or none at all. Asking after the historical environment, one may still add or subtract, as well as leave it alone—for *both* jokes and poems.

As with gestures: one settles, or does not settle, Mother's Goose by inquiring after the sort of human being whose utterance or gesture the words would be, and in what sort of predicament. Construing the verse as the gesture of embittered adults, for example, or of whimsical minds, or both in one shifting medley, makes a palpable difference.

As with cards: choose the other cards of the deck in which you will place Mother Goose. The cards you choose and the game you play will, of course, determine her values. If by any chance you can invent a game for Mother Goose that works perfectly according to the rules of criticism as they exist, everyone will say that you have "discovered" her secret and profound meaning.

When it is found possible, according to whatever principles of justification exist, to throw Mother Goose into a sufficiently rich and varied complex of relationships, Mother Goose becomes poetry; when not, then not. In their different ways, each analogy says the same thing: a poem, or any other work of art, is something one *does.* One makes a great and complex series of decisions not necessarily less well grounded for being decisions or less decisions for being well grounded, with respect to a bit of natural language. The poem qua poem requires setting the poem in proper relations, which cannot be settled a priori but depend upon the process of artistically relevant controversy.

IV. The Poem in the Debate

Terms like "deciding," "settling," or "placing" have been used very freely indeed to denote the way a poem enters or is entered into relationship; yet at least an identification of that process is essential to present the poem in proper relation. However it may have been with the poem itself, when poems are "placed" (or whatever word one prefers) in proper relation within the context of the critical debate, does that "placing" mean "interpreting," "describing," or something else? The answer will be very much affected by whether the context be appreciation, pedagogy, psychology, history, *or* the artistically relevant controversy as such.

Consider an elementary and almost paradigmatic difference of opinion of the sort that arises regardless of critical or metacritical assumptions: the after-theater argument. The theater has offered a performance of the *Hippolytus.*

"A vastly over-rated affair," says one. "Everything done and said, if you take the play on its own merits and without prior prejudice, adds up to a vast to-do over a rather weak-minded Helen Hotchkinson wife 'tempted' by 'Passion' of all things, and driven to hysteria by the shame of it all. How seriously can an unprejudiced person take that sort of thing, especially when he finds at the other two points of the triangle a prig and, perhaps, a latent homosexual? Proper direction would have done the thing as a kind of trans-historical farce."

Says another, "To see the play you must forget the *New Yorker* magazine and a pseudo-sophisticated psychology and place the drama in the Euripidean theater where it belongs. What happens in the *Hippolytus* is, as plainly set forth as anything can be in the theater: in general terms, the breaking up of the human and civil order which Theseus spent his life building and of which he is the legal and proper guardian. Theseus faces 'the destructive element' not outside but in the royal family itself, in himself. That is the specialness. The lady *cannot* help herself. Theseus in the person of his son annihilates the order he thinks himself defending. Hippolytus, no homosexual in any modern sense, sacrifices himself to Aphrodite unavailingly. What would be the point of a homosexual's attachment to Artemis? He would have nothing to give."

It is easy to see that the above embryonic, but radically different, assessments of the *Hippolytus* really do follow on the relationships in which the play has been "placed." It is also easy to see that each side—though it pleads in the interest of "the poem itself"—will need, in offering a defense, to defend a choice of one set of relationships or another, that the pressure of argument in the concrete sets the play in proper relation. This, however, is not the crucial matter now. It has been said before that the poem itself requires the interpretation-description distinction. I want now to say that the poem in proper relation excludes *in the critical debate* that distinction and requires an independent characterization. In my own jargon: the critical object qua critical object is neither the interpreted object nor the described object, but the "constructed" object. The point lies on the surface in the *Hippolytus* debate. For that debate, the interpretation-description framework cannot be taken seriously as though one side might actually be describing the play and the other interpreting it. No doubt each side would claim for itself a "description" of the *Hippolytus* and for the other side an "interpretation," but that seems reasonable to them only because they have accepted the rhetoric of the poem itself. In respect of the actual controversy, all sides, since all sides institute relevant relations for the play, "interpret" or none do. Similarly, if it is decided to allow people to "describe" equally in different frameworks, all "describe," or none. And, indeed, the equal and easy applicability of both terms to characterize the "placing" process suggests that the whole distinction has in the context of artistically relevant controversy lost its point. Why has it?

1. In general, though all works of art presumably admit some physical description, there exists no relevant and standard description of the *Hippolytus* qua drama for which the distinction between interpretation and description may obtain. But since an interpretation *of* anything constitutes an interpretation only with respect to a description, and since it is the dramatic description alone, not the physical description, which interests the disputants and over which they disagree, neither interpretation nor description will serve to characterize the placing in relation of the *Hippolytus.*

2. That a relevant and standard description does not exist for the disputants in the *Hippolytus* argument is patent. Both sides have proposed rules precisely for constructing such a description: (a) to describe the play itself, says one, consider what the play would look like if written today; and (b) to describe the play itself, says the other, consider what the play looks like in the Greece of Euripides. Only *after* a choice is made may they discuss "interpretations": so far they are hardly considering "the same play." To which version shall "interpretations" he attached? Just what shall be "interpreted," "judged," or "taught" as the *Hippolytus?* Some may say that my "versions" are still "interpretations" as, of course, in one use of "interpretation" so they are. Note, however, that *any* "description," according to this way of talking, even in science, becomes an "interpretation" (any description employs principles "placing" the described object in a certain way) and the vital distinction becomes blurred between "interpretations" over which, at a given stage in an argument of a certain sort, "tolerance" cannot be extended without swamping the argument, and "interpretations" over which there is no longer any point debating.[5]

[5] Sometimes it is felt that art is marked by a greater tolerance of divergent "interpretations" than are the sciences. See, for example, Joseph Margolis' "The Logic of Interpretation," in *Philosophy Looks at the Arts,* ed. Joseph Margolis (New York: Charles Scribner's Sons, 1962), p. 116. There are many issues involved but the present argument suggests that Margolis obtains his contrast between science and art at least in part by comparing the interpretations of science ("descriptions") where justification is called for with the descriptions ("interpretations") of art in those moments where there is no need for a decision. So Margolis seems to think that art compared to science has an "odd" way of handling descriptions. Rather, in artistically relevant controversy "description" is never the principal issue.

Both "description" and "interpretation" therefore await a decision between the proposed rules.

3. There cannot be a relevant standard description with respect to which the versions proffered are "interpretations" because, at the same time that a difference of opinion exists to be resolved, all the relevant "facts" of action and communication standard for the difference of opinion are accounted for by all self-consistent versions of the play. This last, that all the "facts" do not suffice when a difference *nevertheless* exists to be resolved, is crucial for understanding that something else is going on in the placing of critical objects, something other than interpreting or describing.

Suppose, then, the *Hippolytus* argument carried on one step further and a claim advanced against either of the versions that it "failed" to show how a certain act of Theseus fitted the specific "structure" of the play, where the rival version indeed "accounted" for that act. (By the "structure of the play" I mean a complete set of incidents in the relationship in which they are given—and assume, for the moment, that one can establish such a set prior to any controversy.) Then, even admitting a "failure" to account for the specific act, a defense is still available against the version that "succeeded": that "failure" and "success" here are Pickwickian. It was not that the act in question went unobserved as an element in the structure of the play; the structure of the play was itself defective and therefore *not* to "account" for the "defect" was a positive virtue. What has been offered as a more detailed and consistent account of the *Hippolytus* is in fact a *face-saving* account.[6] Differences in the explanatory power of the two (or more) versions therefore become intelligible only on the implicit assumption of an identical policy for "taking the play into account." The argument becomes an argument between two proposed descriptions only if it is true that the preferable viewing of a play is the one which accounts for its details and the interrelationships of those details in such a way as to minimize faults. And, of course, one must be able to compare faults.

But consider now the assumption of a complete set of incidents independent of the artistically relevant controversy. Not only would the existence of such a set fail to provide a standard and relevant description, but the existence itself is questionable. Physical descriptions presuppose physical theories other than those immediately at stake in the description, to make agreement possible. For example, a theory of light, a theory of

[6] This kind of point is, I take it, one of the main points of Stevenson's "normative concept of interpretation." See his article "On the Reasons That Can Be Given for the Interpretation of a Poem," in *Philosophy Looks at the Arts.*

optics, a theory of photography, and their appropriate initial conditions settle incompatible descriptions of a star's chemical composition. But it is by no means clear that analogous "lower" level theories exist in the arts, or that if they exist that critics take advantage of them, or that if they take advantage of them that they do so in a manner independent of the quarrel at issue. More, agreement in the abstract on some general way of construing a class of works of art rarely if ever suffices to establish the *relevance* of that way of construing to the particular case, let alone the manner in which it is to be applied. Hence agreement on the incidents composing the structure of a play or the parts composing any other works of art tends, when the controversy is serious, either to be real and trivial, or nontrivial and unstable.

This, I take it, is the sort of situation that often dismays people who hope for some rationality in art and criticism. They have accepted the doctrine of the work of art itself and hence of the work of art as subject to "description." They may well be dismayed. Either there is an alternative to dealing with at least some versions of works of art as either interpretations or descriptions, or artistically relevant controversy is a fraud.

4. There is an alternative, which the remainder of this book will emphasize. If in the critical debate the poem's relations are not "there" to be described, they must be instituted. If they must be instituted, and that institution is at the heart of the argument, then it is not surprising that we cannot settle for the loose tolerance of "interpretation"—as though there were no issue—or the tightness of description, as though basic divisions were settled. To establish a version of a work of art within the artistically relevant controversy is—and the point will recur—rather like the effort of a judge to place a construction upon his case. Obviously, the judge doesn't "make" his cases. But he does "make sense" *of* them. He places, he hopes, "proper" constructions upon them. So for the critic: when he places the poem in proper relation, he places construction upon the poem. Such data as there are, he, like the judge, *uses* in setting up his construction. Not only is the critical object "the poem in proper relation" rather than "the poem itself"; it is also a "construction," rather than an object to be encountered and reported on. The critical object, as I shall henceforth put it, is a "constructed object."

Chapter 4

Constructing Critical Objects: The Construction Argument

That argument in virtue of which constructions are performed I call "the construction argument." Construction arguments, being arguments, and "genuine," are not merely sets of opinions or assertions; they present justifications of whatever it is one "makes of" a critical object. They arise because one doesn't "get" or "understand" or "make sense" of a critical object or because what one does grasp as the critical object has been challenged, as in the *Hippolytus* example. The usually complex conclusion presents the proposed "construction" to be placed upon an object or class of objects and prepares that object or class of objects for "judgment"—which is another and later question.

I. The Issues of the Construction Argument

Construction arguments have formative rules, or the application of those rules, as their issues. The range and force of such rules in artistically relevant controversy has hardly been touched and a brief review of their variety is indispensable for even a rough picture of the construction argument. Formative rules are found, of course, embedded in the discussions of critics, as two such rules were found in the *Hippolytus* discussion: a rule for constructing to maximize the worth of the construct, and a species of expression rule for keeping versions in historical context. Here are some additional rules:

1. *Rules of Relevance:* Discussion may revolve about the appropriateness of introducing an object of a specified sort into artistically relevant controversy. One has to know what to take seriously and what not to. Is such and such a "work of art" or merely "entertainment"? There are formative rules, "rules of relevance," for the objects of artistically relevant controversy. Burlesque, presumably, is not covered. Is "found art"? How such questions are answered contributes something to the kind of thing one makes of critical objects.

2. *Rules of Type:* Most obvious of the issues attendant on placing critical objects in proper relation is the genre issue. Disputes over genre invoke not merely questions of post facto classification; they also invoke questions, as it were, of the economy of art. "Demand of all artifacts having such and such characteristics that they possess such and such others." But what shall one demand? That is the genre issue. One argues the formative rule that fictional works of a certain length in prose have "stories"; paintings, recognizable subjects; music, hummable tunes. Such disputes, about "formative rules of type," when they occur in general form, occur as policy questions in the development of art. When they occur in particular, raising the question whether such and such is satire or sentiment, novel or prose poem, painting or decoration, they restrict the reading, viewing, or hearing that the presented physical object will receive and they determine what sort of work of art, if any, we are going to make of it.

A sufficiently novel object—one admitted to be a fitting subject but which nevertheless presents a problem in typing—would normally be considered to introduce a *new* genre. Establishing a new genre sets up a group of more or less standard and explicit expectations in virtue of which the object becomes "intelligible" and an audience may "understand" it.

Argument, of course, may center around objects that are admittedly members of artistically relevant genres where the admission still does not establish agreement on what to look for. There are formative rules applicable across genre boundaries. Here are some examples:

3. *Rules of Expression:* To someone who sees a painting but doesn't know what to make of it, we may say: "See that painting as the 'expression' of so and so or such and such. You will never get it unless you do. Works of art 'are' expressions." Proposing the employment of a "formative rule of expression" for the analysis of paintings raises a fair question either of the desirability of seeing paintings as expressions or of just whose expression the painting might be, let alone the question of what is being expressed.

The acceptance or rejection of rules of expression constitutes an option, however, on one proviso: that the rules are not required to justify their use in any particular instance by proving themselves for every "work of art." For so, with disastrous consequences to artistically relevant controversy, suppose *both* those who reject rules of expression out of hand (offering counter-examples in which expression rules simply cannot be applied) and those who insist on expression theories of art (asserting, in effect, that critics of the arts *must* raise the expression question even if it is necessary to posit a hypothetical condition or agent to be expressed).

Nevertheless, the dogged refusal of proponents and opponents of expression theories to let the matter lie bears witness to the fact that expression rules are rules, whose use and application must be decided.

4. *Formative Rules of Significance:* These are the rules through which people construct the object to be appreciated by fixing, as they say, on its "significance." "Consider, if you want to understand the work of art and present a *proper* explication of it, the relationship of that object to moral interests, the class struggle, the education of the young, truth, salvation, and on and on." Such rules, despite the evident risks of their application, are in themselves neither "relevant" nor "irrelevant," any more than are decisions favoring or opposing expression rules. The only question, for them as for expression rules, is whether they are used to construct a critical object or to convert such an object into a moral, political, educational, etc., object lesson.

This may seem thin gruel to offer for the vexed questions of truth, morality, and social philosophy in their relations to art; and, indeed, so it is for any larger end than the present one of suggesting the sort of decisions that make a difference in construction. But thin or not, one *Don Quixote* is constructed in relation to the values of truth and significance, and another, though not necessarily an unrelated one, to the values of fantasy.

5. *Formative Rules for Inclusion and Exclusion:* We often receive advice on how to hear, look at, read, or attend some work of art or kind of work of art by noticing one thing deemed plainly "present" or by ignoring another. The justification for the remonstrance is that even when general agreement holds for rules of expression and significance, not everything truly predicated of critical objects rightly claims relevance. Formative rules of inclusion and exclusion say what to include in the perceived object and what to exclude.

Listening to a violinist, does one consider the thud and scrape of horsehair and wood on string part of the music or not?

Observing a painting, does one see the flaking of the paint as belonging to the picture or is it something to be discounted, the unhappier work of time, to be overlooked if possible? And what about the lost arms of the "Venus de Milo," which, it is said, an art lover had dedicated his life to find?

Suppose a poet likes to play with typography, in the fashion of Lewis Carroll or Laurence Sterne or Dylan Thomas, whose poems sometimes take the shape of diamonds and hourglasses—is that part of the poetry or not?

Decisions in matters such as these are no less significant for being made, for the most part, unconsciously—and it is very plain to see that they make a radical difference for appreciation. That nothing is present in the successful work of art which is not also relevant to the construction the good critic will give to it, seems plausible only on condition that one diligently avoids noticing the rules of inclusion and exclusion actually employed. One avoids so noticing, of course, because one takes the work of art on principle as a finished job, ready for the consuming.

6. *Rules of Appropriateness:* Artists and their critics both characteristically combine rules of expression, significance, and type to generate decisions about what may be expected from this art or this and that sub-art or this or that style; and those combinations are often distinctly arguable. So, for example, many people might want to avoid introducing rules of significance for music while keeping them in architecture, perhaps in the form of a rule of social utility; and the distribution seems entirely inevitable until it is questioned in the concrete. Rules of appropriateness formulate such distribution.

While it has already been noted that some formative rules constitute genuine options only on the condition that they are not bought entire, now the point is that there exist strategies for the allocation of resources in the arts and in criticism that determine the direction of construction and have an immediate consequence for valuation as well. Hence Lessing's prescriptions of the limits of painting as a spatial art and of poetry as a temporal art constitute rules of appropriateness in the present sense. In general I take talk of the "requirements of the medium" and of the need to understand "the language" of the medium in which a critical object is encountered, mainly for efforts to formulate and apply rules of appropriateness in the context of a special kind of justification. Media are made to handle rules as though they were pseudo-natural laws, and possibilities as though they were syntax. But I must defer further consideration of media.

7. *Rules for Specific Analysis:* Every particular work of art, people sometimes say, works according to its own rules, not the rules of something that resembles it; and those rules determine the hearing, viewing, or reading granted it. I shall call such rules "rules for specific analysis." When these rules are applied, the various parts of the work of art become distinguishable as parts, fall into the place (or lack of place) in which they fall, or secure the significance they do secure; and the work as a

whole is heard, viewed, or seen as one whole rather than another. Works of art do not "have" their own particular rules but *require* them for construction as particular works of art.

They may tell the musician attempting a "reading" of a score to take the tempo faster here, slower there. In another sense of "reading" they may shift the emphasis from one phrase to another in the perusal of a poem, as in a hearing of music. They may provide an answer to the question of what in the world is going on in the third act (Hamlet's *really* mad, although he pretends to pretend to be). They may appear as the title of a picture, telling us to see the organization of lines in the sketch as "Duck!" or "Rabbit," in Gombrich's example; [1] or they may work as Brueghel's title does for his picture "The Fall of Icarus," which, by telling the viewer to identify the legs in Brueghel's lake as those of Icarus, organize the rest of the characters in the picture.[2] In various ways, then, through identifications as in pictures, by directing attention as in sonnet reading, by providing interpretative principles as in *Hamlet,* even by deliberately frustrating accustomed modes of putting things together, and so on and on, rules of specific analysis provide an appropriate "understanding" of the work of art.

Because they hold over open-ended sets of performances or encounters, they are genuinely "rules"; and whether or not to institute one or another rule for specific analysis constitutes perhaps the central concern of practical criticism and the pay-off for argument about all other formative rules.

Such, then, are the issues that divide people over the construction of works of art in general or in particular: rules of relevance, rules of type, rules of expression, rules of significance, rules for inclusion and exclusion, rules of appropriateness, rules for specific analysis. They are not the only rules over which people take issue, as that peculiar policy rule for maximizing the worth of a construct found in the *Hippolytus* argument illustrates; but perhaps they are the most obvious. There is also a class of rules, not unfairly called "formative," which for profound psychological or sociological reasons critics do not take as issues. Such are the kinds of rules of which Ernest Gombrich in particular has made everyone aware in the visual arts. These may perhaps be called "rules of no option." Rules of no option take us only a small and easily traveled distance toward seeing that it will not do to take the work of art as the work of art

[1] E. H. Gombrich provides a wealth of illustrations, including the one mentioned here, in his *Art and Illusion* (New York: Pantheon, 1960).

[2] For this illustration, although not for using it as an illustration of the general classification of "rules of specific analysis," I am indebted to a lecture of Professor Arthur Danto.

itself. But they work primarily for the understanding of perception and appreciation, and their recognition is a recognition only of the requirements of perception and appreciation. Stop with such formative rules and the problem of artistically relevant construction still remains where the doctrine of the work of art itself left it. So I shall discuss rules of no option no further.

II. The Conduct of the Construction Argument

What are construction arguments like if they are arguments about formative rules? Never mind how they are possible. How are they recognizable? How are they in fact conducted?

Most generally, the following regulative principles control the construction argument and are optional for talking about works of art in the sense that nothing prevents opting for the principles of consumption instead.

Instead of a rule of right, the discussion of the preceding chapters calls for a *rule of impersonality:* "Hold yourself liable to communicate and justify your construction. The fact that *you* chose one thing rather than another does not justify the choice. The work of art does not belong to you."

Instead of the rule of taste, a *rule of use:* "Consider your perception of the critical object the material for your reworking. There is a long way to go. Starting from the way the work of art appears to you, prepare as the controversy begins for a further insight."

Instead of Dr. Rorschach's rule, a *rule of objectivity:* "While what you make of works of art undoubtedly tells a good deal about the sort you are, forget it. Consider what you take to be the requirements of your subject as one work of art among others as you construct the critical object."

If construction arguments are arguments about formative rules under such regulative principles as these, then they are conducted less like arguments over consumer goods than they are like arguments in law. That is the crucial point of this section. The real arguments designated here as construction arguments have been radically misplaced by a fair part of contemporary discussion. Critics who raise questions about the construction or "nature" of an object of criticism raise questions similar to those raised in a court of law over the nature of the case in dispute. For both legal and artistically relevant controversy the construction argument turns about formative rules in such a way that the critical object (case at law or case at art) imposes the task of deciding *which* set of rules applies or else raises a question of the reconstruction of those rules or the relations among them in the light of the specific case. So "the work of art itself" is neither more nor less nonsense than the negligence case that is a case of negligence in itself and, more significantly still at this point, is neither more nor less "subjective" or "private." The job now is to spell this out.

1. If construction arguments are like similar arguments in the law, they must be attempts to justify decisions by the relations sustained to a matrix of other decisions, past, present, and future. They must, in effect, be arguments over critical objects grasped as having the significance of precedent cases, whether or not in making the decision we choose not to reverse our field. *Pace stare decisis.* If *Oedipus Rex* is a tragedy, then is *Death of a Salesman?* You can't have it both ways. Or can you? If so, distinguish! If the Creation is necessary to the Sistine Chapel frescoes, is some "similar" reference necessary to a piece of abstract expressionism? How similar, if similar at all? Decide! Decisions such as these, reached as are these, necessarily generate rules—formative rules—in the process of distinguishing, just as cases generate in the common law the law of torts.

2. Hence, the law and the construction argument both conduct proceedings in virtue of a complex and fruitful relation between formative rules and cases of a sort that modern legal theory has thoroughly exploited and modern esthetic theory neglected. Rules construe cases; cases recast rules. That is the name of the game. The double process, stitching back and forth, marks argument where one encounters rather than the familiar and the finished, the unfamiliar and the problematic. To be a bit more explicit:

Troubled by the application in some particular case of a formative rule of type—by the question, say, "Is this a lyric poem?"—the question raises not merely a classificatory problem in the *history* of poetry, but two intertwined difficulties that may require a high order of critical imagination to surmount: (a) Identifying the poem just read as a lyric or not, saying whether it properly receives the "reading" of a lyric or not, may involve reassessing, perhaps in a wholesale way, the *characteristics* to be demanded of poems having certain other characteristics associated with "lyrics." "What is a lyric, anyway?" (b) Assuming that question answered, at least momentarily, the delicate problem persists of saying how and in what sense the poem under discussion exhibits the lyric marks. "Do you actually mean to call *this* poem a lyric?" Answering, "Yes, I do mean to call this a lyric," will place constraints upon any answer to the question "What *is* a lyric, anyway?" The constraints absorbed, a new response to that latter question leads back to the question, "Do you really mean to call this poem a lyric?" And so back and forth, as long as necessary.

It is vital to see that this kind of interactive, two-directed "feedback" process that characterizes the course of the construction argument may hold not only for the obviously law-like rules of type but, indeed, for all formative rules. In most cases, all that is required is an appropriate substitution for "lyric" of expression, significance, or other phrase demanded by the formative rule in question. In other cases, the formulation is more complicated, but the result the same: "What sort of thing *does* require to be included or excluded in considering a poem (music, sculpture, etc.)? Do you actually think this poem (music, sculpture, etc.) includes or excludes it?" The possibility holds even for rules of specific analysis in the construction argument: "Should all readings (hearings, viewings) actually be organized by such and such principles? Does this or that reading actually organize the poem in a manner consonant with the rule of specific analysis at stake?" By and large it is an old point that what we find in a reading, hearing, or viewing determines the analysis and that the analysis reflects on future findings.

Over time, then, whether the argument occurs only in the mind of the critic or over generations of critics in the working out of a work of art, criticism achieves constructions very much as the law does in its development; and through a sensitive and minute interreaction of rule and case in a field of cases to which the process is responsible, the regulative principles of use, objectivity, and impersonality receive their progressive satisfaction. Nor does the arbitrariness of the starting points, if the starting points of criticism *are* arbitrary, diminish the effect.

3. Add now for the next characteristic of the live construction argument the fact that, as in the law, the conduct of the discussion rarely if ever occurs as though every decision on a formative rule had to make do in isolation from a welter of decisions on a welter of formative rules. It is this which makes criticism difficult as it makes law difficult: the multiplicity of law and the interrelatedness of law, the conflict of laws and the reinforcement of laws, as we seek to say "what the case is." A decision whether to apply a rule of exclusion and inclusion may depend upon the application of a rule of significance; a decision on a rule of specific analysis may depend upon a rule of relevance. No combination of dependencies is a priori disallowed. If sometimes, for example, it seems a mystery why in one form of poetry "truth" is irrelevant and in another (say a modern novel) the object functions as a truth-bearing symbol or

not at all, the reason lies not in the poem itself or the novel itself or in the words they use; it lies in the (changeable) decision to apply one *combination* of formative rules in certain sorts of artistically relevant cases and another combination in another.

Critical objects, then, exist in a skein of rules, always woven or unwoven in that skein, diminishing or increasing. So the critical object assumes in the conduct of discussion an elusive life of its own, always approached but never quite fixed until it dies for us and loses interest; while the rules, to the measure they become more subtle and more just, never finally cohere in the difficult case or entirely account for what may now carry the title, "the work of art itself."

If the construction argument in artistically relevant controversy is conducted by principles analogous to those employed in achieving constructions of cases in the law, then what ought to be expected happens: two separate arguments comprise the construction argument, and the outcome of each bears upon the other in such a way that some considerations that determine the course of one argument may be irrelevant to the other. For any legal structure establishes the law and applies it, uses the dispositions it makes of specific cases to determine the law and the law to determine the disposition of specific cases, while very different considerations may sometimes intervene to justify a legal rule and a disposition under that rule. So the two arguments that comprise the construction argument in artistically relevant controversy are arguments over formative rules and over the disposition of specific cases under those rules; yet they are not logically independent arguments. Arguments rising from efforts to achieve agreement in the first sense I call "formative arguments," and in the second sense, "performative arguments." Formative and performative arguments are both phases of the construction argument, and, obviously, the sort of stitching relationship described for rule and case hold here also.

So it is that endeavoring to institute some critical object in proper relation entails not only modifying, generating, and rejecting formative rules in their relationship to specific constructions in the arts but also, as a matter of fact, invoking the basic perspectives and values of the culture in which the argument occurs. That is why artistically relevant controversy of any depth continually explores the tap root through which art achieves a more than game-like relationship to human life. The very "purists" who construct critical objects in maximum disrelation to any "life value" and drop commitments to significance and expression without qualification, by attributing to the work of art values perhaps more appropriate to the vision of God than to the activity of men, thereby elect to justify their purism as "life values," no less human for going unacknowledged.[2]

Performative arguments, on the other hand, are in their immediate conduct "technical." They relate the complex of formative rules to the shifting, dubious particular case rather than opening out beyond the arts as such, as arguments over formative rules, pressed far enough, usually do. Hence formative and performative arguments can occur independently at certain crucial points, as criticism becomes "philosophical" and the construction argument "technical"; and upon this fact hang consequences of some explanatory value for understanding the facts of artistically relevant controversy.

So, for example, some accounts of what criticism should be propose that its business is purely "explicative"—to discover and state "what's there." Hence, it becomes a mystery why that "ulterior" criticism (philosophical, social, political), which a Blackmur thinks does so poor a "job of work," nevertheless actually affords a degree of illumination. The tap root aspect of the formative argument has been absorbed into the performative argument, then denied. But there need be no mystery if the "ulterior" criticism of philosophy or politics occupies a phase of the construction argument other than that performative phase which exclusively interests the working critic in the last phase of his criticism. On the other hand, the academicism that draws the fire of an "explicative" criticism itself sins by folding the performative argument into the formative, for doing so replaces the concrete work of construction with concepts and principles, history and gossip, stimulated by a cursory experience with art.

Consider, lastly, certain kinds of policy questions arising in criticism: whether, for example, poems are objects such that ethical considerations are or ought to be relevant in judging them. Philosophers often concern themselves with questions of that type. Those who believe ethical considerations to be proper argue that even the purist's way of insulating poetry from "life" makes ethical presuppositions (since to deny the relevance of ethics itself constitutes an ethical decision). Those who believe ethical considerations irrelevant to the judgment of poems or other works of art

[2] Clive Bell writes, "A good work of visual art carries a person who is capable of appreciating it out of life into ecstasy." He tells us that those who know can wring from lines and colors "an emotion more profound and far more sublime than any that can be given by the description of facts and ideas" (*Art* [London: Chatto and Windus, 1914], pp. 29–30). Such language is the language of mysticism for no accidental reasons. The "rules" for the construction of the knowledge of God, in so far as they have been formulated, consist also of a series of denials of reference, genesis, and "life values" in general, and likewise end with an ecstatic but ineffable experience.

seem, on the other hand, equally convincing: they note that a proper criticism introduces considerations in so far as those considerations possess artistic relevance, and only in so far as they do, and that artistic and ethical considerations are surely different things. Should we, like some participants in the ethical relevance controversy, reduce the difference between opposing sides to a matter of emphasis?

It is now possible to arbitrate the conflict without stopping it in mid-air. Both sides not only fail to distinguish formative from performative arguments, they deal with one as though dealing with the other. The proponent of ethical considerations observes that in deciding on formative rules (the formative arguments) ethical considerations always rise; and the person who denies their relevance discovers that in the performative argument, as he confronts a particular poem, only the relation of that poem to a set of formative rules is at stake—hence no ethical question. Does not the entire difference, therefore, rest upon an ambiguity with nothing left over for taste? One side assumes a consideration relevant in the formative argument thereby relevant in the performative; the other, a consideration irrelevant in the performative thereby irrelevant in the formative. Such fruitless discussions arise in the first place because each side imagines it must predicate or withhold the debated values of "the work of art itself." If the target of predication is indeed the work of art itself, then either moral considerations are relevant *to the work of art itself* or they are not, and a logical conflict appears.

III. The Critical Tradition

Talk of the object in proper relation makes sense, it is being claimed, because the construction argument is like the legal argument. Yet it will not do to have the construction argument an individual game for each critic, each critic with his own rules; for then artistically relevant controversy evaporates for real critics in real arguments. A public status needs to exist for the construction argument if critical objects are to have public status. Just as there exists prior to controversy a body of relevant legal materials and relevant legal criticism, so there must exist for the artistically relevant controversy a critical tradition. I must now indicate the sense in which such a "critical tradition" is here alleged to exist, and suggest how it works.

1. Two further regulatory principles, besides those of use, objectivity, and impersonality may now be described on the basis of the preceding section's discussion and extended to make explicit what I take to be the

force of an actual "critical tradition." The extension occurs in terms of an addition of a public domain of formative rules and construction cases.

Rule of Law I: To construct a critical object, paying due deference to the detailed structure of that object as well as to its total import, construe all proposals as though they were precedents for constructions past and constructions yet to come. This case is not the only case. There is a public domain of cases to be taken into account.

Rule of Law II: To construe the critical object as a precedent case in the construction process, construe those cases in virtue of a set of formative rules also in the public domain, both in their general formulation and in their general application to a public domain of cases.

Which cases are in the public domain cannot of course be established by anything quite so official as court records and case collections. Nevertheless, practically speaking, there are always the cases other critics have argued about; there are the publishers' lists, the museums full of pictures, the concert repertoires, which provide as good an initial field of data as anyone needs. To show that an object ought to be included among such data itself requires and receives reference to such data.

Construing cases "in virtue of a set of formative rules also in the public domain," likewise, requires no constitution of art, any more than determining which cases are in the public domain required a court register. This, too, is a question of the equipment of critics and the character of discussion about the cases people talk about, the paintings that are hung in museums, the compositions that are played, etc. The crucial expression is "in virtue of." "In virtue of a set of formative rules" means for every proposed change in the nature or use of a formative rule, or addition or subtraction of a rule, reasons must be shown. Among those reasons will be other "formative rules in the public domain."

Rules I and II are fairly weak requirements for the conduct of the construction argument, but they allow us to perceive the functioning of actual critical traditions in that phase of the artistically relevant controversy called here the construction argument. A critical tradition is a set of formative rules applying to a class of cases, the set and the class both in the public domain—hence of a class of established constructions and their justifications.

2. An earlier discussion of interpretation and description, showed, or tried to show, why the detailed structure of the critical object, let alone the object as a whole, could not be taken as a datum. Now I am adding that a detailed structure and a general import exist in a critical tradition, that the existence of a critical tradition makes construction neither a more

or less arbitrary interpretative process on one hand nor a more or less fixed process of description.

Consider, for a reminder, even the presumably tradition-independent characteristic of internal consistency. Suppose someone in a play says, "John just walked out the front door," and all the characters act as though they agree but we the audience never see anyone going through what serves as the front door; or imagine hearing one character say, "John went through the front door," and another nod in agreement while observing that John went through the back door. Perhaps indeed an egregious forgetfulness has been responsible for "inconsistencies"; but, obviously, given any sort of respect at all for the dramatist, the critic will rather seek to locate some tradition—say, that of Ionesco—in which this sort of thing makes very good sense indeed.

Given a failure, however, given the lack of a pertinent critical tradition, the construction argument ends. There follows the uncertainty and confusion observable in recent encounters with some of John Cage's music, perhaps, or those peculiar assemblages of assorted junk moved by the breeze or an electric motor and passing themselves off as sculpture in motion. The point is not to defend status quo tastes on principle; perhaps changes in the rule of relevance will in time make them "art." But until a critical tradition comes into existence, reasons for constructing them one way or the other—as "music" or "sculpture," for example—carry no weight; and their possible "expressive" values seem to lack artistic point, where all sorts of things other than art are "expressive."

In sum, where whatever one makes of a critical object suffices, the very meaning of being a critic—*or* an artist—goes. Having passed beyond a legal tradition we have passed beyond the possibility of legally relevant reasons and constructions. Having passed beyond a critical tradition, we have passed beyond the possibility of artistically relevant constructions.

3. Yet there are many critical traditions. How, then, can the appeal to a critical tradition grant to critical objects the public status required? Leaving most of the discussion for the claims and reasons questions, in the case of divergent, independent, and semi-independent traditions critics are no worse off than lawyers, and probably better off, even without comparing the plurality of legal jurisdictions.

Critical "traditions" in virtue of which artistically relevant characteristics are instituted for specific objects are, for purposes of artistically relevant controversy, not closed and self-sufficient affairs any more than are the legal "traditions" in virtue of which certain classes of events within a legal system are taken as negligence cases or otherwise. As new cases arise so does a positive necessity for the remodeling of the formative rules and constructions that define the tradition. So argument is possible even in the extreme case when, in Tradition P, "x" has the characteristic "r" and, in Tradition Q, "x" has the characteristic "not-r." What shall be asserted for "x"? The rules of law control the controversy and press the argument to cases agreed upon, to commitments shared, in general toward the giving of reasons with a wider suasion than the reasons advanced originally in terms of the starting position. Criticism, like law, uses differences to open traditions, not to close traditions off.

Further, critical argument has a positive advantage over legal argument, even when traditions prove unyielding in their claims. Sense-making strategies that set the argument to rest still exist, of a sort not obviously available for the legal discussion. For example:

A. Both parties to argument may acknowledge that their disagreement seems irreducible and extol the richness of the work of art that functions so magnificently in two worlds. Read in one way, Hamlet is mad; viewed in another, sane—*that* is the genius of Shakespeare. Viewed in one way, the object is a duck; in another, a rabbit—such is the ingenuity of the draftsman.

B. On the other hand, one party or the other, or both, unwilling to accept the combination, may cry "Fault!" *in the work of art,* fault for a structure so inadequately articulated that it provides equally for what look like incompatible positions.

C. If one party finds an object "meaningless" or "empty"—if, in effect, it can "make" nothing of that object—then, if the other can, the party who cannot may acknowledge the greater utility for a class of works of a certain sort, of a foreign tradition. Sometimes, for example, people may acquire strange arts or strange art forms; they then "extend their sympathies" or "acquire a new language," with no sense of defeat.

D. Lastly, when all such tactics fail, the logic of the construction argument still has a recourse unavailable to the construction argument in the law. What was thought to be "one" work of art may be taken as a blind for more than one. The artist, both parties may agree, has performed a near miracle, like a man who utters a string of sounds that work as different sentences in different languages. Each tradition retires with its own prize.

In sum, the existence of diversity in actual criticism, of precedent and of procedure, leads, in an appropriately conducted controversy, to a broadening of "sensitivity" and the enrichment of criticism instead of to frustration and an infinite series of "subjective" interpretations, as might at first sight be imagined. Less bedeviled by the practical need of sacrificing one interest to another, artistically relevant controversy exhibits a greater rather than a lesser rationality than legal criticism, even though the persistence of multiple strands promotes rather than restricts the growth of the practice for legal controversy also.

I have tried to show here how critics "do" poetry or sculpture or music or what have you. I suggested that they "do" these things through the regulative principles of use, impersonality, and objectivity in their application through the rules of law, that in virtue of such regulative principles critics engage in arguments over formative rules and constructions. Critical objects now as the termini of controlled arguments, hence "construction," constitute what critics take exceptions to, not responses. The first step in the establishment of an answer to the reference question alternative to the normal version's has been taken. Yet I think that ceasing the inquiry at this point would slough over an essential obligation. It is not enough to say that critical arguments are constructions in a genuine argument of a certain sort. It is necessary to say of what they are constructions, and in what sense constructions of whatever they are constructions. For here there are genuine alternatives, depending on how far one has determined to push or restrict the context of consumption for the arts and how far one seriously wishes to account for artistically relevant controversy as it is practiced rather than as the normal version may demand it.

Chapter 5

The Relevance of the Created Object

The construction argument might indeed proceed as though critics were an autonomous community while the artists turned out grist for critical mills. Indeed, by a proper selection of formative rules self-centered critics might ensure a certain relevance to the activity of art as it swept along beneath them—a relevance which, however, was historically determined chance and quite revocable. On such terms, critics might even undertake to find out "what the artist had in mind." They would now be playing the "what did the artist have in mind?" game. Perhaps later they will play something else. They are consumers—the principle that determines their action is their taste, their taste socialized perhaps, but still their taste.

Yet it seems plain that such a picture misrepresents the "good and responsible" critics who are parties to the construction argument. They do not see themselves doing justice to their critical object in so far as it suits their purposes, or defining justice by their particular purposes—they take "justice to" as the essence of their game and conceive their constructions justified, so to speak, semantically. To be sure, a creeping professionalism may sometimes submerge the critic's conception of his relation to a wider enterprise within which he functions, just as professionalism in the law, or philosophy for that matter, may sometimes lead people to talk, or even behave, as though the law (or philosophy) were a strictly autonomous game, nobody's business but their own. Yet when the chips are down the critic of the arts, at least, does not think that it is his role to legislate what the object shall be in anything like the sense in which chess players, for whatever psychological reasons, attribute to an oddly shaped object the properties of a queen. He acknowledges the suzerainty of art; he claims, at least, to respect the object of his attentions. The difficulty is to say what all this means. For given the presumptions of a context of consumption, to acknowledge the demands of art and accord them the respect coming to them becomes a problem in principle to which the normal version dogma of the work of art itself provides the only possible answer:

criticism is at once artistically relevant and autonomous because its objects are not plain old art objects but "the work of art itself." Critics consume special objects—*artistically relevant ones.*

Assuming that criticism neither plays games with counters nor even with works of art themselves, the task of the present chapter becomes to explicate what the dependence of the construction argument upon an enterprise "outside" itself might mean. The import of that dependence, and finally of the "objectivity" of statements about works of art, constitutes the relevance of the created object.

I. The Created Object

Suppose, as in these pages, that one does not assume the authenticity of the normal version's credentials and doubts the dogma of the work of art itself? Then it becomes possible to accept the objects presented to criticism naïvely, in the sense that critics accept them on actual occasions from art dealers, publishers, writers, fellow critics, and the like—which is as an object already entangled in a myriad of involvements, part of a history, with a past and a future.

The whole point is to press the obvious. Whatever they may say, critics know very well that publishers, exhibitors, artists do not give away their products to the critic to be dealt with according to the rule of right unless they have prior reason to believe that the critic will exert his right only in a way appropriate to those objects. Editors do not normally request reviews of the work of art itself. They load their request; they ask for a book review that will say, among other things, what the writer has accomplished as writers accomplish things. Authors do not pare their nails, as Joyce has famously misobserved; they bite them, waiting for the verdict, partly for fear the whole assessment may focus on the wrong things. Objects are offered to criticism specifically as paintings, books, sculptures, music, and unless this is effectively done the critic has great difficulty "making something" of the presented object. Accordingly, while ignorance may be prized as a condition for excitement, and knowledge of the arts in which the presented objects occur dreaded for lessening kicks, the presented object becomes a critical object, an object to be instituted in proper relation given the resources of the critic, on a practical understanding shared by all parties to the practical critical transaction: that what has been presented for criticism constitutes itself a complex construction, with a pertinent career both before and after the critic gets it—a "created object."

Hence what makes a work of art a "created object" in that practical transaction among critic, artist, and intermediaries for which created objects are relevant is hardly that somebody happens to have "created" it—the "creation" over with, a merely causal item or bit of gossip, and the finished object dead in its tracks. That is the normal-version theory of created objects, which makes the amazing achievement that such objects represent a near miracle. What makes a created object for the construction argument is the construction already "present" in the object before the critic.

All people who love the arts have had the confirming experience. The work of art seems to ask to be treated in one way rather than another, in view of its own ends. It asks to be searched out almost as another human being asks to be searched out, to be understood, not fancied. How could a mere thing have an end or advance a claim? The dogma of the work of art itself did not fail because it saw the work of art alive and waiting for the critic; it failed because it did not see that condition as a consequence of dealing with a created object qua created object. Hearers, listeners, viewers are obligated to hear, listen, and see the work of art as hearers, listeners, and viewers of constructions that men have made in an enterprise men are making; if they receive them as only dead weight the very critical role collapses. That is why expression theories never stay dead and artists insist on their need to communicate.

In sum, critical objects are constructions of constructions. That is the final answer to the reference question and the bond that connects criticism to art. They are constructions of those prior constructions to which the critic addresses his comments and which I shall call "performances." The context of consumption dropped, to say what a performance is, is to say what a created object is; and to point more adequately to created objects qua performances must be our task now.

1. Gestures, an old analogue for critical objects, are a species of performance, in that if one asks what has the fellow done the answer is that he has insulted the lady or indicated his affection; but all he has done is wave his arm or tip his hat; and it is this "act" upon which the critic of social behavior comments. On the other hand, of course, if created objects are performances (not just objects that happen to have been created) they are free-er of a particular context and function than gestures, and part of a special domain of performances in a way gestures are not. I tip my hat to assert a particular relationship to a lady, having a particular end in view, and the lady is the proper recipient of that gesture. But a performance qua performance of the sort one would call a "created object" is not meant for any particular individual in any particular

situation, to secure an end. There it is—for an unstipulated audience; performances own a more general status. And the artist who puts on the performance is linked with other artists in a way that does not link the gesturer with other gesturers. There are no professional hat-tippers as there are sculptors, no professional gesturers as there are artists. But the existence of created objects as performances is more important here than their differences from other performances.

2. As performances, created objects differ from the critic's constructions in that the critic in his construction does not, except incidentally, "put on a performance." He presents no object-in-a-construction, as the artist does, or the publisher, or the art dealer; he offers a construction, neither an "interpretation" nor "description," which can be translated into other languages, reformulated, digested, criticized (e.g., for logical inconsistency) as objects-in-a-construction—performances—cannot be.

Another way of putting the difference between the artist's and critic's constructions, "creation," and "criticism" considers the objects with which critic and artist each works. Works of art—created objects—are not the "media" of criticism, unless there is something drastically wrong with the criticism; but the objects with which artists work are fairly called their media. The artist uses material "in a meaningful way"; he makes the media "say" whatever it is capable of "saying" and, given his limitations of skill, whatever he "wants"—in some sense of "wants"—to say. The medium functions as the vehicle for the performance; it does not direct or constrain the artist as the performance directs or constrains the critic, provided that the critic has not succeeded in becoming a normal version critic.

3. Most important, to grasp the nature of the created object as "performance" it is necessary to understand the created object as existing through its constitutive relationships in an artistically relevant matrix—the actual and logically relevant environment of the object that the critic does not invent although he may share in its development. Gestures have such environments, of course, although of a different type. The critic needs to know the relevant environment; but this is not merely to repeat the old point that critical objects exist as such in a field of critical objects and must be "properly" instituted therein. That "propriety" is now the problem, the relationship of the critic-in-his-tradition to an "on-going" enterprise, however problematic, which he has encountered. Hence, instead of "field," I use the expression "matrix" to indicate a moving, generating process in which the artist makes use of what others have done and affects still others, a process in which live problems arise that artists

generate and seek to settle. One would never be tempted to think of the matrix for performances as Eliot thinks of the field for criticism, as though all its objects were spread out in an "ideal" order. Temporality is of the essence. There is such a thing as a relevant art history, in which artists are involved through the production of their work and in virtue of which they perform.

Moreover, the artistically relevant matrix in which created objects possess the characteristics they do has two phases or parts, as I shall propose in order to make the notion of a domain of created objects more concrete. It consists of a "matrix of art" and a "matrix of society." A "matrix of art" designates that historically developing body of rules, implicit or explicit, in virtue of which artists do art and also that body of the accomplished art from which they take off and in which they find significance as they consider and develop their projects. The artist works in some portion of the matrix of art as the critic does in a suitable critical tradition. "Matrix of society" designates that developing net of considerations and problems in which artistic considerations and problems arise, the enveloping and interfusing society in all its complexity of attitudes, beliefs, and emotions from which art springs. Obviously, there are many societies.

In his tradition, the critic explores, organizes, and recreates those matrices. He has no direct access to them. He knows only that neither he nor other critics have invented them and that perhaps they do not seem the same to him as to the artist. Nevertheless, he strives to take those matrices into account; he sees actions as performances within them.

4. In viewing an action as a performance, the critic of course only views physical phenomena. Artistically relevant characteristics accrue to performances in virtue of the way certain physical characteristics occur in a matrix of art and of society.[1] Those "artistically relevant characteristics" are the "values" of which critics are always discoursing—"values" as when people refer to "the values" of a painting without committing themselves necessarily for or against. Physical characteristics, I shall then say, possess values in a matrix of art and of society. The "same" characteristic may have varying values according to how it appears in the matrix, but every value of every performance must have a physical characteristic to show for it. A point of some interest follows.

[1] Literary objects have physical characteristics also, of course; only, here between the physical characteristics and the artistic performance the rules of a natural grammar mediate, so that it is more convenient to deal with poems as performances in virtue of linguistic characteristics. With this understanding I shall, for simplicity's sake, talk of "physical characteristics" instead of "physical and/or linguistic characteristics."

Physical descriptions of even the most elaborate and complete kind cannot state artistically relevant characteristics ("values"). Values require just the kind of descriptions which in fact performances receive and which trouble philosophers: description in an "esthetic" discourse wherein physical characteristics and structures (groups of such characteristics) are said to possess "elegance," "lucidity," "dynamism," and so on through the dictionary with the only qualification that where the dictionary defines such a term physically that definition will not do. People now talk of "esthetic values."

The normal version, having taken due note that physical descriptions do not as such provide for "esthetic values," and depriving itself on principle of any matrix within which to define such values, transforms them into "reports" of what transpires in the psyche. But if the present account of values as values of performances holds, then, whatever the ultimate accounting for secondary qualities, the significance of such values and of the language that expresses them turns no more mysterious than how a card may have the value of trump in a game of pinochle. That clubs are trump does not even *aim* to report psychic events, no matter how often a peculiar mental condition accompanies trump.

There is now a sense in which works of art may properly be said by critics to "have" their values "independently" of the critic, for the proper locus of the work of art itself lies in the performance. Only, in the performance, it ceases to be "the work of art itself"; it becomes the work of art in a relevant matrix of art and a relevant matrix of society.

5. Created objects as performances in such matrices provide, therefore, the ultimate grounds on which values—"esthetic values"—are correctly predicated by critics of created objects. If they do indeed provide those grounds, then the relevant characteristics of a presented object will in fact be determined, both for the critic in the construction argument and for the presenter of the performance, by much the same kind of rules and decisions controlling the artist's activity. Regardless of what weight the possessive case deserves when the work of art has been identified as the *artist's* performance, to what would the critic appeal if he wanted to give evidence that he had rightly attributed a property to some critical object, except the matrix of art or society? His tradition provides a way of seeing and dealing with those matrices; and though the relation is nothing so simple as mirror reflection, the characteristics the critic identifies are characteristics of the sort that concern the artist, as artist. In any effort to show how performances acquire artistically relevant characteristics for the critic to manage, the very convertibility of those characteristics from

characteristics asserted in constructions to characteristics asserted of performances, and back again, will testify to the depth of the involvement of criticism in the artistic enterprise.

I doubt that it would be necessary to make such a point were it not for the normal version presumption of a disparity between consumption and production.

II. Formal Values

The distinctive "values" of works of art which critics employ to describe those works, are commonly separated into "formal" and "nonformal" values. To be sure, critics designate in what seem like most esoteric ways all sorts of things as "forms," "formal values," or possessors of "formal characteristics"; and no one can discern any physically denotable characteristic common in a proper and nontrivial way to the objects so designated. "*What* form?" the skeptic inquires. And how is it that so-called experts disagree whether an object "has" some "form" or "formal" value, whatever that might mean? It is not surprising that when critics begin to talk of "nonformal" values they become more unintelligible, if anything. Nevertheless, I would like to suggest, critics are not necessarily talking nonsense when they distinguish the values of works of art between those which are "formal" and those which are not. Examining the distinctive values of art works as values, not of the works of art themselves, but of performances, will show how specific criticism can indeed possess a subject matter capable of making claims upon it, and clarify the sense in which the language of formal and nonformal value has a semantical dimension. First, "form" and "formal" value:

"Forms," then, for present purposes, are physical characteristics or sets of such characteristics regarded as having formal values or as capable of having them. When the arts change, forms once thought to have considerable formal value may become dead or neutral. When the process goes too far the object lapses into a historical curiosity. Conversely, historical curiosities may develop unexpected formal values. Obviously, "formal value" is itself vague. However, formal values designate those values usually distinguished as "formal values," the ones most easily associated with "the way" things are put together, "the way" things are said, "the way" acts are performed. One talks of things as put together, said, or performed, in perhaps a "fresh," "elegant," "powerful," "clear," "muddy," "harmonious," or "abrupt" way.

1. Physical characteristics, I propose, then, acquire formal values in the arts as modes of dress and manners of behavior acquire the values of

fashion (which, of course, does *not* mean that art lacks values other than those of fashion). "Fashions" are physical characteristics to which certain "values" adhere, notably the value of being "fashionable." As fashionableness and its associated values accrue to fashion in the matrix of fashion (which a little sociology soon identifies), so formal values accrue to the formal structures of performances in a matrix of art. The force of the analogy will be partly familiar from the earlier discussion of the work of art in proper relation. How is it that "form" and "formal values" are so often so hard to see? For the same reason that nobody understands a fashion qua fashion simply by regarding the configurations of clothing that is supposed to be in or out of fashion.

The man sees the color, the shape, the size of the object as well as his wife does. He "likes" or "dislikes" it, just as his wife does. "Of course!" she says. "He just doesn't understand fashion." What is it that he does not understand but that his wife does? If he persists in thinking he has missed a quality of the object, like "redness," he is in trouble; he will conclude that either the quality is special and mysterious (like "significant form," in some renditions) and not for his eyes or that the whole thing is a fraud (as philosophers are tempted, hearing people talk of "formal values"). But the primary fact is his missing of last year's fashions, which he missed for the same reason he missed the fashion of the year before last. He has looked at "the hat itself"; he has overlooked the whole fabric of relationships in which the hat relates to a preceding year's (and, of course, to a number of other things as well, such as the elite who wear the hats). Putting aside such considerations as who wears the hats, considering the problem of fashion from the point of view of the style setters and promoters, there is never a possibility of explaining the year's fashions independently of those the year before.

Form and formal values in arts, as in fashion, are in that way completely arbitrary: one sees the continuity with and departure from a predecessor or, when experience has deepened sufficiently, with a successor. How does one get into the dance from the outside? One talks oneself into it; one is persuaded into it, manipulated into it, as women are into fashion, or people are into any language. Then one "gets" it. The mistake is to think, as unsympathetic males think, that the arbitrariness as such of the fashions of this year and the year before preclude significance to the relationships among those fashions. Given that arrangements of objects become at any time "fashions" in virtue of their relationships to preceding arrangements (and "unfashionable" in virtue of their relationships to successors, or, perhaps, "fashionable" again) it is possible to see how "casual," "formal," "plain," "showy," and the like are predicable as "fashion-values" of objects that otherwise seem, and are, utterly incongruous:

through a *shift* from one fashion to another perceived in a domain of shifts by a properly sensitivized and conditioned organism.[2] So with the formal values of the arts: they exist as the *values* of performances in virtue of the continuities and discontinuities of performances with other performances; and they are perceived as "formal" precisely because they characterize physical characteristics that would lack such values outside the matrix of art.

The formal values of art are also like those of fashion in a respect not intimated earlier in the discussion of the work of art itself. Not only do created objects as performances possess certain formal values in relation to other performances, but also, as in fashion, it is possible and legitimate to assert at time "t" that a given performance actually possesses certain formal values rather than other possible ones in the complex and changing matrix of art. For to the question, "Does something possess the values of fashion, and what are those values?" one answers that indeed it does and they are such and such, *regardless* of the fact that, obviously, the object will not be fashionable next year and that the same physical characteristics would have borne different values in years before. The assertion of fashion is justified by present reference to present performances.

Similarly, I propose, performances—the objects of critical constructions—may be attributed certain values in terms of a present condition, the present (at time of attribution) state of the matrix of art in which the performance occurs. This is obviously so for contemporary art but the same observation holds for a Rembrandt or Praxiteles. If I ask what are the formal values of either, I do not mean what *were* those formal values in Holland or in Greece, regardless of the connection between today's artistic conditions and those of an earlier date, or whether those conditions ought in some sense to be incorporated within present critical traditions. What those values were is an historical question. Nor do I mean what *will* those values be a hundred years from now, which is some other kind of question. I mean to inquire after the values that the Rembrandt or the Praxiteles possesses now, which is to say, in the condition of the matrix of art within which present artists work and to which, with whatever emphases, critics refer when they take the work before them as a presented object. And this is not a matter of history at all, not even of current events, but of the Rembrandt or the Praxiteles as a performance now going on.

Cultural relativism swamps the performing of the created object in the

[2] Something of the sort may partly explain how the "peculiar" language of poets acquires its texture and richness, its character and power, quite apart from what it "says."

mere fact that it has been performed, is being performed, and perhaps will be. But the proper analogy for predicating formal values of performances is not with historical predication but with legal or scientific predications. There, too, it is true enough that something was thought to possess a legal value or a truth value, or is thought to possess one, or will be thought to possess one. But it is also true that, asking whether something is indeed legal or indeed true, we assess the relation of the object to the state of the legal or scientific matrix in which we are involved.

To know, then, what are indeed the values of a created object—what those values "really" are—the answer has to be found in the state of the arts at the time of judgment. And this is as it is in fashion.

2. I do not, of course, deny that there are also significant disanalogies between the way formal values accrue to performances in a matrix of art and the way the values of fashion accrue to performances in a context of fashion. So, for example, characteristically, fashion defines itself in relation to its immediate predecessor, the preceding fashion. The formal values of artistic performances, on the other hand, while they include rather special values that are indeed determined by relationship to an immediately preceding performance, include values determined in relationship to the whole domain of artistic performances. Hence the difference between the formal values of art and the value of fashion performances does not lie, as may be supposed, in the freedom of artistically relevant forms from "arbitrary" conditions but in the enormously greater range of conditions for formal performance in art. In both cases, the arbitrary is the necessary. But there is no comparing the depths and richness of the matrix of fashion with the matrix of art. In the condition of the matrix of art at any given time great stretches of work may be, and are, presupposed in that anyone who wants to understand the conditions for the performing of art must understand them. So "conventions" extended and differentiated, developed and projected, ought to be expected to lend to performances in the arts, as the analogue does to performances in language, the possibility of subtleties and distinctions otherwise unmanageable.

It may be claimed that the present exposition of how values accrue to performance in a matrix of art is not a *sufficient* explanation of how values are generated in artistic performances but only of how values are generated in the performances of fashion. Yet, of course, I have not sought a sufficient explanation of formal values in art performances, only of their language-like or "formal" aspects. And just the same qualification holds for fashions. Subliminal instincts may conceivably guide fashion, but that is not relevant to what makes the outcome distinctively "fashionable." Why the performances of art are not simply conventional even on the formal side must wait briefly for the discussion of performance in a matrix of society.

In any event, one ought not overextend the distinctions between art and fashion. There is no intrinsic reason why the concerns of "fashion" may not approximate art. What Baudelaire called a "serious devotion to the frivolous" [3] is by no means a logical impossibility; nor did he necessarily talk nonsense in terming dandyism "the last gleam of heroism in times of decadence." [4] Extending fashion to the center of life against all use and function absorbs life into style, he thought, and "defeats" nature. All this has an old-fashioned ring, which goes to show that making heavy distinctions between art and fashion may only be a new fashion.

The second objection to overplaying the difference comes from the side of art. For if the values of fashion are above all those associated with "novelty" and "freshness," even those are not nearly so trivial for the arts as may be supposed. (Neither, of course, are the values of being "plain" or "showy," or the like, trivial; their importance goes uncontested.) A high valuation on novelty and freshness emphasizes the expansion of the arts; their devaluation by an academic taste for "eternal" values tends to emphasize the stablization of the arts, which is death on art that is neither derivative nor irrelevant to the times. Hence a criticism that rejects on principle the fashion values of novelty and freshness as merits of a performance worth considering, will have carried the artistically relevant controversy a fair distance from the matrix of art toward archaeology. Perhaps the easy assumption of the inherent superiority of the latest in an onward and upward progress of the arts damages both art and criticism. Still, an esthetic puritanism practiced on the fashion values is at least as deleterious, and kills a large part of the fun for the sake of preserving the rites of the work of art itself.

III. Nonformal Values

Nonformal values, like formal values, are artistically relevant characteristics of things or events in a certain matrix. If "being a picture of the battle of Waterloo" is artistically irrelevant, then "being a picture of the battle of Waterloo" does not constitute a nonformal value of the work.

In general, the class of nonformal values is extensionally equivalent to

[3] Charles Baudelaire, *The Essence of Laughter* (New York: Meridian, 1956), p. 48.

[4] *Ibid.*, p. 49.

some subset of the class of "life values." "Sexy," for example, is not ordinarily considered a nonformal (in our sense) value of a created object qua artistic performance. But critics pronounce novels or plays "insightful" or "superficial" and not as though they were doing so according to some private set of rules, but as judgments about relations somehow true of the object. Similarly, paintings are sometimes supposed to convey tidings of "reality," although it is rarely clear what those tidings are. Music allegedly exhibits "greatness" or "religiosity" or "tenderness" or, perhaps, the value of a great but unspecifiable "momentousness" or "import." In fact, it is hard to imagine a lexicon that would sharply distinguish formal from nonformal predicates, once artistically irrelevant predicates are excluded from the class of nonformal predicates. It seems hopeless even to attempt such a lexicon, remembering that we might equally well say that the sculpture "exhibits" an intricate form as that it communicates the character of intricateness. Nevertheless, I shall urge that the distinction amounts to more than a matter of language or, in some vague way, of "emphasis," since it is rooted in the condition that created objects have as performances.

What follows is an account of nonformal values of works of art seen as characteristics of performances *through* a matrix of art but *in* a matrix of society.

1. That nonformal values accrue to works of art through their formal values—that is, through their characteristics in a matrix of art—provides the basis for a distinction which has *both* formal and nonformal values artistically relevant. I refer to the obvious, if cloudy, truth that works of art have their "meaning," "say" what they say, "communicate" what they do, by their forms. In contradistinction, some commercials, not being "works of art," "mean," "say," or "communicate" what they do in forms that aspire only to make their messages the more acceptable and the harder to forget. Commercials are Platonic art, with weak minds. But artistic performances do not have their forms for the packaging and their messages for the content; their nonformal values are not "content" in this sense at all but the values of values. Rudolf Arnheim has written,

> Some painters of the nineteenth century insist on this conception of the world [that] things are not stable in their mutual relationships but are rather in a state of constant change . . . by gathering within the frame of the picture figures that seem to have little or nothing to do with each other. [The relationships among the figures in Degas' "Cotton Market in New Orleans"] may appear scattered over the canvas at random, but again it is only by the standards of an older order. . . . They cease to appear accidental

and become compelling and unchangeable as soon as we recognize that the lack of a common purpose, the atomization of society in an age of individualism, is precisely the theme of these pictures.[6]

"The atomization of society in an age of individualism" in the above interpretation constitutes a "nonformal" value of the picture; figures having "little or nothing to do with each other" represents a formal value. Though we have yet to see how it is possible, clearly "within the framework of the picture" the picture has the nonformal value it does "through" the formal value, and only through that formal value along with any other formal values that might be found. And it is possible to generalize the distinction between formal and nonformal values in a way pertinent to the construction argument: because formal values have values of a higher order under certain kinds of yet unstated circumstances, artistic performances may fairly be said to "mean," "say," "convey," or "refer." The distinction between formal and nonformal values is a distinction relative to value level in the analysis of the values of any performance. Performances are said to "mean," "say," "convey," or "refer" in so far as values are being distinguished as values *of* values; but there is no intrinsic reason why any artistically relevant characteristic ("value") may not function as a "formal" value for any performance, where "formal" values are discriminated in the manner described in Section II. The "second order" value constitutes what the "first order value" signifies.

Hence, an understanding even of literature in terms of formal and nonformal values is within reach. "Form" in literature, that is, need not mean something as package-like as novel form and, hence, the "nonformal" something as content-like as doctrine. Dostoevsky's views of the Russian Orthodox Church in *The Idiot,* for example, would constitute his starting point, without either formal or nonformal value as such. The specific way that view was worked in the novel to produce certain effects—certain tensions, certain resolutions, certain character combinations—would now constitute the "formal values" of the novel. (Of course, he makes use of much besides his orthodoxy.) Yet the use of the materials of religious orthodoxy to establish certain kinds of novelistically relevant values—the "formal values" of his novel—might well be held to illuminate "the condition of man." The "condition of man" would now constitute a nonformal value of the novel, one of the things the novel "means," etc. But if a novel contained a lot of talk about "the condition of man," that talk would not as such constitute a nonformal value of the

[6] Rudolf Arnheim, "Accident and the Necessity of Art," *Journal of Aesthetics and Art Criticism,* Vol. XVI (Sept. 1957).

novel any more than would Dostoevsky's talk of the Russian Orthodox Church. One would want to know how the novelist used that talk of "the condition of man" and what he wanted to "say" by means of it. The relation of formal to nonformal value is the relation of use, within a certain context.

"Formalism," then, is either a misunderstanding based on a confusion of nonformal characteristics with materials themselves artistically neutral, or a prejudice against using certain kinds of materials, or a prejudice against higher level values in any performance.

2. I have spoken of the relation of "use" within a certain context. That context is, of course, the matrix of society. Nonformal values accrue to created objects having formal values, within a matrix of society.

Everything depends upon differentiating the proposition that created objects exist as such in a matrix of society from the banality that social conditions "produce" all works of art and that works of art "reflect" them. It is the former proposition that is held here to illuminate nonformal (and, indeed, formal) values; the banality is indeed irrelevant to the critical construction of performances. Only the confusion makes the thesis seem coarse and unresponsive to the condition and function of art.

Yet the basic phenomenon is actually quite familiar. People are married; property is exchanged; flags are saluted. These are all social performances not just in the weak sense that social conditions cause them. They have the significance they do—the "values" they have—as functionings in and of "society." To emphasize that that same situation holds for created objects I have adopted the pedantry of referring to created objects as existing "in a matrix of society" rather than more simply as "social performances," which, given normal version predilections, would suggest merely the genetic point. But social performances all involve physical acts which become "performances" only if certain specific steps are undertaken, steps that are "right" in certain "matrices" that define the proper "formalities," steps that, in virtue of those formalities, sum up to produce, in a given society, values—"non-formal" values—of the most surprising significance.

The society in which facts exist as artistic performances, in which they possess the formal and nonformal values they do, is any group functioning as an entity for the purposes of that act. In art, "humanity" is sometimes taken as the society for which the performances of art exist. "Humanity" is a possible society; so is a clique. Whether the created objects (of art, of course) are "universal" or not is no issue now. In any

worth of the performance, not what the performance is, but what values it may have.

3. How is it possible for a certain arrangement of formal values to mean so much, to exhibit those ultimate and terminal affairs I have called nonformal values? The same way in which it is *possible* for that set of dances to have the values it does in the Indian celebration. Obviously, the facts of biology and psychology are always necessary. Yet, surely, their necessity cannot account for what is done with them. Many are the dances, fewer the steps. Some try to handle the fact that arrangements of physical characteristics may carry a profound import by supposing that works of art designate values by having those values themselves. But the difficulty is just how objects do "have" values. It has become almost truistic that even representational values, assuming them artistically relevant, are hardly to be dismissed as structural isomorphisms recognized for what they are—that "isomorphisms," useful though they may be in explaining on one level how objects "have" values, themselves constitute complex constructions. Taking society, therefore, not as a web of custom to put on and cast off almost at will, but to include the constitutive rules for feeling and apperception that mark an inner membership in a society, one says that the performances of art acquire their nonformal depth through the way they use the matrix of the society in which they occur. Formal structures do not need to "mean" the inexpressible and near inexpressible nonformal things they do, semantically, as it were. They may mean in the same way war "means" death. They may in virtue of a matrix of society touch and move the strings of human personality in this time and this place. In one sense, therefore, it is correct to say that works of art mean what they are and are what they mean.

But what are they? That is the burden of the construction argument; and only concrete knowledge can afford an answer, knowledge of human beings and their art. Let a responsible and self-conscious critic testify to the point as he speaks for the "ultimate meaning" of *Hamlet:*

> The anagoge, or ultimate meaning of the play, can only be sought through a study of the analogical relationships within the play and between the world of Denmark and the traditional cosmos. There are the analogous actions of all the characters, pointing to the action which is the underlying substance of the play. There are analogous father-son relationships, and the analogous man-woman relationships. There are the analogous stories, or chains of events, the fated results of the characters' actions. And stretching beyond the play in all directions are the analogies between Denmark and England; Denmark and Rome under "the mightiest Julius"; Hamlet's stage and Shakespeare's stage; the theater and life. Because Shakespeare takes all

> these elements as "real," he can respect their essential mystery, not replacing them with abstractions, nor merely exploiting their qualities as mood-makers, nor confining us in an artificial world with no exit. He asks us to sense the unity of his play through the direct perception of these analogies; he does not ask us to replace our sense of a real and mysterious world with a consistent artifact, "the world of the play." [12]

That is precisely it. Seeking that "ultimate meaning" or "anagoge" that is the central nonformal value of the play drives the seeker to that matrix of society in which that ultimate meaning or anagoge functions as a performance. One has to know the nature of the "world of Denmark and the traditional cosmos." "Stretching beneath the play in all directions are the analogies between Denmark and England," and one has to know them. Presenting such analogies presents the "meaning" of the play. In an appropriate sense of the word, one "discovers" that meaning: for the play has its meaning in "a real and mysterious world," not as a "consistent artifact" presented to viewers, to tourists. This is the understanding on which informal predicates become manageable, nor does it in any way imply transcendent powers.

And now a specific class of nonformal predicates gains intelligibility. Most people feel, but find hard to explain, the importance and the relevance of calling works of art "spontaneous," "authentic," "contrived," "false," "unreal," and the like. The point is that such predicates work directly to say something about the relationship of a created object to its relevant society, to "the constitutive rules for feeling and a perception that mark an inner membership in a society." They are at once esoteric and implausible only if you drop out the performance and consider "the consistent artifact." How indeed could a mere tourist, as tourist, say whether a dance was "authentic"? More important: why *should* he? Assertions of authenticity or of seriousness say whether or not the life of a society comes off in a performance, and how effectively it does. Nor is there anything more, or less, mysterious here than the judgment that certain gestures "express" a man or group or disguise that man or group from himself or others. Once again, for art as well as gesture, the verifying criterion consists in knowledge of actions and of men in their worlds. The incredibility of judgments of authenticity and the like comes from the endeavor to apply such judgments to the work of art itself.

4. It ought now to be plainly visible why the works of art presented for criticism are granted by critics to possess the nonformal values they

[12] Francis Fergusson, *The Idea of a Theater* (Garden City, N.Y.: Doubleday, 1953), pp. 152–53.

do. The same considerations hold that held for the acknowledgment of formal values. That a presented object "possesses" a nonformal characteristic means not that it once possessed such a value, nor that in the future it will possess such a value, nor even that now it possesses that value for some people. That is all history. The force of asserting a nonformal value lies in the analysis of that value within a selected matrix of society, the matrix of society within which the judgment is made. That selection constitutes a decision: it is the best, the "right" selection, on whatever grounds. Because of it, the critic can, within limits, presume to speak of the "real" or "true" significance of the object given him to criticize.

IV. The Rule of Respect

Embedded in the very language of artistically relevant controversy and in the very processes of the construction argument one perceives a basic regulative principle, which may perhaps be called a "rule of respect." The rule says, "Take seriously the object before you as a created object, as a performance." So it must be if the constructions of critics are indeed constructions of performances. So it must be if criticism acknowledges (and to the extent that it acknowledges) the suzerainty of art—if it acknowledges, in effect, that all its animadversions must be artistically relevant, not just critically relevant. Yet the basic question is how to go about taking created objects seriously as performances, and how seriously to take them. And the next question is, what does it entail for the commitments of criticism to take performances seriously, what kind of thing may criticism then become? Answers were simply assumed when it was acknowledged that the most respectful criticism furnished no mirror image of performance and that a genuine problem existed in making appropriate selections within a matrix of art and of society for the bland and quiet objects there before one.

1. How, then, in practice, does a party to the construction argument pay his debt to the rule of respect? Not by any application of a categorical rule, I suggest. He does so by placing a minimal weight upon each of certain particular policies in the construction of critical objects such that the considerations those policies sponsor constrain the argument to the degree of the weight placed upon those policies. No policy possesses absolute weight; none, therefore, can impose an unqualified constraint upon a respectful construction. Which policy possesses greater weight, which less, will be a question of critical style and strategy; but anyone who follows the rule of respect must grant some weight to each policy. A

policy, and hence its consequent considerations, has a minimal weight if determinative for constructing a critical object one way rather than another unless and until another policy and its derivative considerations weigh more heavily. Hence there will be many ways to exhibit a proper respect toward created objects, which is as it should be. Such as these are in fact the policies of respect:

A. The Policy of Physical Respect: Many people will say that in placing a construction upon a performance one ought to consider only those physical features actually present and ignore those which, perhaps, ought to be present but are not. Otherwise, performance or not, the created object has not been respected. The situation, however, is not so simple. Sometimes what is physically present is the work of accident—the weathering of time, the mistakes of copyists. At other times what is physically absent might perhaps be filled in—or, if not literally filled in, the absence might be taken into consideration in appraising what is present. So while it is plain that a proper respect requires heeding what is present and what is absent in a construction, it is not at all plain that a heedful policy may not be overridden. As a policy of respect, the policy of physical respect possesses "some" weight, a weight that is never zero in artistically relevant criticism.

B. The Policy of Appropriateness: In general, no one would be said to respect a created object as a performance unless, determining the relevant characteristics of the object, he placed a value upon selecting the historically appropriate matrix for the created object. So, for the social performances of art, a policy of appropriateness means placing a certain weight in construction upon such considerations, avoiding anachronisms and allowing for the artistic problems the created object was set to solve. To place *no* value upon such considerations would surely show an absence of *all* respect. Observe, however, that placing less than infinite value upon those considerations is perfectly compatible with respecting them; and that a policy of appropriateness, therefore, need demand nothing so absolute as the constraint placed upon critics by the dogma of the work of art itself, which allows the historically relevant matrix no claim at all. The policy merely asserts that if anyone wants to know what values a presented object has when that object is a social performance in a matrix of art, the answer will be bound by considerations of appropriateness—*ceteris paribus.* Anachronistic constructions, constructions remote from anything the artist dreamed, are not necessarily disrespectful though they may be departures from a policy of appropriateness, *provided* other respectful policies call for such constructions.

C. The Policy of Respect for Art qua Art: Anyone who wants to understand the formal and nonformal values of a created object is expected to respect that object qua art. This is the policy upon which the proponents of the normal version focus with such unqualified concern. Considering the created object *qua art* they wish to feel free to select that portion of the matrix of art and of society which suits the object best, or to imagine a matrix that does—where "the best" maximizes the artistically relevant good of which such an object is capable.

On the other hand, while the *policy* of respect for art qua art acknowledges that you respect a thing when you take it at its best, and that lacking any inclination so to take it you are lacking in respect, the policy only requires *some* inclination to so take it. Provision exists for considerations of physical respect and of appropriateness to limit the respect for art *qua art* and so save criticism from that indulgent fantasy which is the very reverse of taking created objects seriously as performances.

D. The Policy of Respect for the Present: Objects are always being characterized by their relevance to the problems and tendencies of the contemporary arts, to the "forcing edge" of art. The decision to make such characterizations does not necessarily depend upon the greater "esthetic value," whatever that may mean, which juxtaposition into the forcing edge of artistic activity may uncover. Often enough, such respect as this may reduce esthetic value. But just as no one respects anything unless he considers it *in some measure* relevant to where he is now, and just as exhibiting relevance exhibits respect, so parties to the construction argument continually exhibit their respect for the work of previous generations by considering it under the aspect of the present—by showing the expressionism in Goya, surrealism in Romanticism, abstractionism in El Greco, or the theater of cruelty in Diderot, and so on. To be sure, criticism then claims to be noting "predecessors." But predecessors are noted as predecessors because they are considered under the aspect of the present, not the other way round.

Observe now that there is nothing inevitable about respect for the present. A man might conceivably take his stance in the court of good Queen Anne and estimate things from there; or he might abstain from asserting esthetic predicates in cross-temporal ways. But if these endeavors seem peculiar, positively requiring justification, the reason must lie finally in this: that once relevance to the present activities of art [13] is seen as a

[13] The present activities of art are not, of course, "equivalent to the matrix of art in its present state," but constitute a relevant part thereof. The "matrix of art in its present state" includes paleolithic cave drawings; in the future it may not.

matter of indifference, criticism fractures into the variety of uncommunicating alleys, which the ideal of criticism as construction of construction ought to prohibit. If the present is no common ground, what will be? The person who, come what may, sees art from the court of the good Queen Anne does not take art seriously; he takes himself seriously, his quirks and idiosyncrasies, against which Eliot warned.

Still, it is plain that the most the policy of respect for the present can insist upon is a prima facie weight—a weight, for example, limited by a policy of appropriateness.

E. The Policy of Conceptual Respect: With the evolution of performances a parallel critical activity constructs a body of concepts that articulates the structure and dynamics of performances and compares performance with performances. There is such a thing as a critical theory of created objects, partly in the sense that Frye seeks a theory of poesis. A policy of conceptual respect is for criticism what a policy of empiricism is for the sciences. The policy of conceptual respect says (a) that no concepts will be used in the construction argument that do not articulate the structure and action of actual performances and (b) that no concepts that do are to be ruled out of the construction argument. *Ceteris paribus,* of course. Obviously, also, the policy has a conservative effect upon the construction argument.

In regard to (a): If a Martian visited an art museum he might come with an intellectual equipment completely alien to any that might reasonably be supposed to rise from specific contact with our art works. With the best will in the world he could have no proper respect—he would encounter objects, not voices. We are not to act like Martians, without sufficient reason. Of course, it might be useful to be just a little bit a Martian—but again, not without sufficient reason. New concepts must prove their worth partly in terms of the conceptual frameworks available.

In regard to (b): If a critic or his adviser turned aside lock, stock, and barrel the concepts of authenticity, genuineness, seriousness, and the like, as normal versions of criticism dispose him to do, then he would have shown a lack of conceptual respect. Hence, since granting a positive value greater than zero to each policy is required by the rule of respect, the popular objection to what I perhaps may call predicates of authenticity shows a positive disrespect of the created object as performance. Normal version critics could not, of course, care less. But the point is that the policy of conceptual respect does not preserve the relevance of concepts as the normal version preserves the principle of their irrelevance—it merely says that they are relevant unless and until there is good ground not to use them.

So we have at least seen five of the ways through which criticism shows its respect for art in the business of the construction argument. It is only because such policies as these have in fact been followed by our "good and responsible" critics that it is fair to talk of critical objects as constructions of constructions. And it is because the rule of respect functions in the open way described that a major job remains to the critic no matter how respectful a man he be. Because of that open way, created objects come to him, in the metaphor already employed, as voices, dimly understood, to be made out, to be "interpreted," rather than as sounds on one hand or messages on the other. That is, they come as constructions.

2. What, now, is the construction argument up to, and criticism in general, when performances are taken seriously, in accordance with the rule of respect? The answer hangs upon a crucial fact that has emerged from the specification of the rule of respect in terms of policies: a man might take seriously the created object as a performance in accordance with the *rule* of respect and nevertheless in some specific construction run counter to a given *policy* of respect. Since by hypothesis he is by no means indifferent to the created object as performance, or to any of the policies comprised in the rule of respect, to overrule considerations required by any policy of respect means offering to reconstitute the created objects under inspection, as performances. Far from such a specific disrespect's committing criticism to a separate existence outside the enterprises of art, under the rule of respect specific disrespect has criticism taking performances seriously indeed; while specific deference to each and every policy would often constitute a vote against the possibility of reconstruction. Such is the general answer to the question of what criticism is up to when it takes created objects seriously as performances according to the rule of respect. Specifically:

A. If, for whatever reason, someone finds a denotable physical characteristic irrelevant to the performance, or an absent condition (like the arms of the "Venus de Milo") relevant, and his standard of relevance rests upon respect for the created object, he has found that the physical object constitutes a marred token of the performance. One of the legs of the "M" has been broken off, but it is *really* an "M," performing as such in the alphabet. Such a "disrespectful" man wants to reorganize the performance of the "Venus de Milo" from the way in which that performance has been organized by literal-minded people who see the "Venus de Milo" armless. Perhaps if he could find the specifications he would refit the lady's arms. His fascination with the policy of appropriateness has led him precisely to providing a "new" "Venus de Milo." "This is what the 'Venus' is really like. Now state her artistically relevant characteristics."

B. Wrenching the created object from its historically appropriate matrix, doing violence to the policy of appropriateness, may, under the rule of respect, lead to the assertion, "There! Now you can really see the work of art," or perhaps even, "the work of art itself!" As a social performance this object was old pottery from the eighth century B.C. Now a policy of respect for art qua art, or perhaps of respect for the present, has led to the "revelation" of a performance previously unsuspected. Criticism now hopefully drops another pebble into the matrix of art and of society. Everybody had thought this was just a nice pot. Not so.

C. Indeed, it may be said, so much respect for the created object according to the policies of respect for art qua art has in such and such a case led to the most monstrous process of "reading in" meanings, that critics will set themselves up as artists unless they let it go. "Why make big things of small things? You are missing the actual performance, which is thus and so." Respect demands a hold upon the policy of respect for art in the interests of the independence of the matrix of art and of society.

Or the interest of the policy of respect for the present might induce one to say that what works to produce "esthetic values" in an outdated segment of the artistically relevant matrix—like classical sculpture in the museum these days—has ceased to be a performance of art. Let the matrix of art now exclude classical sculpture, whatever historical stuff it may include. Fill it in dead or neutral, no voice but a sound—archaeology. Let its merits be considered no more.

Under the rule of respect, neither of these judgments restraining the policy of respect for art qua art is a judgment aimed at and holding for critics of art as critics and only for them. If properly respectful critics attend such judgments, *they* do so at least because those judgments aim at and hold for anyone, critic, artist, or historian. Here, as in all cases, specific disrespect calls for reconstituting in a suitable way the matrix in which created objects come to be what they are.

D. Any party to the construction argument might exhibit the profoundest disrespect for the policy of respect for the present. Diderot is Diderot, he might claim, not an embryonic Beckett; and he would hold that art in its contemporary phase is quite inadequate to do an adequate performative job on Diderot. But then, assuming Diderot worthwhile, does not such a view hold up, at least for inspection, the limitations of the context of activity within which the matrix of art and society now functions? Since the matrices of art and of society at any time in their careers include or take up a whole domain of performances other than contemporary ones, in ways appropriate to their stage and purposes and in rather a Hegelian manner—since, indeed, it is only in this way that formal values can be defined—a break in a specific instance with the policy of respect for the present (where, it must be remembered, the policy has been granted *some* weight) means a recommendation to reconstitute the matrix of art and of society as they stand. That is why the critic says, "Diderot *is* Diderot!" He wants certain values of Diderot accepted as focal points; perhaps he rather hopes that contemporary literature will in consequence take a different tack.

E. Suppose, lastly, that a party to some construction argument introduces a concept that in whole or in part, and most likely in part, corresponds to nothing or to little in the historic matrices of art and of society. *Under the rule of respect* he has duplicated in projection that process by means of which the arts themselves develop new forms and implications. His disrespect asks to re-perform sectors of the arts; his disrespect presents new possibilities for artists. Provided only the regulative principle of respect has not been disregarded, our not-so-hypothetical party to the controversy has exhibited the potential in the present, the "real" in the "accidental," and shown criticism relevant in being reformative.

Indeed, just this has been the point of the relevance of the created object to the artistically relevant controversy: under the rule of respect, and in the necessity of overriding specific policies, criticism explores potentialities in the matrix of art and endeavors to contribute to the achievement of those potentialities as legal scholarship of a certain type explores the potentialities of legal systems, or as political science of a certain type explores the potentialities of political institutions. Every construction asserted, every formal or informal value predicated of a performance, represents such an exploration and, contested, such a testing of potentialities in the practice itself. So the final relevance of the created object to the actual construction argument is to set the critic up not as a tourist among performances, tasting here, tasting there, but as a participant in his peculiar way; and the critic accepts the suzerainty of art over criticism in the sense that art engages him rather than in the lesser sense that he admires art and enjoys art and considers art important to him, though no doubt he does. Not his own choice, necessarily, but the thrust of controversy has driven him to an involvement that, perhaps, caught in his own pleasures and purposes, he never contemplated.

What kind of relation does the rule of respect have as a regulative principle to the formative rules discussed as the issues of artistically relevant controversy (Ch. 4, Sec. I)? And what of the other regulative principles of that controversy? Perhaps the necessary distinction and relation among all these "rules" is something like the distinction between primary and secondary rules in the law. Formative rules could then be taken in the sense of primary rules of law, distinguishing the kinds of cases there are, what is appropriate to them, and so on, while the rule of respect in the construction argument would constitute something like a rule of recognition, adjudication and/or change in H. L. A. Hart's formulation.[14] It is certainly tempting to take notice of the regulative principles of use, objectivity, impersonality, and law as rules of adjudication and change. Formalizing the relations among the various kinds of rules would of course mean making some radical revisions in the classification of what were listed as formative rules; no doubt it would also cause a considerable stretching and changing of the notions of "primary" and "secondary" rules, which in the light of our specific discussions, seem over-simple. But in this book it is enough to get some initial insight into the functioning of various rules in the actual controversy.

V. The Terms of Esthetic Discourse

Understanding how formal and nonformal values work in a matrix of art and society as characteristics of performances, illuminates the use of esthetic terms in the discourse of the construction argument; for esthetic terms are the predicates used to refer to formal and nonformal values. Here is an example of a bit of criticism in which esthetic terms are predicated of objects in a way that presumably everyone would admit is characteristic of esthetic discourse. Roger Fry considers Greek sculpture:

> Such a figure as the Theseus is clearly a type figure. But the unknown creator's feeling for rhythm has enabled him to conceive a perfectly free and natural pose. The movement has extraordinary ease and there is a profound feeling for plastic unity, for rhythmical transitions and oppositions of planes. Though the forms are very much simplified, the simplification is neither so extreme nor so wilful, as in the Olympian sculptures. There is far more subtlety and variety in the curvatures, and though the artist still clings to an almost logical exposition of the main divisions of the body, as for instance where the thorax articulates with the stomach and the stomach with the thighs, this no longer appears as a schematic abstract; it

[14] H. L. A. Hart, *The Concept of Law* (New York: Oxford University Press, 1961), Chapter V.

is filled out with a far more penetrating sense of the minor modifications within the different areas which he has marked out.[15]

1. Suppose someone says "no" to Fry. He doesn't think, for example, that the Theseus shows "far more subtlety and variety in the curvatures" than the Olympian sculptures. He does not find "a far more penetrating sense of the minor modifications." Might he not, in saying "no," actually disagree? When he speaks of "finding" might he not mean, not merely that such and such is what he, unlike Fry, finds on inspecting the sculptures in question, but that in some appropriate sense Fry is mistaken? Could he *never* significantly disagree, even if for one reason or another, in this case he could not? Let us assume that if he can disagree anywhere he can do so here. Then, unless he can, the possibility of an artistically relevant construction argument goes down the drain where we would like it not to do so. There exists a construction argument only if Fry does *not* simply answer, "I find those curvatures subtle and varied and I would like you to do so also."

If, however, Fry takes the man who disagrees with him seriously—and why should he not, at least in some cases?—there is no real question at least of the kind of thing that Fry will offer by way of an answer. He will provide a guided tour through a whole domain of elegant performances, in which similarities and dissimilarities with the troublesome sculptures are demonstrated. He may even talk about the appearance and functioning of ideals of "subtlety and variety" in the curvatures of human figures in relation to various socially constructed personality types. In effect, he will try to place his sculptures in a certain way in a matrix of art and society. He will, in effect, as at least a first step, try to show that his judgment is not fantastic, but a possible judgment about performances. Nor will the necessity that Fry's interlocutor be capable of "following" him, of "appreciating" his points, separate Fry's argument off from argument anywhere else.

If the interlocutor now claims that he sees what Fry means but the demonstration of a meaning is not a proof, will Fry necessarily be forced to reconstrue his remarks merely as the articulation of his own developed sensitivity? It seems clear that this is not the case. He would still have the option of retracing his argument and drawing agreement after agreement on the specific judgments he suggested all along. I do not wish here to examine in any detail materials properly discussed when we come to the reasons question. But it does seem plain that Fry is not necessarily making the remarks he does make merely to tell what he sees in the history of

[15] Roger Fry, *Last Lectures* (Boston: Beacon, 1962), p. 199.

sculpture and humanity. He *may,* at least, make the implicit claim to have been guided by the regulative principles of impersonality, objectivity, use, law, and respect. Perhaps he will invite his interlocutor to consider the weights they place in their use of the rule of respect. It seems odd to say that Fry has presented no arguments but that he merely appeals to the other's sensitivity, despite the fact that to secure *assent,* he is indeed appealing to that sensitivity.

"I see," says the opponent, "how you have reached your judgment on the subtlety and variety of the Theseus' curves. Your perception is deep, informed and sensitive. But I still find the curvature no more subtle and varied than in the Olympian sculptures." But is this opponent not also, like Fry, required to support his holding or withholding of esthetic terms? Unless he does support his view Fry has the *right* to shrug his shoulders. If the fellow does support his judgment, they may indeed find themselves at an impasse, or they may find room for further argument. There will be considerably more to say about such further arguments. But the point is now that even if an impasse is reached both sides will seek to support their perceptions by placing their remarks in a matrix of art and society according to the regulative principles of the artistically relevant controversy. Their perceptions, their judgments of the appropriateness of esthetic terms, have now become *views* to be defended as best they may be.

One notices a further feature of the discussion. Suppose, on hearing Fry's presentation, the other fellow said, "Everything you say is true. Clearly, what you call subtlety and variety I call by some other name, and conversely." Assume three things: (a) that the response makes more than a trivial verbal point, (b) that a further analysis of the matrix of art will not change the fellow's mind, and (c) that he really was able to "follow" Fry's line of thought. Then he may be expressing the *desirability* of a wholesale change in the construction of the general framework of the matrices of art and society. Trusting to the strength of his perception that these particular objects do not have the values of variety and subtlety which Fry says they have, he accepts the consequence and he accepts it even though he "sees" what Fry is driving at.

Now I do not wish to deny that such a line is possible, merely that it does not therefore follow that the construction argument has been precluded for esthetic terms. For, notice, the fellow is "trusting" to the strength of his perception. Some trusts are misplaced. May this one not be? Is not his education perhaps faulty in matters of this sort? But if he trusts because he is convinced of the *desirability* of a wholesale change in the construction of the matrices of art and society, he may be called upon to show that the change he proposes is indeed desirable. Underlying the construction argument for formal and nonformal values there are clearly assumptions of desirability. Just what such assumptions amount to and how they are made good is another issue, which will arise again later in the discussion of artistic merit. At least it *seems* clear that artistically relevant arguments do occur about such issues.

2. That we commonly take esthetic terms as arguable in a construction argument—even esthetic terms other than those which designate formal and nonformal values—may perhaps be made clear by an example. Should I call Harry fat and dumpy? He *is* fat and dumpy, you insist. Why should "fatness" and "dumpiness" *not* require taste or perceptiveness for their application? Merely possessing a certain weight and figure does not *as such* make Harry fat and dumpy; it merely proves that he possesses a certain weight and figure, not another. Even so, your perceiving him as fat and dumpy does not make him so, he might claim; if you perceive him as fat and dumpy that merely proves that you perceive him that way. Do you perhaps *trust* in your perception? Then it is required that those quasi-formal but quite esthetic values, fatness and dumpiness, be Harry-relevant. And that means that Harry is fat and dumpy with just that fatness and dumpiness that are his in virtue of the relations in which his figure stands to those of fat and dumpy people. Not knowing the history of fat and dumpy individuals and generations, you are disqualified from asserting or denying that Harry is fat and dumpy. You are not disqualified as incompetent to achieve an end grasped but beyond your powers, although perhaps you do lack the required visual and tactile sensitivity; you are disqualified as not understanding the force of the predicates in their usage within a construction argument. You are not competent to enter the argument, assuming that something rides upon the argument and there is a point in having one. Of course, more often than not nothing rides upon the argument and there is no point to it. But in such cases it is this fact which makes fatness and dumpiness unarguable, not their esthetic character.

That part of esthetic language, then, which deals with formal and nonformal values, if, indeed it is not the whole part, is art-relevant and controversial in approximately the way in which talk about Harry may be Harry-relevant and controversial without being descriptive either of Harry's physical characteristics in the manner of physical descriptions or simply of the quality of one's response to those physical characteristics. In the case of formal and nonformal values, as of fatness and dumpiness, we are dealing with an object in a matrix the assessor never made, even though, admittedly, Harry is not a created object in quite the same sense as the "Discus Thrower." But perhaps fatness and dumpiness are ways in which Harry performs in the world.

3. Someone might say that an esthetic term as it appears in esthetic discourse is a word or expression "such that taste or perceptiveness is required in order to apply it" and then present a discussion of esthetic terms as the discussion of "an ability to notice or see or tell that things have certain qualities," in contradistinction to a discussion of questions "which center upon expressions like 'a matter of taste.' "[16] He might, in effect, argue that there is a (proper) non-normal version account of taste terms which makes unacceptable the kind of account I have offered of how such terms function in artistically relevant controversy.

The essential point is that there are two pertinent and crucially related senses of noticing, seeing, or telling, not one. In sense 1, I tell you what I see or notice and in doing so say what I have in fact found. It is true that I am not then dealing with what I say, tell or report as a matter of taste. In sense 2, I tell you what I see or notice and I am making an *assertion* about a subject matter. If there is no possibility in sense 1 of making, noticing, telling, or saying statements contestable in the manner in which I have held attributions of esthetic terms contestable, it does not follow that therefore such statements are incontestable in that manner in sense 2. But if there are no contestable statements (contestable in *some* such fashion as I have indicated happens in the artistically relevant controversy) for seeing, telling, or noticing in sense 2, would we not in fact say that in seeing, telling, or noticing I am merely exhibiting my taste, that I am not seeing, telling, or noticing in sense 1 but merely pretending to? If sense 2 is impossible, so is sense 1. Statements in sense 1 become statements "as you like it" or "as it appears to you," to which it is perfectly appropriate to answer "*de gustibus. . .*" That sense 1 statements are indeed not *de gustibus* is the consequence of the *possibility* of sense 2.

From a slightly different point of view: The "*justification*" of tellings, noticings, seeings in sense 1 will obviously not be the same as the justification of sense 2 tellings, noticings, seeings, even though *unless* there are sense 2 justifications one will not be able to distinguish sense 1 statements of the sort from *de gustibus* statements. Precedents and rules must indeed be irrelevant to sense 1 tellings, noticings, and seeings if

[16] Frank Sibley takes such an approach in his essay, "Aesthetic Concepts," in *Philosophy Looks at the Arts,* ed. Joseph Margolis. The quotations in this sentence are, respectively, on pages 64 and 65. 1 and 2 of this section have obviously been written with Professor Sibley's remarks in mind, although how much they break with and how much they simply diverge from those remarks is an open question. 3 is intended to accommodate more directly, if only partially, his observations with my own points.

indeed the point is to tell it as you see it. "Argument" and "reasoning" with other people can, indeed, only be to "get" people to "see" things as you see it. To justify will be to "get" people to see. But it does not follow even if sense 1 tellings, seeings, noticings are "ultimately" necessary to justifications in sense 2 that procedures irrelevant to justification in sense 1 are irrelevant to justification in sense 2, or that justifications in sense 2 of tellings, seeings, and noticings are somehow wrong in principle.

It is possible, I have been saying, to have artistically relevant controversies over the use of specific esthetic terms—like "subtlety and variety" in Fry's remarks—because formal and nonformal values exist in a matrix of art and society and esthetic terms refer to them according to the principles of the construction argument. Yet I must emphasize that any light cast upon the use of esthetic terms by this notion of the values of a performance depends in the long run upon suitable answers to the claims and reasons question (taken to include questions of desirability and artistic merit). Of course, the terms of the metacritical inquiry set out in the first chapter entitle me to assume that that there are indeed answers to the claims and reasons question suitable for the purposes of artistically relevant controversy. Moreover, I have in the present section remarked upon the pre-analytic expectations of discourse like Fry's that support the use of esthetic terms as terms in controversy. Nevertheless, just as to ground upon Harry the fatness and dumpiness which esthetic terms require finally demands some claim, some issue, for which it would make sense to contest that fatness and dumpiness, so to ground the predicates of formal and nonformal values upon performances requires some claim or issue in the interests of which it would make sense to affix such predicates. The three parts of the metacritical question—the reference, claims, and reasons question—are mutually dependent.

Chapter 6

The Claims Question and the Dogma of Estheticism

Now that the reference question has been considered, it is time to turn the artistically relevant controversy so that the claims question comes uppermost and ask what kind or kinds of claims divide people who differ in their judgments of works of art. Judgments, whatever else they may do, assert claims. They claim agreement, to be sure. To *what* do they claim agreement? Nothing? What commitment does the judgment require of those who assent to it? So the question posed here aims at no general survey of the nature and functions of artistically relevant judgment—of the psychology of judgment, of the pedagogic functions of judgment, of the linguistic peculiarities of artistically relevant judgment—though all of these matters and others may be incidentally relevant. The question asks for the content of claims presented in artistically relevant judgment, rather as one might ask for the content of claims projected in some legal judgment. In order to signalize and stress as much, the claims question is called such rather than the "judgment question." If there was a basic difference possible over the use of esthetic terms the reason was an implicit difference about what was *claimed* in making a judgment that used them.

Two dogmas, held simultaneously, define the normal version: the dogma of the work of art itself, which poses an answer to the reference question and which has been treated, and what I shall call "the dogma of estheticism," which poses an answer to the claims question. The problem of this chapter is to assess what the normal version of artistically relevant controversy asserts when it asserts the dogma of estheticism and to say why that dogma will not serve for an answer to the claims question. For while it is true that the procedure explicitly adopted in the book for posing and answering the metacritical question requires approaching the claims question through the normal version, there is more to beginning with the dogma of estheticism. The dogma, if not always in the blunt form in which I shall first present it, runs deep in what is perhaps still the dominant way of regarding the arts; and unless at the start it is understood and can be shown false for the artistically relevant controversy, the truth and point of the answers previously given to the reference question must remain hypothetical.

I. The Force of the Dogma

The dogma of estheticism holds the following: (a) all artistically relevant judgments of the sort which any critic of the arts qua critic of the arts would care to make are directly or indirectly esthetic judgments or they are not artistically relevant judgments of that sort at all, but shams; (b) esthetic judgments advance the claims of taste, are judgments of taste; and (c) if there is an artistically relevant controversy that controversy must have esthetic judgments as issues. So if we want to know what critics "argue" about, what's at issue among critics, not just the subject of the argument, the answer will be matters of taste.

Obviously, therefore, some who adhere to the dogma will take arguments, including the construction argument, more seriously than others. Some will try to patch the doctrine up so that there is something which resembles a "genuine" argument in the sense of Chapter 1, some will not. Some will formulate the dogma in "subjectivist" terms, some avoid that formulation. For all formulations,[1] however, a *dogma* is asserted, by

[1] C. J. Ducasse provides an excellent (subjectivist) illustration of how, in the normal version, artistically relevant controversies reduce to "esthetic" differences. "All rules and canons and theories concerning what a painting or other work of art should or should not be," writes Ducasse, "derive such authority as they have over you or me or anyone else, solely from the capacity of such canons *to predict to us* that we shall feel esthetic pleasure here, and esthetic pleasure there. The feeling judges the rule not the rule the feeling." Accordingly, "the difference between the criticism of professionals and laymen is essentially that the former are able to trace the esthetic pleasure or displeasure which they feel, to certain features of the object, while the latter are not able to do it. From this, however, it does not in the least follow that the evaluation of the professionals ultimately rests on any basis less subjective and less a matter of individual taste than do those of the laymen." Hence, technical knowledge is positively dangerous. "Listening to the comments of artists and of some critics on a picture will quickly convince one that, strange as it sounds, they are as often as not almost incapable of seeing the picture about which they speak. They are thus often not more but less capable than the untrained public of giving the picture *esthetic* attention, and of getting from it genuine esthetic enjoyment" (*The Philosophy of Art* [New York: Dial Press, 1929], pp. 292–94). It is, I propose, one of Ducasse's virtues that he follows the consequences of his choice of consumption for the interpretation of criticism to the bitter end: "Is there then no such thing as the refining and educating of taste?" he asks only a little later, and answers, "Certainly there is—and there is also such a thing as perversion and depravation of taste. But the question in any given case is, 'Which is which?' No observer so far as I know has yet pointed out any way of answering this question otherwise than arbitrarily and dogmatically."

which I mean that in taking esthetic judgment as a matter of taste and artistically relevant controversy (here, as always in this essay, in the sense relevant to critics of the arts qua critics) as being about esthetic judgments, a substantive choice is made for dealing with works of art—a choice which need not necessarily be made, but which is dealt with as though there were no alternative. In seeking to understand the dogma we shall be dealing once again with the context of consumption, although this time from the point of view of judgment as such rather than from the point of view of the object of judgment. So there will be some belaboring of points already made, "in essence."

1. Let me first comment on the specific content of the notions of taste and esthetic judgment. The force of the dogma of estheticism depends upon that content.

A. Historically, the decision to judge the class of objects called works of art as objects of taste, and hence, to make esthetic judgments, is a concrete choice, which I shall call "estheticism." Since it is a concrete choice, estheticism may, unlike the dogma of estheticism, if one believes the dogmatists, meaningfully be refused. Even those who accept the dogma and say that anyone who makes any choice other than estheticism necessarily plunges himself into confusion, do not deny that people did not always, and do not always now, either make or judge objects of art as objects of taste. Primitive artists, Gothic artists, metaphysical poets, critics of a certain stripe, reach remarkable consequences in the pursuit of irrelevant ends. They chose "y" when they should have chosen "z" and—lo and behold!—choosing "y" led them to "x," the same destination to which "z" leads.

Appraisals and valuings of actual art objects, then, became judgments of taste, and works of art were construed as objects of taste rather than, say, of religious value, utility, or private amusement when, as a consequence of appropriate social conditions,[2] those objects became affairs to be collected and viewed as collector's items. People no doubt have always collected things. But they do not always conceive their collection as something to be placed on some sort of exhibition. Taste begins with the collection and the museum, when, in order to be displayed, objects are wrenched from the environments in which they had come to be and had their being.[3] Certain people become experts in that sort of object. Stamp

[2] See, for examples of such conditions, Katharine Everett Gilbert and Helmut Kuhn's *A History of Esthetics* (Rev. ed.; Bloomington: Indiana University Press, 1953), Chapters IV, V, X.

[3] For an account of the significance of the museum, there is, of course, André Malraux's insightful "museum without walls" in *The Voices of Silence* (Garden City, N. Y.: Doubleday, 1965), p. 19.

collectors, art dealers, headhunters, librarians, "apart from any interest," become professionals.

Not the object, then, as the normal version likes to pretend, but the very special placing of the object in frames, under glass, in files, on poles, demands judgments of taste and creates the thing itself to go with those judgments—a placing that would make inevitable the distinction between mere manufactures (objects not in museums or the equivalent) and "works of art," objects of taste. So the isolation, the "framing" of the art object as the "esthetic object," and the autonomy of the faculty which judged that esthetic object did not happen because suddenly the esthetically blind received a great light. There was no need for such a light, not with collectors and connoisseurs on hand. On the contrary, there is still something anomalous about setting out to create paintings for museums, books for the library. One paints pictures, which are placed in museums, writes books, which are placed in libraries. The artist who sets out to create an object of taste misses the boat. He is no "real" artist, except, perhaps, for those persons of taste whose taste it is to set up second-order museums of objects found in museums, for objects-in-museums.[4]

B. "Art proper," art as the set of objects appropriately judged by "men of good taste" in particular, emerges only when objects stolen or purchased advance from the status either of trophy or proof of wealth into an indication of "refinement." The notion of refinement is revealing: when direct and immediate evidence of status becomes inadequate, either because such evidence is too widely shared or long since taken for granted, nothing will do but a further step, a further discrimination. The penalty for not taking this further step is "vulgarity." "Vulgarity" means, being translated, a state of no longer serving the essential purposes of collecting things and exhibiting them. Simply "showing" has become "showing off." "Showing off," obviously, will never demonstrate the justification of the membership one holds in a status class nor will it justify membership in a class to which one aspires to belong. Some proof of refinement is far more useful for that, and the idea of "fine art"—of art for the refined—is abroad.

C. Immanuel Kant has put very clearly the relation of estheticism to the split between possession and use, and the connection between taste and status. "Only" he writes, "when men have got all they want can we

[4] It is not germane to press the point here, but the connection between "work of art" and "curiosity" must be close, "in a context of consumption." "Curiosities," be it noted, are also things which are as curiosities separated and require a special taste—a collector's taste, significantly enough. Of course, all curiosities are not works of art. But that does not prevent all works of art in a context of consumption from being curiosities.

tell who among the crowd has taste or not.[5] What else would "taste" be but "the faculty of estimating an object or a mode of representation by means of a delight or aversion apart from any interest"? [6] Whatever the psychological difficulties of talking about "delight or aversion apart from any interest," on the level his critics seem to miss Kant was saying something specific and something true: Judgments of taste embody the point of view of someone who buys pictures, attends concerts, reads books only because he "favors" them—not because he needs them or has any objective except to satisfy his taste. The theory of esthetic judgment declared the right and independence of the connoisseur in his court.

Thereupon Kant needed a principle for his esthetic magistrate, for his man of good taste, or no one could tell the man who qualified as a judge from the *nouveaux riches*. For the *nouveaux riches,* aside from pretensions, also have all they want from one point of view and they also have their preferences. Kant, along with all estheticians of taste, must show, as it has been put, that a "pleasurable feeling can partake of ideality"; he must find a basis for taste which was not mere preference or there would be no discriminating. Tolstoy, for example, did not misunderstand, nor did he make a simple error in principle, when he fought his classic battle against estheticism in the arts—despite the excessive price he let that fight impose upon him.

At any rate, defining a criterion for refined consumption has constituted a problem ("How is refinement possible?") in philosophy of art only on the acceptance of an optional way of regarding the arts. Of course, I do not mean that only class, status, or, generally, "social decisions" generate the esthetic way of handling artistically relevant judgments. People who make the choice of estheticism—estheticians, naturally—do seek in that process to find, despite Tolstoy, a place for Tolstoy. And besides providing a meta-criticism of refined taste, theories of esthetic judgment, most emphatically including Kant's, have responded to prior philosophical conditions and perplexities. But the history of the intellectual origins of estheticism is another and very long story; here my concern is merely to find a few rough reminders that a historical choice has had specific content, and hence was a real choice.

2. The following summarizes the "logical" force of the dogma of estheticism:

A. Observe, first, that the *dogma* does not simply happen to have a content. If the dogma of estheticism, holding all artistically relevant

[5] *The Critique of Judgment,* trans. by J. C. Meredith (Oxford: Clarendon, 1952), pp. 49–50.

[6] *Ibid.*, p. 50.

judgments esthetic judgments, is to advance something better than a verbal recommendation, to call a judgment artistically relevant (artistically relevant as such, of course, whatever "as such" might mean) and to call it "esthetic" must mean different things; and this will be so even though in fact the species of all such artistically relevant judgment may be co-extensive with the class of all esthetic judgment of a certain sort. So the normal version in proposing the dogma wants of us something of the sort that we need not necessarily yield, although perhaps we ought; and the synonymity of "artistically relevant" and "esthetic" in the ordinary dictionary counts merely as proof of the normal version's influence, not of the truth of the dogma.

B. Normal version "esthetic judgments" constitute highly special judgments offered in the process of applying the *rule of taste* in an appropriate manner. Obviously, there will be many "theories" of "esthetic judgment" and of how it differs from other sorts of judgment. But what will provoke them all, as normal version theories, will be the commitment to a particular choice—the choice of refined consumption, which means the choice of the rule of taste for formulating judgments of what works of art are and what they ought to be, where works of art are understood to deserve peculiarly sophisticated tastings.

Therefore the normal version alleges through the dogma of estheticism not simply that artistically relevant judgments state claims that *arise* from a certain kind of immediate involvement with an object, historically called "taste." The normal version characteristically claims that all artistically relevant judgments *assert* or *express* "taste" as their content, in the sense that when people differ they differ in tastes. If they differ in anything else, to that extent they do not differ over esthetic judgment. In legal or scientific judgments, which are not primarily forms of esthetic judgment, differences in taste are incidental. One can say that nothing hangs upon them and for the most part be right. In esthetic judgment the situation is reversed. Taste is of the logical essence and nothing hangs upon it, except what may be invoked by the rule of Rorschach.

C. There is, then, something in the normal version dogma of estheticism which makes a primary difference between esthetic judgments or judgments of taste and assertions of judgments of taste. The taste itself does not call for its assertion or justify one assertion to another, if by an assertion is meant something someone else is supposed to accept. It is not for nothing that silence or a gentle, non-assertive expression (the pun is important) has always been held to mark the man of taste. In the wings of the normal version theater stands inevitably a *persuasive* theory of the issue in artistically relevant *controversy*. The only point to *asserting* tastes is to get somebody to preserve or change his taste. But that is not an issue of esthetic judgment.

D. If there is no direct issue possible in asserting an esthetic judgment except "getting someone to see," there may, of course, be the claim that no specific esthetic judgment makes, as such, a choice to which anyone else might provide an alternative. The traditional identification of judgments of taste as judgments of beauty gives away the game. Regardless of his intentions, when Kant finds judgments of beauty judgments of taste he in fact presents one very particular and questionable historical ideal of art: a systematic preference for harmony of the sort the Renaissance approved and found absent from the "Gothic." Beauty may indeed be the proper object of a rational taste, but the statement is something more than a tautology because "beauty" means more than "the proper object of rational taste." So there is, in fact, a specific taste to preserve or to be changed, which a judgment of taste as a judgment of beauty advances and refuses to acknowledge. That is the reason why judgments of taste are normative.

E. Observe now what happens when the normal version proposes that artistically relevant judgments in the arguments of critics "are" esthetic judgments. Those who make the proposal do not simply *opt* to assert judgments of taste of works of art and then propose that others do also. That would not be philosophy. They want also to say that anyone who fails to opt for refined consumption in controversies over works of art has made, rather than a poor choice, a mistake in principle. *Artistically relevant judgment must, properly, be "esthetic judgment," just as previously the critical object had to be "the work of art itself."* From the perfectly real decision made about the arts, "*Let* the proof of the pudding be in the eating," the normal version moves on to, "The proof of the pudding *is* in the eating." Equipped with the "truth" of that declaration it then denies the very intelligibility of any alternative—and estheticism is established as a precondition for rationality in the arts. No one *can* say of works of art, if the proof of the pudding "is" indeed in the eating, that their judgment "ought" to be anything else but "esthetic," unless he fails to grasp the "nature" of artistically relevant judgment. Accordingly, I understand by "the dogma of estheticism" the view that a person commits an error in principle by denying that the concrete judgments of criticism which everyone acknowledges, directly or indirectly, to be artistically relevant, are "esthetic" in nature.

F. There are, then, *two* distinct positions advanced in the normal version of artistically relevant judgment, which, despite the tactic of the normal version, must be discriminated: the first position is the *choice* of refined consumption; the second is the characterization of artistically relevant controversy—that artistically relevant judgment *as encountered* is esthetic judgment. The failure to discriminate the two constitutes the source, perhaps, of many a philosophical gloss on the nature of "esthetic judgment," as the philosopher tries to show that artistically relevant judgment *must* be what he has already decided it ought to be.

In order to evaluate properly the normal version response to the claims question I propose now to consider (1) how the rule of taste, which constitutes the principle even of refined consumption—of the choice of estheticism—fails to square with the practice of artistically relevant controversy; (2) why that rule of taste cannot be made right; and (3) how some specific attempts to make it right fall flat. Only then will it be permissible to leave the dogma of estheticism to those who cannot imagine judgment without estheticism and to move on to examine directly the kind of claim advanced in an artistically relevant discourse open to exception.

II. The Discomforts of Estheticism

The normal version of artistically relevant controversy will not do, not because works of art prohibit dealing with them as objects of taste—they clearly do not—or even because it is always and necessarily undesirable to deal with them so, but because considering artistically relevant judgments as judgments of taste makes hash of that practice of controversy this essay seeks to understand.[7] Here, then, are some of the reasons why no one can be entirely happy identifying artistically relevant judgments with judgments of taste.

1. There are certain incoherencies that look like paradoxes of art and criticism but are actually the incoherencies of the normal version.[8]

Consider, for example, an imitation of a painter's style and normal subject perfect enough so that no merely visual inspection suffices to tell the imitation from the paintings "known" to have been done by the imitated master. Van Meegeren's "forgeries" of Vermeer attest that the

[7] Chapters 2 and 3, of course, have already considered the rule of taste from the perspective of the reference question. Considering it again from the point of view of the claims question may entail belaboring a target perhaps sufficiently damaged, but the requirements of the claims question leave few alternatives.

[8] The choice of consumption, of course, is to opt for the rule of taste—the choice of refined consumption, a species of the genus: to opt for a rule of "discriminating" taste.

trick can be pulled at least for a while. Yet very few, if any, of the men of refinement said, "What luck! Here's somebody besides Vermeer who can do Vermeers!" Though they ought to have done so, if the normal version holds. By *their* hypothesis, Van Meegeren painted the "Supper at Emmaus" to make no perceptual, hence no artistically relevant, difference compared with other works by Vermeer, and until that hypothesis is refuted they have consequences to face. For it is certainly clear that the historical question "Who painted the Vermeer?" has nothing to do with "the work of art itself." Something has gone radically wrong: is it criticism or the normal version?

For something of the following sort seems to be what actually happened. Before the disclosure of fraud, few competent critics felt the "Supper at Emmaus" artistically inferior to any picture of Vermeer's. After the disclosure, instead of commending the esthetic value of "the work of art itself" and allowing its financial value to fall independently, people marveled over the skill and ingenuity, the technical resource, exhibited in a painting that so precisely duplicated the effects of Vermeer; nor did they consider seriously how to make sense of the claim of Van Meegeren to be Vermeer reincarnated, which would at least have saved esthetic face. Face forgotten, they evaluated the "Supper at Emmaus" qua imitation, located the artistically relevant values in the "original" Vermeers and the value of the Van Meegeren in its service as a reminder—either that or they discovered defects in "the *work of art itself*" never previously apprehended.[9] Either, that is to say, people exhibited the usual dishonesty over responses they would like to disown or they let honesty take the place of consistency and for the duration of the controversy forgot the normal version.

The problem, of course, is to account for what happened in terms of our picture of criticism in general. Obviously, one *might* persevere in the normal version and (and assuming no subsequent *relevant* esthetic difference) say that in the Van Meegeren instance critics went wrong, not the normal version: "Van Meegeren's pictures are precisely as good as Vermeer's is a *true* esthetic judgment. There was *no* call for an esthetic revolution." No one can dislodge anyone from the choice of consumption if that is the choice he is committed to make, and he is willing to pay the price. Only, the more tightly held the choice, the *greater* the need to

[9] Do we not suspect what would happen if the "Supper" turned out to be no forgery after all? If the "Night Watch," which has turned out to be the "Day Watch," turned out the "Night Watch" all over again? Examples may be multiplied infinitely. All go to suggest that commitment to estheticism has some of the inconveniences of commitment to the party line.

legislate to the artistically relevant controversy (in the interests of what is nominally a second-order theory but in fact a choice of stance).

But why *not* "legislate" to the controversy openly, honestly, in the interests of the rule of taste; why not opt to pay the price, turn critics into pure consumers, and, where necessary, tell critics what they *ought* to have said? The way, I repeat, is open—but that does not make it a desirable way. "If my right eye (Vermeer is better than Van Meegeren), offend me, pluck it out!" constitutes a perfectly plausible policy, provided one does not push it, and an increasingly strenuous one as situations occur requiring its extension. And there's the rub. A *host* of occasions for the exhibition of normal version virtue rise up when one occassion is disposed of. Why, for example, do people value so lightly "derivative" works of art? Or derogate the poem or novel that sensibly employs a proven style for ends of proven value while the works of art that established the parent patterns are represented as masterpieces? Because the later artist does less well? Perhaps. Yet can we even conceive someone redoing Shakespeare, only better? Or Bach or Praxiteles? It is very unfair to the imitator to pretend an impartial judgment knowing very well that *nothing* he can do will make his performance equal. And what, after all, does one have against Illiac? The weight of sacrifices that the dogma of estheticism requires, the pressure of consistency upon consistency (an eye here, an eye there, this nostril, that ear, on and on), can have but one end—which, again, *can* always be accepted—namely, the systematic violation of the practice of criticism.

That is why I have been speaking of the "discomforts" of estheticism. Anyone who tries to hold on simultaneously to the rule of taste and the practices of critics will need constantly to hew away at one or the other; there is no rest in it; and for the metacritical question, no solution.

2. Nowhere, to the best of my knowledge, has the theory that artistically relevant judgments are judgments of a consumer's taste been more explicitly confronted with the discomforting facts of criticism than in a small book by Konrad Fiedler, that eminent critic of a not too remote generation.

> If esthetic feeling is called upon to judge a work of art, it is named taste. In familiarizing oneself with works of art, one acquires taste, and yet its cultivation and refinement are presupposed in order that it may be able to distinguish between good and bad. The same work of art may arouse any degree of dis-satisfaction or pleasure, from disgust to highest admiration, not only in different persons but even in the same observer. However, if it is the dominant characteristic of the cultivated taste that it provides a reli-

> able yardstick for the value or the worthlessness of works of art, then wherein does he who by his sensation is led aright differ from him who seduces to error? Is the former in possession of another, a greater esthetic sensation than the latter? Or is not rather the capacity of feeling the same in both of them, except that a different insight acquired apart from that feeling supplies different material to different persons? One can only refer to the fact that he who wishes to arrive at a sound judgment about works of art must from the beginning repress his esthetic sensations, and that he must, on the contrary, acquire in a particular way a capacity for a sure judgment. . . . When he has reached this state, in which his esthetic sensation is only aroused by the good and the significant aspects of works of art, whereas the non-significant and the bad aspects incur his displeasure, he has attained artistic judgment. But such judgment is the result of his acquired capacity, not the result of his original, uncultivated esthetic feeling.[10]

What, then, does Fiedler tell us? Something about the first-order activity of critics, I propose—something to be dealt with regardless of any second-order explanation Fiedler himself might propose: [11] that the critic seeks as part of his essential business and predicament to *break* with the rule of taste,[12] to deny that "esthetic feeling is called upon to *judge* a work of art." For, "he who wishes to arrive at a sound judgment about works of art must seek from the beginning to repress his esthetic sensations."

All of which, of course, does not mean that the critic *uses* something other than "taste" in making his judgments, or that he will not strive constantly for the improvement of that "taste" *through* which he judges. The point is finally a point about judgments: that for the intelligent and sensitive critic, aware of the flux and discord of his own and other people's tastes, taste is no sacred cow, and judgment, no matter how "sincere," is not beyond question. The critic's problem is not to *have* taste, but consciously, wisely, to transform it; for he, more than others, realizes that change it will, in any case. Therefore, for the working critic, to control transformations in an adequate manner is the ultimate mark of "good taste." Nor is it necessary, in order to perceive the manifest conflict between the rule of taste and the practice of critical inquiry as Fiedler

[10] *On Judging Works of Visual Art,* trans. H. Schaefer-Simmern and F. Mood (Berkeley: University of California Press, 1949), pp. 7–8.

[11] Fiedler himself seems to have supposed that art represents independent, cognitive activity and that the critic's role *amounts,* therefore, to an attempt to discriminate an always valuable creative power rather than to apply previously developed standards to the unique creations vouchsafed by the artist.

[12] It might be useful here to compare Fiedler's extensive remarks with observations in Chapter 1 about the nature of artistically relevant controversy. Fiedler's remarks constitute a way of referring to that discussion in a brief and confirmatory way.

does, to suppose that the appreciator of the arts *never* employs the rule of taste. For he may, indeed; only, not at the point where he seeks to reconcile differences of opinion, or, more accurately, to state the terms on which to seek that reconciliation.

Needless to say, the same qualifications that turned the "incoherencies" of the normal version into the "discomforts" of criticism, rather than refutations of a context of consumption, obtain for assessing the force of Fiedler's practical point. There is nothing to prevent anyone wedded to the normal version from simply cutting off criticism at those points to which his position will not stretch. Once again, the drawback will be the sense of increasing discomfort as Procrustes, regarding his handiwork, scratches his head and wonders whether he really likes what he has left after his improvements.[13]

3. To conclude my reminders of the discomforts of the normal version's commitment to the rule of taste, let me mention a discomfort that most philosophers, given their normal version assumptions, have been prone to take rather lightly. Estheticism's employment of the rule of taste distorts not only the critic's behavior but the correlative activity of the artist; and it does so, in effect, by defining the artist's job for him as the satisfaction of market demands (which remain market demands no matter how elite the market). It is this implicit definition, may I suggest, which generates much of the force of contemporary attacks on "leveling" processes in art, culture, and religion; critic and artist, laboring with the normal version, seeking in status and tradition what seems the only way to rescue art from vulgarity, *stratify* the market. Moreover, may I also suggest, it is this same normal version description of artistic activity that produces so much discussion of the "alienation" of the artist from society. For under the persuasion of the normal version the artist thinks he *ought* to be "selling" (appealing to "taste"), notices that he is not, cannot see how he could do much differently in his productive work, and ends blaming *both* the market, "society," *and* himself—which I take to be "alienation." It is terribly hard to be an artist and to hold the rule of taste seriously; and in the concrete, if not generally, nearly everybody knows so much when reminded.

Consider, for example, the following sort of remarks addressed to an artist in judgment of his work: "I like that. Someday I think I may like it

[13] It is, of course, also possible for the normal version adherent to seek to modify his bed to fit the patient, without producing any "essential" change in the bed; and he might attempt such modifications not only to allow the transformatory functions of an active criticism but to manage the "incoherencies" discussed on pp. 103–05. Why *this* is an unpromising tactic Sections II and III of this chapter seek to show.

better, although of course I can't be sure. You keep it up and I'll attend your next exhibition (read your next book, etc.)." The phrasing, of course, is particularly raw. But that's just the point: to present the rule of taste undisguised. Will not the artist—*ought* not he, as a man who respects himself in his capacity as an artist—answer that the speaker's *feelings* are irrelevant and their expression impertinent, that he denies any judgment has been rendered, even a right one, merely because the response is "favorable"?

"I am *not* your servant," he will surely answer if he thinks he can get away with it. "I couldn't care less whether my work tickled you. If you like my work show me the justice of my decisions. Explain to me the surely splendid things I have accomplished. Show me what I've *done* to your taste. But if you want to tell me what you feel now, or what you might feel if things were different, ask my indulgence. Be humble. Recognize that you are merely offering me responses, which I may or may not consider in my next opus."

Some such answer has surely been on the lips of every bedeviled writer, artist, actor, or musician, and would surely have found expression were it not for self-doubts, metacritical assumptions, or the need to make a dollar. Yet this answer amounts to arrogance only on the dogma of estheticism, and on the assumption of the priority of the market. For, as a matter of fact, the creative artist, as we call him *for that very reason,* is the person perhaps most directly involved of all, more directly even than the "responsible" critic, in *making* audience "taste"; and the audience, or portion of the audience, which forgets that, forgets, precisely, its place. He is "involved" with taste in more or less the same way that Aristotle's legislator is "involved" with the pleasures of his citizens. He stands responsible for them, to perpetuate them or alter them. Though either an act of legislation or an act of art incapable of giving satisfaction to any human being would lack value, yet that circumstance never eliminates the need to decide *which* "pleasure" the legislator will encourage, *which* "esthetic sensation" the artist will choose to promote.

The artist, then, may not be "the unacknowledged legislator of the world" in the sense that Shelley imagined him; but only under the normal version is the artist necessarily unacknowledged as a legislator of artistic values. The artist's own work leaves him no choice but to put in for the active role. To take some conventional examples, how could a Schoenberg, Joyce, or Picasso do his special job and at the same time follow the tutelage of the cultivated public *before* the cultivated public learned to look for what he had to offer? *They* cultivated the "cultivated" public, which alone could judge them. That this much is truism is precisely the discomfort of the normal version. Accordingly, the chief trouble with taking art in a context of refined consumption, as the object of judgments of taste, under the rule of taste, consists in this: that to do so abrogates the creative role and the legislative functions of artistic endeavor in the total artistic enterprise.

The point has sufficient importance for the overall discussion of a context alternative to consumption to warrant some small elaboration on the obvious objection that not all artists have been movers and innovators of taste. I would merely suggest that a master is no less a master in making use of given arrangements than in turning the house upside down, that there are two ways, not one, in which an artist exerts his mastery of the status quo in taste. For, obviously, sometimes it will be convenient to employ available modes and "languages." At these times, the artist will seem to become more available, more serene, as impersonal as the moon and the stars, to the "man of taste"—who now comes into his own and shows his "classic" taste, his preference for "beauty" over mere innovation.

But the important thing is to avoid confusing the adoption of conventions for an artist's own artistic ends with the adoption of a prevailing "language" in order to say what others want to hear, because it will delight them to hear it. No longer mastering taste, the artist has been mastered by it. (And I may add here that under certain circumstances the attempt to turn prevailing modes inside out may manifest just as sure a subordination to the rule of a taste when, come what may, it insists on change.) Hard as it may be on occasion to determine which kind of relation to the rule of taste the artist sustains—ascendancy or dependency—and certain as it is that these things are rarely all-or-none affairs, one ought not to adduce the grave legitimacy of the classic mode of composition to support the pretensions of a mode of commerce.

4. But if, lastly, it is asked just why it is so important to do justice to artistic activity and its aspiration, *why* the price of forfeiting the role of maker and breaker of tastes and standards is the *life* of the arts, I shall refer the reader to two final and related esthetic discomforts.

A. First, it should be observed, a merely apparent unpretentiousness springs from that basic confusion between mastering taste and being mastered by it. It is this pseudo-hardheadedness that seems to characterize Mr. Somerset Maugham when, backed by a staggering circulation, he informs us that stories are or ought to be constructed to entertain people and that whether or not those stories entertain constitutes the sole justification of the storyteller's art. Having carried the normal version to its limit he has ended by identifying art with entertainment. Such is the final outcome of the "choice of a context of consumption" when the last inhibitions are removed: the artist as a man in the art business, and the product to be sold as the customer's entertainment. There is no need to be snobbish about entertainment to see that something important has been missed, that somehow art is a serious though not ponderous affair, that in one way or another the identification of art and entertainment has crossed categories [14]—and that it won't do unless, of course, one hardens one's mind and says it *will* do.

B. Having stripped the artist of his effective, taste-making role and made of art a more or less high-falutin' entertainment, there arises that modern embarrassment: a "science" of art. Under the suasion of the normal version and its dogma of estheticism we come to dream of a "science" in which human psychology and techniques for the manipulation of materials will be mastered so successfully that at relatively small price the spiritually naked, as it were, may be clothed and reclothed. Nor does there seem to be any a priori reason why a fair amount of human ingenuity might not devise cheaper and more efficient means to meet the requirements of even an elite market.

Let me characterize the resulting discomfort (following what is by now, apparently, ordinary usage), "the discomfort of The Machine." It is a discomfort because neither artist nor normal version critic will hesitate for a moment to construct metaphysical roadblocks in the path of technology, to exorcise the competition of "The Machine." Nevertheless, it is a discomfort of the normal version, not of critical nor artistic activity as such, and certainly has nothing to do with the limitations of technology. Its source is that fact that in a society of pure consumers the mode of production makes no difference.

To put it another way: though all the computers in the world were to put their circuits together to provide a moving image of perpetual and absolute beauty, though they were to satisfy in the highest whatever interest the work of the artist might finally satisfy—and there is nothing in principle against such a possibility—they might thereby bring about paradise and the kingdom of heaven, but not art. The reason is simply that men want out of art not a servicing, but some kind of human doing

[14] R. G. Collingwood, of course, has examined this particular crossing at some length and, as I would think, with considerable insight. See his *The Principles of Art* (New York: Oxford University Press, 1958), Chapter V. I do not here examine the particular sense in which a crossing has occurred largely because the primary aim now is to refer to first-order facts about the arts, as it were, but also because the entire argument of this book would be required to provide the premises for the distinction on a metacritical level.

in which men may involve themselves and *change* themselves. We have, on the whole, had enough of being serviced; and the domain of art constitutes one final domain in which men stand some chance of being born again, their own progenitors, so to speak, directly and immediately.

All that wanting is, of course, the merest prejudice, but one deeply rooted, which does not set well with approaching the arts in a context of consumption according to the rule of taste.

III. Why Estheticism Cannot Do

Nevertheless, of course, few except those in the entertainment industry and their spokesmen, and probably hardly any philosophers, have ever wished to carry to a complete conclusion the reduction of art objects to objects of consumption. The point has not been that the estheticians were vulgarizing art. If they were, we would have nothing to say to them. The trouble is that, having chosen the prime rule of the context of consumption for examining art, they have still wanted to save criticism. Having said "a" they have endeavored above all things not to say "b." Here lies the "antinomy" that generates so much of the driving force of philosophical discussions of "esthetics": the endeavor to show that though judgment be a question of taste we need *not* rest with the conclusion that one judgment is no better than another where artistically relevant controversy requires saying that one judgment *is* better than another. The discomforts of estheticism are, for the estheticians, genuine discomforts: something, the esthetician wants to say, *is* wrong about the Van Meegeren paradox; critics *do* reconstruct taste; artists *do* have their dignity; neither entertainment nor the computer is an alternative to art. Although in one sense all tastes are equal, he holds that in another some tastes are more equal than others. Committed to some form of estheticism people wish at the same time and in the same respect to keep their standing as good consumers and to account for the arguments of critics and artists.

Now I should like to make explicit why the trick *cannot* be worked, why something *must* give, given the demands of the artistically relevant controversy as standard. With all prior commitment to estheticism hopefully eliminated, or at least suspended, I shall very briefly recount three related considerations pertinent and crucial for judging the rule of taste as the principle of judgment in the arts. Brevity is possible because all three considerations are entirely familiar.

1. *Judgment and Decision:* Reaching a judgment about any "nonpractical" or "immediately valuable" object in the sense of the good consumer means, of course, tasting and tasting again and attending to one's

responses and then perhaps having another go at it and then voicing one's "opinion." That is a perfectly good sense of decision: "decision" means "deciding" what one likes. Judgment then constitutes a complaint or an approval addressed to a producer for meeting or failing to meet the claims of taste, that it be satisfied; and this, again, is a perfectly legitimate sense of judgment.

Only, it does not therefore follow that because "judgment" in artistically relevant controversy has been addressed to the same "immediately valuable" objects "judgment" *must* be employed in the above senses—unless one begins with a context of consumption for approaching that controversy. Otherwise, of course, one can begin with the rules of the artistically relevant game in determing how to judge the objects one likes (or dislikes) and in determining the force of "judgment" upon them.

The question is, therefore, whether the rule of taste indeed determines the issue of the controversy; and here, indeed, it seems, from our discussion of the reference question and of the discomforts of estheticism as well, that it does not, that the sense of decision which troubles critics when they need to "decide" among conflicting claims is not the sense of decision which a critic of Martinis or puddings confronts when he "decides" whether he likes the thing or not. For now, as has been pointed out, the critic must "make up his mind," must *reach* a decision rather than simply report a fact. Precisely this *taste* is in question, and nobody knows it better than the critic engaged in an argument. That is why people distinguish between "taste" and "good taste," and philosophers strive to distinguish between "normative" and "factual" principles, whatever the merits of the way they put it.

If, therefore, to decide as one pleases, even as one "really and truly" pleases, serves as a legitimate rule for consumer judgments, it will be perfectly useless for purposes of artistically relevant controversy; and the attempt to make the rule of taste do the job of the rule or rules of art (and in the discussion of the reference question I sought to give a partial idea of the kind of rules required) cannot conceivably succeed.

2. *Differences in Judgment:* Sometimes people shudder when someone interjects into a critical discussion, "Well, anyway, I know what I like." Partly they shudder because they know they now have to face an unassailable opponent; partly because "I know what I like-ism" usually coincides with the most questionable likes. But also they shudder because, while very likely he *does* know what he likes, nobody asked him. I propose now to restate directly in relation to the problem of judgment the criticism of the rule of taste already advanced in connection with the

reference question.[15] In civilized differences of opinion, self-revelations, except perhaps as grace notes to acknowledge personal *limitations,* indicate that the fellow who makes them lacks a sense of the critic's business.

However it may be with the rest of us, that is, the critic tries to consider the work of art as an object lying in the *public* domain. This means that differences must be reached in a public manner and be stipulated in that manner. A purely personal way of regarding a work of art—however delectable—would therefore have nothing to do with the judgmental function. Somehow the critic must make "his" way of regarding the critical object good for others, and argument proceeds over whether or not he has succeeded. Similarly, *he* asks about the work of art whether the *artist* has "succeeded": has the poet presented the kind of structured, "interpersonal" fact regarding which one judgment will not do as well, and hence as badly, as another? Otherwise, there will be no point in "differing" about the artist's job, and people will say he has "failed" to communicate.

Accordingly, the rule of taste necessarily misses as a rule for determining artistically relevant judgment because its prime function is to generate intelligible "*personal*" rather than "social" differences. For, notice, I do not contest the rule of taste on the ground that there *are* no "personal" judgments. Personal judgments make perfectly good sense—and differing over them may bring conflicts among people who do not share them. That is why people often, though not always, argue "personal" judgments strenuously; regardless of how it may be with drinks at the dinner table, the economy of the world *may* not permit the simultaneous satisfaction of differing tastes.

But it seems clear that differences of judgment over works of art in artistically relevant controversy are not of that "personal" sort at all. No one takes people who differ in an artistically relevant controversy to be competing over the demands to be exacted of a finite economy. In fact, one says that in the artistically relevant controversy the question of how to allocate resources depends upon *settlement* of the differences.

3. *The Relations of "Esthetic Judgment:* But, of course, not all "personal" differences are "esthetic" differences, in that they constitute differences over appreciations. Differences over appreciations are special. Yet in the respect that they are regarded as "personal" they are over "tastes." There arises the familiar and unavoidable disqualification of the rule of taste as a principle of artistically relevant controversy all over again: if one judgment "offers up" or "states" my taste as appreciation

[15] See above, Chapter 3, section I.

with respect to an object, then where another man's judgment offers his, his appreciation and mine have no logical relation. Taking artistically relevant judgments as judgments *of* taste, then if I say, "*War and Peace* is too long," and you say, "Not so, it's just the right length" (I "appreciate" its length; you do not), we argue the positions as contraries only by forgetting certain implied prefixes to *both* our statements: prefixes such as "in my view," "according to my preference," "to my taste," "in my judgment," and so on. We have tried to deal with assertions in indirect discourse as though they were assertions in direct discourse. When we place "esthetic" judgments in their proper frame it turns out that we have made logically independent statements. We ought no more to argue over appreciation of works of art than we argue over the virtues of Manhattans versus Martinis, which we nevertheless do and in proportion to our seriousness.

Therefore, the rule of taste cannot be the rule of artistically relevant judgment unless I have been mistaken and there *is* some way around this difficulty, and the other, too.

IV. Some Artful Dodges

The ways around the extremities of estheticism are quite familiar. Many of them, in fact, have already cropped up in the discussion of the principles of consumption. Yet so prevalent are the evasions of estheticism that if ever we are to be in a position to examine the language of esthetic discourse and its claims freely we must again accept repetition and find some assurance, in specific relation to the problems of artistically relevant judgment, that those evasions do not succeed.

1. The first of the network of evasions that concern us here—for evasions do indeed come in networks, one evasion in its last moments appealing to another—has a classic illustration in Mill's distinction between "higher" and "lower" pleasures within the context of a kind of ethical estheticism. Knowing that people do distinguish among pleasures and believing one man's judgment better than another's, Mill tried to distinguish among the *intrinsic* values of pleasure; given pleasure as the sole standard of value, he had no choice. He did so, as everybody knows, by appealing to a public acquainted with *both* the allegedly higher and lower pleasures; and he picked for the "higher" pleasures the pleasure that public preferred.

Listen now to an esthetician seeking to differentiate judgments in humor: "If," argues this writer, given a person with maximum capacity for sensing and enjoying all the different kinds of humor, "such a person preferred one to another comic object, it would not be because he was limited in capacity or viewpoint but because being able to experience all the kinds in all the ways, he would be more able to compare. And what he chose as more comic would be likely to be more comic in an eminent sense just because of his qualifications." [16]

Now it seems to me that the notion of a privileged public will not work to explain controversially relevant distinction in judgment for the arts any more than it did for rules of ethical behavior. The first of the difficulties, of course, is explaining just what one does when one's elites split. Just as Mill in effect dodges the crucial question of establishing a criterion for distinguishing among his pleasures by assuming a uniformity of agreement among "qualified" observers, so the appeal to a privileged public amounts to an evasion of the interesting problem of deciding how to patch up significant disagreements. One notes that where people *agree* there is no problem.

Moreover, there remains the question, even assuming agreement among the elite, of what "agreement" amounts to. For if it means only that people of given "qualifications" will decide in a certain way, then asserting that one pleasure is "higher" than another or one object is more "comic" than another amounts either to a tautology or a mystery that reference to "an eminent sense" in no way dispels. The judgments of those who judge otherwise in either case remains, in all logic, unaffected. Nor will it suffice at this point to ring in the qualifications of "true" or "experienced" judges in training, sensitivity, information, and so on. For (a) these advantages lend authority only when it is possible to show that they lead to a high incidence of right judgment; and (b) simply making qualification a guarantee of correct judgment leaves the controversy wide open to the double problem of determining just what, in the concrete, and not merely rhetorically, those qualifications are and of saying (assuming they are agreed upon) when they have properly been employed. Concretely, any critic of spine and sense confronted by an elite who differ with him will either doubt the adequacy of their training, sensitivity, maturity, information, etc., or else marvel at how even Homer nods. Someone may tell him that, of course, the public of the wisest and best cannot be granted unquestioned authority; that there are times we must risk defying it and reach out on our own responsibility toward a public more "ideal," not knowing but only trusting that something really possible is there to support us.[17] But he will wonder, while agreeing that no "public" is entirely to be trusted, how a "public of the wisest and the best"

[16] Albert Hofstadter, "On the Grounds of Esthetic Judgment," *The Journal of Philosophy*, LIV, 22 (Oct. 24, 1957), p. 685. Each of my alleged evasions is persuasively argued here by Professor Hofstadter.

[17] *Ibid.*, p. 686.

assumes even *tentative* authority when there exists no independent possibility of verifying their wisdom and what, therefore, it *means* to talk about a public still "more ideal."

In sum, if one begins with judgments of tastes one ends with them; and the upshot is one large ad hominem: "See how much more refined I am than you are"—an ad hominem which just those persons whom Mill and his esthetician imitators would introduce as authorities in the matter of the higher and the lower would probably be the most reluctant to push. For who would know better than such a one that when he asserted his preference for *New Yorker* humor over Bushman humor, knowing both intimately as he does, he is merely pushing his *personal* taste? Precisely in questions of taste, to understand is to forgive. That is how civilized persons know it is merely a question of taste.

2. The next evasion requiring attention is the closely allied Aristotelian evasion, except that Aristotle himself probably never committed it. For if Aristotle was right in telling people who wanted to know what it meant to be good to ask the good man, so it would seem that those estheticians also are right in referring people who seek good taste to the man of good taste.

Now the point is that the solution seems to hold good in virtue of an equivocation concerning the level of reference. The pedagogue or the legislator, whose vantage points chiefly concerned Aristotle in both his ethics and politics, indeed depends upon the fact that some people are better than others, and he uses those persons, their characters and decisions, if not their opinions, as models. Furthermore, it is also true that the people whose language and practice one examines in order to understand *the kind of thing* virtuous action consists in, will, at least, include the good people, although one would prefer it to include the wicked as well. But the pseudo-Aristotelian rejoinder to the problems of the rule of taste requires *more:* that anything the virtuous man does is ipso facto virtuous, which is considerably more than Aristotle wished to say. Knowing that virtuous men could lapse from virtue, he attempted so far as he could to organize a concrete theory of the practice of a "rational" life. And *there* lies the moral for inquiry into artistically relevant judgments. For what we (and Aristotle) want to know about the virtuous man, in so far as he serves as a model for the man of good taste, is by what communicable procedures he comes to his virtuous decisions, procedures such that, should he fail, then on the recollection of a more tranquil moment, he can tell himself that he has. Aristotle's men of virtue were men whose virtue consisted finally in the way they achieved a practical reason, not Christian saints whose examples not only defied reason but were analyzable on no rational principle.

3. There exists, however, a third and rather more popular evasion of the predicament of estheticism. One turns esthetic judgments into "verifiable" affairs. One denies that esthetic *judgments* are reports by making them predictions of the occurrence or nonoccurrence of certain kinds of "values." Suppose you say Bach wrote better music than Tchaikovsky and I disagree. You answer, "When you're older and more mature and have listened to more music you will be more capable of perceiving values in Bach you miss now, and learn to prefer them." *If* your answer states the issue (assuming one can explain the sense of "perceiving values in Bach you miss now") then indeed one of us is wrong, assuming the music not of equal value, and a logical relation has been established between esthetic judgments in a context of consumption.

Yet, surely, it is obvious enough that a prediction about future responses is no less a sentence in psychology than is a statement about a present response; and if one really wants to argue that there are no artistically relevant judgments, only sociological or psychological statements, one ought to say so instead of pretending to give a theory of what the critic or artist wants to do when he judges. Why, then, should anyone hold that artistically relevant judgments are predictions about consumers in a certain area?

Because, I would suggest, the simple substitution of a *prediction* for a diction does not finish the predictive theory's mistakes at all. There exists a mistake which makes the mistake credible—credible because that underlying mistake is not a mistake as such, but only for the prediction theory of artistically relevant judgment. For people normally do try to adjust their decisions to what they suspect of the future; predictions of eventualities in an area of action are always relevant as evidence for or against some decision. Why then, some ask, will predictions not also serve as evidence for discriminating a good taste from a poor one? Such is the leap of the pragmatic theory of artistically relevant judgment as that theory coalesces different ends: the end of consumer fulfillment and the end of effective action. But it is logically impossible to apply the logic of action to a domain of "judgment," which, on its own hypothesis, is entirely consummatory, the domain where action reaps its rewards; nor does the insistence on the "esthetic" or consummatory as an "aspect" of a continuous action change the situation, if it is the esthetic qua esthetic which we now wish to judge.

Concretely, then: in appealing to my musical future, at the moment you take moments of consummation as ultimate in judgment, telling me that eventually I will prefer Bach no longer states any consideration pertinent to my preference for Tchaikovsky. When the very force of the "esthetic" judgment inheres in the way the object strikes me, why should a future "now" legislate to a present one? Why should we hold it against a "pro" or "anti" sentiment that it comes earlier in time than its successor? In truth, it is to proposals that the future is relevant, not to tastes. Proposals tie times together; tastes are delighted to take things, one way or the other, as they *are.* And unless we can develop artistically relevant *proposals,* predictions about the course of our tastes will either prove irrelevant or, if relevant, relevant to a nonartistic controversy as we urge how fostering one kind of taste or another will ruin a character, strengthen it, etc.

It is plain how the argument about my bad taste in preferring Tchaikovsky to Bach will continue. You say that I will prefer Bach when I am older, more mature, and have wider experience in music. "I see," I must answer, "you want me to give the future a little push." For I have encountered this sort of transition, in which prediction smuggles in a decision, more than once before and not only in discussing criticism. "I will be glad to oblige—but only *if* Bach is indeed superior to Tchaikovsky. If he is, then the prediction that I will prefer him in the future indeed predicts an increase in maturity, knowledgeability, and so on. But if he is not—and, of course, it seems to me he isn't—then no matter how true your prediction about the course my taste will follow, far from making me change my mind *now,* it merely gives me further reason to lament the sadness of my lot: that after the fires of youth I should, also, come to settle for the pallid exercises that appeal in middle age!"

4. Apparently, the evasion of prediction evokes the evasion of "maturity." Maturity, used as a weapon, is always something that "will" happen, so that the appeal to maturity seems to rest on a prediction. Nevertheless, the heart of the argument consists in distinguishing a "real" ("mature") taste from an apparent ("present," not "mature") taste. "When you are more mature you will prefer the *Divine Comedy* to the *Rubaiyat,* even though you differ with me now. Therefore, work toward that end—don't fight it." A man's "true" judgment reflects his fully developed taste. Some people manage to contradict their real esthetic selves. They oughtn't.

The only difficulty, of course, is determining when in fact one is working toward maturity in esthetic taste and when not. So in the artistically relevant controversy that continually engages the diligent critic, maturity—like war guilt—is always determined by the victorious side; and he observes the depressing alternation in the favors of fortune. Clearly, criteria of "maturity," however they work, will work only with familiar objects judged by accepted standards, and for the controversy itself maturity lies hidden like a homunculus in the bottom of the mind.

There is reason to think, then, that the normal version is not adequate to settle the divisions that divide people in an artistically relevant controversy, if only because its conception of the claims which divide them is faulty. The claims that critics put forward in their judgments no doubt concern taste, intimately and essentially. But there are many senses of "concern" and the artistically relevant controversy might invariably raise questions *about* taste without therefore being a question of taste. Maturity, predictions as such, the qualities of an elite do not, as they are supposed to, save the normal version from the consequences of its choice of a context of consumption, since they either presuppose the artistically relevant judgments they exist to justify or turn out irrelevant to any artistically relevant claim.

V. The Context of Production

Therefore, to avoid the difficulties of the dogma of the work of art itself and the dogma of estheticism, there is a grave need to consider not only the reference question but the claims question in terms of a choice of context other than the choice of a context of consumption. And since the proper analysis of reasons in artistically relevant controversy might reasonably be expected to depend upon the nature of the object such controversy addresses itself to (the reference question) and the nature of what is at stake with respect to such objects (the claims question), we must in time be able to formulate a suitable interpretation of what reasons are like in a context alternative to consumption (the reasons question). "A context alternative to the context of consumption" is a long and much too bland phrase. Henceforth accepting the risks which attend the expression, I shall speak instead of a "context of production." [18] All artistically relevant controversy over the arts occurs in a context of production in the sense that the conduct of that controversy exhibits regulative principle of a certain kind, not, of course, in the sense that that context commits anyone to a special brand or style of criticism (the "productive" criticism). It is, of course, to a context of production that one would need to turn, insofar

[18] For the expression "context of production" but not for its content or the wisdom of its use here, I am indebted to Professor W. V. Quine, who in conversation several years ago characterized the position I was taking then as a proposal to consider the arts "in a context of production."

as that context is construed for the claims and reasons question, to make good, among other things, the analysis offered [19] for esthetic terms.

In a context of production the parties to the construction argument function according to the regulative principles remarked so far: the rules of use, impersonality, objectivity; the rule of law; and the rule of respect. The first three were offered to replace the consumption rules of right, taste, and Rorschach; the rule of law said something about how arguments are actually controlled in the construction argument; the rule of respect established a system of constraints by means of which critics might achieve their announced ends of objective reference. Such expressions as "work of art in proper relation" and "the construction of a construction" showed those rules operative in contradistinction to the normal-version dogma of the work of art itself. For the rest, our principle task will be to exhibit the rules for claims and reasons (and not only for the construction argument but for any other arguments which may comprise the artistically relevant controversy) through a similar juxtaposition against the rules operative in a context of consumption. For such juxtaposition, after all, is the point of proffering the context of production as a context *alternative* to a context of consumption.

But at the moment I want merely to show what justifies the use of the expression "context of production" and what I definitely do not mean by it. Obviously, the expression indicates something considered important about the principles which define the context so named.

1. Let it first be stressed that a "context of production" for the analysis of artistically relevant controversy does not shift judgmental authority from those on the consuming end to those on the producing end, on the ground that authority rightfully belongs to the latter qua producers.[20] The conduct of the construction argument in its current description plainly requires no allocation of authority one way or the other. Further: "Production" is for the sake of "consumption." A prime trouble with the context of consumption was just that the rule of right did hold in that context, not that the context of consumption had it wrong. It would be absurd to say that if only one examined the artistically relevant controversy seriously enough, consumption would turn out to be for the sake of production in a consumption-production situation, and only because this time production was the production of art.

[19] See Chapter 5, Section V.

[20] Nor, of course, are artists necessarily better critics than critics so that critics ought to get their opinions from artists. On the whole, I think it probably true that artists, despite their foibles, make better critics than the people who get into the criticism business. People in the criticism business are fond of pointing out the wild mistakes of artists. They are less fond of pointing out their own absurdities.

A "context of production" is asserted for the critic qua critic regardless of who the critic might be: artist or, in the formal sense, "critic." It is precisely that interpretation of criticism which founds criticism upon a division of labor between those who produce and those who consume (and therefore judge) which setting up a context of production as an alternative to the context of consumption refuses. The most elegant of connoisseurs occupies no higher logical ground in the artistically relevant controversy than does the merest artist; and it is certain that the artist occupies a higher ground than the mere voyeur, if that is all he is—for at least the artist has a piece of the action.

> The more venerable academic element, still under the sway of Trilby, looks upon an artist as a mad genius. This group believes, and I think the public joins it, that an artist has no idea of why he paints; he simply has to. Among the younger and more advanced collegians, the New Criticism has taken over, but the artist himself fares no better. For according to this very avant-garde view, it makes little difference what an artist paints or what he himself happens to think; it is the viewer who really accounts for the meaning of the works, and even he would flounder were it not for theorist, or critic. In his hands rest all the clues to art; he is the high priest of the art process.[21]

I have used the expression "context of production" to side with Ben Shahn in his polemic against the normal version construal of artist and critic, most particularly of critic, although, of course, Shahn need not accept the assistance.

2. Polemic aside, however, the following considerations constitute the chief reasons for considering criticism in a "context of production," and they determine what that inclusion may amount to in general.

A. First, considering criticism "in a context of production" signalizes the reality and significance of the construction argument. It signalizes that the task of criticism is not simply to register tastes and impressions, or to decode codes, but to prepare the object presented for appreciation. The critical object is precisely the incomplete object. The critic completes; and he has that share in the preparation of art for public consumption.

Some people, of course, considering the critical object finished, complete, and waiting, conceive that criticism can only "interpret" what has been presented. They face the problem of attaching an "interpretation" to an object which, so far as it is indeed completed, needs one interpreta-

[21] Ben Shahn, *The Shape of Content* (Cambridge, Mass.: Harvard University Press, 1957), p. 21.

tion no more than another. What I have called the construction argument has been cut off from its base; its very point as well as its logic have come open to questions "in principle."

Under these circumstances, to speak of the construction argument "in a context of production" as a "making" or a "doing" kind of decision process calls attention to the ways in which disputes over what would otherwise be considered "interpretations" become fundamentally relevant. They become so (even forgetting for the moment the rule of respect) through the rules of use, objectivity, law, and impersonality, which ensure that the construction argument does not come to a confrontation of private fantasies.

The critic really does "make" something of a critical object. He makes, through the process of argument, an object at once determinate and public. It is the process of the argument which justifies the use of expressions like "production" and "make." All arguments are not of that sort.

B. The next, and perhaps most essential reason for taking criticism in a context of production has already been intimated in connection with the polemical point. It concerns the centrality of the rule of respect (for created objects) in artistically relevant controversy. The critic not only makes something of an *object,* he makes something of an object conceived as a created object, as a construction—the outcome of a specific artistic and social matrix. The critical activity is not self-sufficient activity but a dependent one, dependent on the rules and problems of actual artists. It is this dependency of critics upon the doing of art which is expressed by the provision of a "context of production" for the artistically relevant controversy.

C. As will be seen in more detail, the "good and responsible" critic functions in "a context of production" because the justification of his decisions does not differ in type (although, surely, critics and artists often differ over specific artistic decisions) from the justification of decisions in the process of artistic performance. There is not one set of formative rules for the critic as such and one set for the artist as such. And the following common agreements signify that justifications are not normally considered to differ in type, theoretical considerations aside:

Everyone would say of a critic who would establish a difference in justification that his criticism is no longer artistically relevant. Of an artist who would do the same it would be said that his justifications lack "esthetic" significance, that they fall outside the scope of art.

If a decision on the nature (or value) of a work of art contradicted, in some sense of the word, an artist's decision in putting his performance together, we would say that both decisions could not be right, and vice versa.

There are not two kinds of reason, one for art and one for criticism. That criticism is not a self-sufficient but a dependent activity perhaps explains why. At any rate, how judgments and reasons also call for and define a "context of production" will be seen in detail as the argument proceeds.

D. The last reason for speaking about a "context of production" in contradistinction to a "context of consumption," despite the obvious risks of misunderstandings, is to link in a, hopefully, fruitful way considerations of the artistically relevant controversy with the consideration of other kinds of things. Substantially, we "understand," in a sense of "understanding" particularly appropriate to philosophy, what we are about when we see how whatever it is we are about compares with other activities. The use of expressions like "consumption" and "production" constitutes an invitation to seek analogies and disanalogies of a particular sort. Asserting that the rules and principles of artistically relevant controversy occur in "a context of production" rather than "a context of consumption" summarizes the results of a wager: that those rules and principles are less like those employed in certain sorts of consumer activities (more of which later) and more like those employed in legal and scientific activities (in which warranted criticism is criticism of the activity with respect to the ends and criteria of that activity.)

The sense of a fundamental metaphor noted, then, let me return to the general problem of this book, which is to present a picture of criticism in a context of production, criticism as it is rather than as the normal version presents it.

Chapter 7

Consumer Claims and Artistically Relevant Claims

The last chapter compared artistically relevant criticism with its normal version, criticism with metacriticism. The present task is to compare criticism with criticism, to show how even when a consumer criticism and an artistically relevant one deal with the same object (the "Mona Lisa," the Parthenon, Humpty-Dumpty, a happening, the Late Nite Show) they in fact treat them differently and ask different things of us. The normal version aside, consumer criticism is genuine enough. To differentiate artistically relevant criticism from consumer criticism, to the extent called for, I shall assume there is no intrinsic mystery in what critics are demanding in particular cases and seek the warrant for what rules and distinctions may finally emerge from whatever may be found concretely to be said. For in the differences between consumer and artistically relevant discourse, as those differences function in practice, lies the crux of the issue between the normal version and attempts to formulate "a context of production" for artistically relevant controversy.

The following, then, are examples of critical discourse, most, though not all of which, would ordinarily be taken as artistically relevant:

A. R. P. Blackmur judges Hardy: "Hardy is the great example of a sensibility violated by ideas; and perhaps the unique example, since Swift, of a sensibility great enough—locked enough in life—to survive the violation." [1]

B. Roger Fry again, on Greek art and sculpture: "It is open to anyone to prefer the elegant precision of the Greek line to the plastic power of the Chinese, only we must take note that all those who are revered as great draughtsmen from Giotto down to Degas, with the possible exception of Albrecht Durer, have followed the Chinese and not the Greek method." [2]

[1] *Form and Value in Modern Poetry* (Garden City, N. Y.: Doubleday, 1957), p. 31.

[2] *Last Lectures* (Boston: Beacon, 1962), p. 185.

C. Tennessee Williams adds to his description of a director's criticism: "In the case of Cat [*Cat on a Hot Tin Roof*] he [E. Kazan, the director] was shown the first typed version of the play, and he was excited by it, but he had definite reservations about it which were concentrated on the third act. The gist of his reservations can be listed as three points: one, he felt that Big Daddy was too vivid and important a character to disappear from the play except as an offstage cry after the second act curtain; two, he felt that the character of Brick should undergo some apparent mutation as a result of the virtual vivisection that he undergoes in his interview with his father in Act Two." [3]

D. Yeats in judgment on contemporary poetry:

> "Irish poets, learn your trade,
> Sing whatever is well made,
> Scorn the sort now growing up
> All out of shape from toe to top,
> Their unremembering hearts and heads
> Base born products of base beds.
> Sing the peasantry, and then
> Hard-riding country gentlemen,
> The holiest of monks, and after
> Porter-drinker' randy laughter;
> Song the lords and ladies gay
> That were beaten into the clay
> Through seven heroic centuries;
> Cast your mind on other days
> That we in coming days may be
> Still the indomitable Irishry." [4]

And again:

> "Shakespearean fish swam the sea, far away from land;
> Romantic fish swam in nets coming to the hand;
> What are all those fish that lie gasping on the strand?" [5]

E. Francis Fergusson summarizes *The Skin of Our Teeth,* "the marriage of Plato and Groucho Marx," and explicates his adverse judgment on Wilder a playwright: "A reading of *Our Town* and *The Skin of Our Teeth* suggests that Wilder's extraordinary freedom and virtuosity in the theatre is gained through eluding rather than solving the problem which most playwrights feel as basic; that of embodying form and

[3] *Cat on a Hot Tin Roof,* (New York: New Directions, 1955), p. 151.
[4] *The Collected Poems of W. B. Yeats* (New York: Macmillan, 1958), p. 343.
[5] *Ibid.,* p. 236.

meaning in character and language. . . . But Wilder has seen how it is possible to leave the 'greater number' in peace with the material understandable to it, and Plato in peace in the super-temporal realm of the Mind of God. He is thus able to be 'for' Plato (as politicians of every persuasion are for Peace, Freedom and Prosperity) and at the same time devote his great gifts to entertaining the crowd or 'group mind.' "[6]

F. Mr. Frank Alston, in the *New York World Telegram* and *Sun,* criticizes *The Body Beautiful:* "A Wow! This is a real fun show, one for the gang. Get a ringside chair, Mac."[7]

Let us now examine our illustrations for the sense they might make to critic or layman who would presume to say he got their point. The idea is to do so independently of the reference question and its results.

I. Artistically Irrelevant Criticism, Consumer Style

Everyone will admit that Mr. Alston's happy talk lays down a sort of judgment on *The Body Beautiful;* it presents a simple but a genuine enough criticism which, regarded naïvely, leaves small doubt as to what it has in view:

1. *The Body Beautiful* is a "Wow." Mr. Alston thinks that the show has done so well in the entirely informal competition of entertaining people that it is entitled to be called a "Wow!" But the fact that the statement, "X is a Wow!" shows enthusiasm and, hopefully, generates enthusiasm does not justify a purely emotive theory of Broadway reviewing. "X is a Wow!" is a statement in stimulus-response psychology: "If you see it, you will say 'Wow!' as I did."

2. "This is a real fun show." Mr. Alston has now specified somewhat more clearly than he did in calling *The Body Beautiful* a "Wow!," the respect in which the competition, presumably with other shows of the sort, was waged and won. If you come to the performance looking for a good cry or for deep wisdom, you will not find them. But if you come looking for fun, you will.

This *is* a "fun show"; and a "real" "fun show" because if you come looking for the right sort of thing, it is predictable that you will find it.

3. "Something for the gang." Mr. Alston has now specified the group for which his production holds true, the elite who will really get what is

[6] *The Human Image in Dramatic Literature* (Garden City, N. Y.: Doubleday Anchor Books, 1957), p. 59.
[7] Feb. 2, 1958.

to be gotten from *The Body Beautiful:* namely, "the gang." The fact that "the gang" does not necessarily possess much social status regarded from the outside in should not lead to the supposition that it lacks such status looking from the inside out. The "gang" is the public that "ought to be" interested in *The Body Beautiful*—as the market is a group of people who "ought to" buy your product.

4. "Get a ringside chair, Mac." Who is a member of that relevant public? "Mac," obviously. People who feel themselves referred to in an acceptable manner when called "Mac" are the people for whom *The Body Beautiful* has been composed. They and they alone are qualified to judge, and they judge the adequacy of Mr. Alston's criticism by going to see *The Body Beautiful* and seeing if they don't find it a "real fun show."

Someone may perhaps find the imperative mood of what is after all an injunction to Mac, slighted so far. Indeed, it would be foolish to deny that Mr. Alston constructs his remarks about *The Body Beautiful* to induce people to come and see it. However, those remarks assert for *argument* nothing more pretentious than a prediction of how a market of Macs will respond. If, therefore, someone differed with Mr. Alston's criticism of the "fun show" and proposed that Mac avoid getting a ringside seat, it would be understood all around that the difference in advice ("Buy!" or "Don't buy!") was derivative of a means-end claim, settled as soon as it could be settled whether *The Body Beautiful* was a "Wow!" or not. For, and this is the primary point, nobody ever *legislates* to a market conceived as a market. One *appeals* to it. Therefore, the injunction is "derivative." The *market* decides, not Alston.

If, then, his claims illustrate the claims of consumer criticism—of criticism in a context of consumption—we may generalize as a formative principle for making judgments of the consumer order: "Let all your judgments be claims to knowledge." The claims that generate controversy in matters of consumption are cognitive claims. For the fact that among the members of Mr. Alston's market nobody contests the rule "*de gustibus* . . . ," far from removing the possibility of criticism such as his, states merely the condition for its functioning: that people be *free* to find *The Body Beautiful* to their taste or not.

Accordingly, a second characterization of consumer discourse follows. By providing the condition for verifying consumer critiques, the rule of taste indicates the particular kind of cognitive status appropriate to consumer claims. For with respect to the ends of taste, the cognitive claims of Alston-style discourses are technological. They include what Kant would have called a maxim of prudence. Once such a maxim is formulated, it does not matter whether the end to be achieved is the excitement signified by "Wow!," or shelter from the wind and rain, or the national defense. Taste functions as a standard for the institution of a technology.

Lastly, it is plain that Mr. Alston poses no mere hypothetical rule for his considered judgment, but an assertion about an existential state of affairs as well. His judgment asserts a market—a market of Macs. If *he* talks to no one, he is a bad critic. Accordingly, the final mark of such cognitive criticism as Mr. Alston's, hence the defining characteristic of judgment in the bald context of consumption, remains the prediction that under specifiable conditions a real market will be happy. On *that* strictly cognitive basis hangs Mr. Alston's demand, advice, or persuasion to buy.

In sum, then: not only do we have the rule in a context of consumption for formulating judgments, "Let all your judgments be claims to knowledge," we have also the modifying rules, "Let all your claims to knowledge be prudential," and "Let all your prudence be the prudence of the market." The characteristics of a genuine consumer criticism follow from those regulative principles. But no one, including Mr. Alston, would ever dream that he had presented artistically relevant discourse or that, in disagreeing with him, one would differ with respect to an artistically relevant claim about *The Body Beautiful.*

To be sure, maybe *The Body Beautiful* "is" art. Nevertheless, it was not discussed "as art." And one might treat the Elgin Marbles as so many "body beautifuls." In what way do the treatments differ?

II. Artistically Relevant Criticism: The Difference

The ways the critical remarks of Messrs. Blackmur, Fry, Williams, Yeats, and Fergusson differ from Mr. Alston's provide the distinction between an artistically relevant and a consumer criticism.

1. Mr. Alston has, more than obviously, given his approval to *The Body Beautiful* in a "rave" review. "Go see it," he says. "You can't miss." He might easily explain, as an old hand at "show biz," what made the show so enjoyable that he and others adjudge it "A Wow!" But he does not judge *The Body Beautiful* a "Wow!" because he has discovered the tricks of the trade through which *The Body Beautiful* secures its effects. He rather looks for the tricks, if he does, because *The Body Beautiful* gives people so good a time. If he himself liked *The Body Beautiful,* he might ask himself, "Now why in the world did I like it?" But if he did *not* enjoy the show, he would merely look for the *explanation* of why he did not and no collection of explanations of what went on could ever conceivably convince him that he *ought* to like it. The show makes you

go for it, or it does not. The question is a factual one, "in stimulus-response psychology." In each of the other instances, however, if you asked the critic why he approved or disapproved, and if he felt the question worth answering, he would support his judgment by no causal explanation of why he or anyone else might be expected to approve, but by a reason for "liking" or approving, however inconclusive the reason. So, for example, Yeats, finding Shakespearean and other fish swimming at different depths, does not explain *why,* as a matter of fact, anyone in particular actually approves Shakespearean over contemporary poetry; he proffers, rather, a reason for preferring Shakespearean poetry, regardless of whether, on encounter, one actually prefers it or not. And until you see that there is something "wrong" unless you prefer the living fish to the dying ones, that therefore you "ought" in some sense to prefer Shakespeare to the contemporary, you have missed the point of Yeats' little poem.

In sum, findings follow approvals for *consumer* discourse; but for the other examples, with the possible exception of the director's criticism of the Williams play, of which more later, it would seem that approvals follow findings. The difference in the order of criticism reflects the difference between a technological and what now looks like a nontechnological mode of discourse. In a technological discourse, ends or approvals admonish construction; in the nontechnological discourse of artistically relevant criticism, construction admonishes ends or approvals. Hence if consumer discourse advances *predictive* claims, artistically relevant discourse advances *prescriptive* claims, and it constructs or "produces" through its prescriptions, the "taste" that it approves. Of this difference even a normal version account must manage some explanation.

To be sure, one ought not to draw the difference too sharply and without obvious qualifications. Even in the criticism of the arts technological questions occur about how critical objects actually achieve their effects upon audiences. The point is, they occur subordinately, not as standards, but as interesting considerations to be manipulated in the construction of taste or approvals, as data rather than ends. Also, of course, prescriptions for construing critical objects one way or another ("This is a real fun show!") occur in the "technological" discourse of consumer criticism. Still, they merely specify the conditions for the market's attaining *its* end, and hence finally preserve the consumer order of appraisals and approval.

2. While Mr. Alston would have *failed* as a critic of his peculiar sort had he contented himself with diagnosing the nature and structure of *The Body Beautiful*—and *justifiably* lost his job had he not made it unmistak-

ably clear that *The Body Beautiful* was the kind of show that the market would approve or disapprove—the other criticisms seem to stand as criticism regardless of any inferences to approvals or disapprovals either of critics or specific markets. It is merely requisite that the respect in which a critical object is appraised or, ambiguously, approved for what it is, be judged somehow significant. Therefore, critics of the arts deem an "explicative" criticism genuine even when they prefer a more "judgmental" analysis; but Mr. Alston, as a consumer critic, would be absurd "explicating" *The Body Beautiful* except to a group of technicians in *The Body Beautiful* manufacturing business. Concern with production and consumption are rightly distinguished in one form of criticism, consumer criticism, in a respect in which they are not rightly distinguished for artistically relevant criticism.

That difference in concern is further emphasized by the consideration that, while Blackmur (quotation A) gives no summary judgment of Hardy's work (one can say only that he finds "values" in it) and Alston leaves no question of his "judgment" of *The Body Beautiful,* it would be absurd to say that Alston is a better or worse critic than Blackmur. But ought he not be better or worse unless both critics were situated differently with respect to appraisals of what they found? Such *would* actually be the conclusion of anyone unfamiliar with the kind of thing literary criticism is: "Come now, Mr. Blackmur—get to the point. Is the stuff something for the eggheads or not? Did you or did you not, egghead as you are, go for it?" There would be a failure to understand that this sort of harassment would constitute a radical misunderstanding, that Blackmur is a different *kind* of critic than Alston, neither "better" nor "worse." In calling attention to something perhaps not seen before—"Look at the way experience is artificially compressed by dogma and yet breaks through!"—Blackmur has indeed performed "a critic's job of work"; and that job of work properly induces us to approve the *importance,* however determined, of pointing out the sort of thing pointed out, rather than to approve or disapprove the critical object for being to our own or anyone else's taste.

Accordingly, Blackmur and others achieve what Eliot perhaps intended when he argued in favor of a criticism that would be "impersonal." Such "impersonality" has nothing to do with a colorless language, but merely with the fact that Blackmur is *not* concerned to "judge" Hardy in the sense that Alston is concerned to judge *The Body Beautiful.*

Similar considerations hold for Fergusson's judgment on the drama of Thornton Wilder, even though Fergusson's own position is more apparent than was Blackmur's on Hardy. Despite Fergusson's disapproval of

Wilder, it matters hardly at all to his critical claim whether or not we like or dislike Wilder's plays. He has simply tried to show how those plays operate and what, from one point of view, they amount to. Who would deny that his reference "the marriage of Plato and Groucho Marx" amounts to a literary judgment? Yet the remark does so not in so far as it is funny, which it is, and turns us away from *The Skin of Our Teeth,* which it does, but in so far as it *cuts.* Such, precisely, is *The Skin of Our Teeth,* under the skin. It would constitute the weakest possible rejoinder to answer, "Oh, you just don't like the play, that's why you talk that way."

Consider, now: do we go to the drama or not after reading Fergusson? Do we read Hardy after reading Blackmur, assuming we have not read Hardy before? It is clear why such questions cannot concern either Blackmur or Fergusson as critics, regardless of any incidental interest they might possess in educational uplift. For as critics of poetry and the theater they can rightly and sensibly disclaim *ulterior motives.* What you do with their criticism is your own affair; and here is another way to see the difference between Alston's kind of talk and theirs, since what you do on the basis of his criticism is precisely Alston's affair, every bit as much as your behavior is not for Blackmur and Fergusson.

"It is open to anyone," says Roger Fry, "to prefer the elegant precision of Greek line to the plastic power of the Chinese."

Artistically relevant criticism is "objective" [8] in the sense that (whatever the feeling of its deliverer) it seeks to present certain states of affairs for inspection while rejecting as inessential, at the least, approvals qua my-approval or your-approval, along with the causal relations among such facts. As for the approvals that allegedly exist in the "order" of criticism, Section III will consider them, for I have by no means said that the only possibilities for an approving critic are *consumer* approvals.

3. Nevertheless, it is obvious that in certain fundamental ways artistically relevant criticism differs decidedly from what people consider "objective" discourse. Criticism in the arts not only employs "value" terms; it

[8] Consider how even the very *force* of Yeats' lines, its poetic value, its "hardness," derives from the fact that we take this appraisal of Shakespeare and the others as "objective" rather than mood-engendering. So it *is,* says the poetry: the weakness of modern poetry has the reality of those fish gasping on the strand; it is part of the very order and state of nature. What is the poetry for if not to make us feel in our bones that Yeats does not aim merely to tell the way he *feels* about poetry or the way he thinks the various types of poetry will meet his readers' tastes? I am, indeed, tempted to argue further that not only the subjectivity of critical discourse but the subjectivity of poetry itself constitutes so much hog-wash. For some discussion of this latter point see my article, "Sin, Science and the Dry, Hard Style," in *Philosophy and Phenomenological Research,* XIX, 2 (Dec. 1958).

employs them neither in a mere descriptive or referential way nor technologically (as Mr. Alston might employ his value language to show how certain consumer effects depend upon doing thus and so). But *still* it does not follow that "esthetic" values are strange phantasms requiring a special vision to appraise them.

Briefly, then, people may "find," in appraising, that objects possess certain "values," much as a judge or a board of arbitrators or the assessor of home values would "find." They *decide* on values; they assign them and are nonetheless held liable for their decisions' being, as they readily admit, "responsible" and "objective" ones. Therefore it is always open to critics not only to describe the appearance, conditions, and consequences of human values, but also to prescribe them. Listening attentively to Fry or Yeats or Blackmur or Fergusson, one hears not just *descriptions* of "values" found, but *prescriptions for* "values," guidelines for making new value "findings," and the capacity to discriminate these findings determines membership in a proper public for the work of art under inspection.

Putting the matter traditionally, the non-Alstonian critic asserts for the "values" of a critical object not what *will,* necessarily, be found, but what *ought* to be found. Yeats does not mean that anyone will necessarily take his findings of Shakespeare, the Romantics, or of the moderns—he merely proposes that anyone, someone, see what he sees. Similarly, Fry discriminates a particular feeling for different sorts of draftsmanship, Fergusson for the "meaning" of *The Skin of Our Teeth,* and Blackmur for Hardy's poetic talent. Such and such, they say, are the significant things, the artistically relevant "values" of the critical object. Never mind how they justify their conclusions. Still, our non-Alstonians do not simply pick out things the audience already observes and call attention to them, as an Alstonian criticism might well do; they organize values, they "create" meanings that perhaps no one ever previously imagined. Their criticism is, or hopes to be, "creative."

That discourse is "value-bound" when the "values" to which critical discourse of the artistically relevant sort calls attention occur "actively." An "active" employment of values in a discourse "attributes" values to things in the sense of deciding on a construction, and *uses* the repertoire of "value" *descriptions* open to a consumer criticism, in its own "creative" way.

We may now state on the level of specific linguistic function that overall distinction between consumer and artistically relevant criticism which, misunderstood, seems to generate the most pervasive normal version perplexities, and perhaps gain new insight into those perplexities:

What marks off artistically relevant discourse in respect to findings or appraisals from the artistically irrelevant discourse that addresses itself to what seem roughly like the same sort of "values" is (a) precisely the attempt to preserve the "objective" and "impersonal" features noticed both in our discussion of the "Harry-relevance" content of esthetic content of esthetic concepts [9] and in subsection 2 of this section; and (b) the "value-bound" characteristics noticed here in subsection 3 along with the "noncognitive" order of criticism observed in subsection 1.

What characterizes artistically irrelevant discourse (again, artistically irrelevant discourse of that criticism which shares the largest vocabulary and frequently the same objects, consumer criticism) is the combination of an inactive use of value language plus "cognitive" discourse with the "subjective" and "personal" features of the rule of taste.

The normal version in its attempt to differentiate an *outright* consumer discourse from an artistically relevant one located the "objectivity" and "impersonality" of artistically relevant discourse in the rule of taste, and the "subjectivity" and "personal" characteristics in the "Harry-relevant" and decisional functions of critical discourse—in sum, systematically confused the two criticisms. It is small wonder that an endless supply of philosophical problems are generated, as people seek ideality in taste and taste in ideality, "objectivity" in a peculiar "subjectivity" and a peculiar "subjectivity" in "objectivity," "truth" in "beauty" and "beauty" in "truth." "Artistically relevant discourse" has very literally been misread in a "context of consumption."

4. We come to the apparent counter-example to the previous discussions of appraisals and their relations to approvals in consumer and artistically relevant criticism. For in the order of Kazan's reported criticism, findings seemingly follow disapprovals, the intent appears overtly technological, and value discourse seems to occur inactively. Yet it seems unduly harsh to call that criticism artistically irrelevant.

A tempting solution of the difficulty blames the failure to fit the pattern on Kazan's proposing a *director's* or, generally, a participant's criticism rather than that of an observer or judge. There are *two* kinds of criticism, the solution affirms: artistically relevant observer's *and* artistically relevant producer's. The kind of production-consumption dichotomy this essay has chiefly concerned itself to attack seems to be required after all. It is apparent that Kazan might have made the same observations from a seat in the orchestra after a performance of the *unrevised* play, and with equal warrant, as he explained what characteristics of the play

[9] See Chapter 5, Section V.

he, as a good observer or judge, found wrong. And it is equally apparent that if he had watched the revised play *after* Williams had made the requested revisions, far from venturing on a logically irrelevant enterprise, he would have taken his responses as confirmation or disconfirmation of his original suggestions. So if Kazan's criticism has the characteristics it seems to have, even the nondirector's criticism cannot have the characteristics attributed to it here, at least not always.

The resolution of the Kazan quandary, which seems to make it necessary to surrender what has been won or to deny the artistic relevance Kazan seems to have, lies, I propose, on the very surface of his remarks. Those remarks, themselves, as is so often the case, are ambiguous. Reading them, one sees that there *is* a practical doubt whether or not Kazan takes exception as a producer out to produce a play that will go with a Broadway audience, as the *Cat* did; whether he is a technician examining a product to test if it will do the job; or whether, as the cliché goes, his criticisms display an interest in drama. What, then, does Kazan *mean* when he says that "Big Daddy was too vivid and important a character to disappear from the play . . . after the second act curtain," or that "the character of Brick should undergo some apparent mutation"? Only that question settles the puzzle over Kazan's criticism.

For the question does not actually concern Kazan's motivations, rather the point of his specific utterances. That point would appear, presumably, in further questioning and make possible a decision whether his remarks were artistically relevant.

When Kazan "feels" that Big Daddy is too vivid and important to disappear, does he justify that feeling by what he finds in the play or does he interpret the play to account for his feeling? For, of course, it is justification that has been the theme all along in discussion of the order of criticism, not the critic's psychology (which might very well begin with an approval or disapproval and seek to make it good).

Why should Brick's character undergo some apparent mutation? Because the mutation constitutes the means to the market's approval and Kazan is an expert on what the market will approve? Then we have an illustration of "technological," Alston-like criticism. Should the character undergo the mutation in order to be true to psychology? "Most people would behave in such and such ways." Then, while his remarks have as such ceased to be restricted by marketing ends, they are nonetheless descriptive, rather than artistically relevant, in the sense that one says that a particular description does or does not constitute a psychologically true or useful case study. But if, for example, Kazan had said, "Let us do plays so that the mutations characters undergo will be the probable ones," or, "Let us do plays so that they undergo mutations when such and such a kind of person does," then, whatever the proposal's worth, we would think his criticism showed signs of artistic relevance.

When Kazan talks about vividness and importance, does he want to say something like, "When you read the typed version of the play, you will as a matter of fact find Big Daddy vivid and important," or "When you read the typed version, you ought to find Big Daddy vivid and important, and such such and such is the kind of vividness and importance I want you to find for such and such reasons"? We do not know. To the extent we do not know we are hard put to determine the artistic relevance of his appraisals, although we may *surmise* that very likely he meant to say both. Hence we would have to inquire further to discover whether his criticism at this point amounted to a consumer criticism (a finding of how people will react) or to artistically relevant criticism (a prescription of how people ought to find, given the circumstances, with or without the additional assertion that some of the circumstances ensure that the people will indeed so find).

III. Critical Differences Continued: Significant Approvals and Disapprovals

A fact that has been on the periphery of the discussion so far must now be brought to the center: overtly or not, regardless of critical doctrine, and with whatever emphasis, the critics of our illustrations do say as critics, "I like that," or, "That doesn't suit me," or, "That won't do"; and the artist who hears or overhears such comments may regard them as the justification (or damnation) of his labors. Therefore, *all* approval functions of critical discourse cannot be artistically irrelevant, not even all those that *sound* like consumer-type comments. What kind of "approval" or "disapproval," then, is "meaningful" in artistically relevant discourse? How does it compare with the kind Mr. Alston bestowed on *The Body Beautiful?* We must look to our examples; and I shall argue that only an unnecessarily dogmatic reading of critical discourse presumes that all the critic can be doing when he says, "I like that," is to record his taste; that the artist is *not* wrong to look for a different sense in which the expression "I like that" might signify a "dry" sense, a quiet, an "impersonal" sense.

"Dry" approvals, "impersonal" ones in contrast to "damp" ones, "personal" ones, "romantic" ones, to take a small leaf from Hulme's notebook (for Hulme's categories apply to criticism as well as to poetry), follow from taking seriously the basic approval-appraisal order of criticism discussed in subsection 1 of the previous section. Any "good and responsible" critic, when asked why he approves or disapproves, will say pretty precisely *what* he approves or disapproves. He will present appraisals of the critical object, "construct" the critical object, in support of his "liking." If you take Fergusson up and announce that you see through him after all, that when he talks about the marriage of Plato and Groucho Marx, you at least can tell he *really* disapproves of Thornton Wilder, then his retort is obvious: "Of course I disapprove of Thornton Wilder. But not necessarily because I didn't enjoy myself in the theater. Rather because I judge that anyone who mistakes the business of the playwright, as I have described it in my other excerpt, is a poor playwright." He, like any other critic, will want to emphasize the impersonality of his approval.

Nor is there anything novel or self-contradictory about an impersonal approval. Approving impersonally was what Hume, with considerable force, said we were doing when making moral judgments. Perhaps even that "disinterestedness" which Kant ascribed to the experience of beauty, properly taken, signifies the property of artistically relevant judgment in virtue of which the claims of "beauty" are not arbitrary but, somehow, controlled affairs. The nature of the reasonings—whether they are more like Hume's or more like Kant's or more like neither—that establish impersonal approvals does not enter now. It suffices that artist and critic both know that the spectator's responses, as personal, do not constitute criticism, that a personal reference proffers itself only in the guise of criticism and hence is "presumptuous."

What happens, then, when a critic approves or disapproves, and does so as a critic, "dryly," "impersonally"? I suggest that he makes a kind of proposal, and that the proposal does not simply say "Please me!"

Consider once again the account of director Kazan's criticism of Williams' play. Suppose that Williams took Kazan's approval and disapprovals seriously, as he did. Then, if Williams takes Kazan's remarks as artistically relevant, Williams will surely find the approvals and disapprovals expressed in those remarks interesting for the advice they give, advice that, knowing Kazan, he thinks to be very likely correct. A series of proposals constitutes the arguable element in Kazan's responses. Regardless of the ultimate "ground" of the proposals, it is inevitably the proposals—"Do such and such rather than such and such"—over which Kazan and Williams would have argued. That is what Kazan's approvals and disapprovals claim, and "I like such and such" in practice means "Do" or, of course, "Don't, but keep things as they are." The same kind of analysis works for a "dry, hard" approval in every instance of artistically relevant approval, even when the approver does not occupy the directorial chair.

Whatever the ultimate interpretation, when Fergusson disapproves of Wilder "for eluding rather than solving the problem which most playwrights feel as basic" (namely, "embodying form and meaning in character and language"), his disapproval proposes that playwrights do one sort of play rather than another. "Don't do as Wilder does, in this respect!" Suppose someone disagreed with Fergusson's recommendations; then he would find Fergusson's disapproval ill-advised. And suppose he approved rather than disapproved Fergusson's recommendations; then, if he agreed with Fergusson that Wilder was doing what Fergusson alleged, he would, all other factors equal, thereby disagree with Fergusson's recommendations. Whatever one wishes to make of the fact, Fergusson's artistically relevant approvals project specific demands.

Similar considerations are true down the line: when Blackmur talks about "a sensibility violated by ideas," he more than simply expresses his dislike for events called "violations"; he warns poets against a trap by the very selection of the term "violation"—and his warning may be read to apply to critics also, as an adjuration to take a certain kind of phenomenon into consideration when in the future they evaluate poetic works. There lies the *argumentative* force of his disapproval. And even Fry, in his delicate way, though, unlike Fergusson, addressing himself primarily to the connoisseurs of art rather than its producers, enjoins all good connoisseurs to forego their habits of appreciation for the moment and attend to incompatible practices among the people they consider "great draughtsmen"; so that the whole point of his approval is to recommend that artists follow the Chinese rather than the Greek line and that critics encourage them in that choice.

In effect, therefore, critical discourse suggests a reversal of the usual interpretation of "emotive" language.[10] Where the quarrel is all, "emotive" language seems to function *logically,* rather than, in that horrible misuse of the word, "poetically." For the emotive language in which approvals so frequently appear actually works to give notice that something is herewith proposed, somewhat in the manner of an assertion sign. Then the critic's apparently quite personal "I like that" signifies that a

[10] See, for an example of that interpretation, John Hospers in his book *An Introduction to Philosophical Analysis* (New York: Prentice-Hall, 1953), p. 3. "There are emotive words," he tells us, "words which do not stand for things but serve to please certain feelings in the speaker and/or evoke certain feelings in the listener. The purest emotive words are the interjections: 'hurrah,' 'phooey,' 'whoopee,' and so on. Most emotive words are also used to stand for things, and therefore are impure examples of emotive words: 'nasty,' 'beautiful,' 'contemptible.' " Words, of course, do as Hospers says; but, I am suggesting this "subjective" interpretation of emotive language exhausts the force of such language in very few contexts and misses the pertinence of such language entirely, in critical discourse.

certain critical object satisfies the kinds of proposals a critic wants to make for an art form, style, or even, under appropriate circumstances, for the structure of a specific work of art. So the bite of critical approval or disapproval becomes explicable: the artist finds in a "dry, impersonal" approval a place for his line of work, a plane which expands the sense and import of that work, and in a disapproval a displacement which contracts that sense and import. And such things are not trivial, as will be a particular individual's enthusiasm or lack of it, expressed in "emotive" language, except to those concerned with the individual himself. In critical approval there are great issues at stake, and this fact calls for the subordination of individual response no less than in science, law, or politics.

Therefore, critics have perhaps mistaken what they rebelled against when they sought to substitute pure explication for approval. They thought themselves rebelling against approvals and disapprovals as such when they rebelled against the identification of approval and "personal approval."

One last word of somewhat greater significance: the difference between the approvals of Alston-like consumer criticism and of artistically relevant criticism may now be more correctly understood. Mr. Alston's criticism, if taken as communicating the approval of a man doing a certain sort of critical job, does not, though it refers to "personal" approvals, communicate them as its point. The critic's own feelings do not really count (as they may indeed for a man tasting puddings), though he may use them as barometers of the entertainment weather. "Buy, buy now!" is the objective claim of his criticism; and it is this with which another consumer critic would take issue. In fixing upon a "dry, hard" sense for artistically relevant approvals, therefore, one does not necessarily mean that consumer criticism invokes a wet, soft kind—not where the consumer critic, unlike many a critic of the arts, knows just what he's doing. Alston-like approvals convey their recommendations to potential audiences in the hope of satisfying that potential audience. But artistically relevant approvals tell no one to buy and no one how to prepare saleable products. Hence they address their proposals neither to audiences as such, with their given characteristics, nor to producers as such with their market aspirations, but to actual or would-be participants in the practice of art. Let Alston tell such persons what the "show" *should* be like, hence how to govern their enjoyments, and not what an audience *will* enjoy—then to that extent his approval of *The Body Beautiful* will have turned artistically relevant. The question of what part actual audience responses will play in that telling is another story, a story of evidence and the reasons question, not quite a story of claims.

IV. The Two Criticisms and the Two Contexts

It is now possible to summarize the distinctions so far encountered among critical approvals and disapprovals by means of regulative principles for formulating critical discourse in a given mode. Such a procedure will show distinctly the nature of the choice between talking about the *same* objects "in a context of consumption," Alston-style, or in a "context of production."

1. Three such "rules," the reader may recall, function to control the criticism Alston offered of *The Body Beautiful:* "Let all your judgments be claims to knowledge," "Let all your claims be prudential," and, finally, "Let all your prudence be the prudence of the market." [11] If this sort of rule formulates criticism in an explicit and unmodified context of consumption, what rules do the equivalent job for the context of production?

A. First, as a prime prerequisite for artistically relevant discourse that makes sense of disagreement, there seems to be some sort of rule for specifying the physical characteristics to which the criticism refers. That was the point of the discussion of Harry-relevance and art-relevance. Very naïvely, the objects critics talk about, and the respects in which they talk about them, are not affairs in anybody's mind at all—not "esthetic objects" at all—but, in an epistemologically neutral sense, "things out there." Hence the first prerequisite for formulating critical judgments, which in practice no one would think of doing without, is, simply, "Specify just what you are talking about!"

Even in theory nearly everyone would admit the pertinence of such a "Rule of Specification" for Alston-like consumer research criticism. The discussion now breaks with certain theories in the "esthetic" tradition in regarding such a rule as *also* a rule of artistically relevant criticism.[12] The dogma of estheticism rejected, it turns out that consumer criticism and artistically relevant criticism are in this respect quite alike, equally "materialistic," equally "physicalistic."

[11] These rules, let it be observed, are held to be distinctive and by no means sufficient for consumer-relevant discourse.

[12] Croce, for example, might be taken as an extreme instance of the attempt to do without a "Rule of Specification"; and Ducasse, in our earlier example, will serve as a less radical example of the attempt to distinguish artistic criticism as the criticism which pushes off specifications to a minor (and distracting) role.

B. Though artistically relevant discourse advances no cognitive claim as such about the relations of certain objects to certain responders, it does not, therefore, differ from a sharply consumer discourse in some merely "emotive" sense (so that Consumer's Union says something about you and the product, but Fry or Blackmur merely emote or persuade). Instead, artistically relevant discourse follows a kind of "Rule of Construction" for the assertion of its claims: "Having specified what you are talking to, so construct your account that, whatever factual statements you may advance in the process, the force of your remarks will consist in a set of recommendations not just to like or dislike the specified object in a specified respect, but in a set of recommendations for constructing or construing those specified objects and respects." It is interesting to see that the very notion of an artistically relevant approval leads to the rejection of the dogma of the work of art itself.

On the other hand, is it not the simple (esthetic) *case* that Shakespearian fish run deeper and further out? Tell it as it is! But with the best will in the world, unless simply expressing how one feels, one has to make large proposals for poetic oceanography and say how to measure uncaught fish. And where's the strand?

C. It is also evident from the comparisons of different samples of concrete discourse that a kind of "Rule of Responsibility" guides the formulation of artistically relevant discourse: "When you formulate your account, talk about the critical object; neither about your own responses or anyone else's." [13] Using rules of prudence of an Alston-like formulation marks a primary failure in intent.

More specifically, we may state the Rule of Responsibility through two related "rules": (1) "Let the weight of your discourse be value-bound so that values are *used* rather than described or their origin talked about; and, (2) "Let your discourse *establish* the conditions for the existence of relevant publics for works of art under criticism, rather than minister to the requirements of previously determined audiences." That is what it means to "talk about the critical object; neither about your own response nor anyone else's."

The "Ideal Public" or "Spectator" theory of artistically relevant criticism follows from the attempt to assimilate the Rule of Responsibility to the Alston-like Rule of the Market: one ends with an imaginary public and wonders how to know when one belongs.

[13] I hope it will be clear that the Rule of Responsibility is no rule for proper rhetoric. The most "subjective," "it seems to me" type of rhetoric might defer to that rule in import; the most frigid and ex cathedra discourse might simply serve to tell about oneself or others.

D. Lastly, to finish slicing the last section's critical pie, I propose a "Rule of Referral" for the "dry, hard" *preference.* That is to say, if anyone asks a critic of the arts what his preferences are supposed to signify, he will not retort that they signify his likes and dislikes, or relative "personal" approvals and disapprovals—that would add nothing. Rather he will do two things: first, in order to establish the significance of his preference, he will say how such and such is done here, how there, how it might have been done and wasn't, and so on; and second he will indicate which of the suggested courses he would *propose* in such and such circumstances for the particular artist or for the art in general. Such, I would suggest, is what he will say to us his preferences mean in so far as they are artistically relevant. How to support such proposals—whether, for example, the critic's proposals rest "finally" as the normal version would have it on "personal" preferences—is another story. At least, "dry, hard" preferences function to advance claims to action that one may choose to grant or not, for whatever reason.[14]

The Rule of Referral may, therefore, be restated as follows: "Let all your expressed preferences, approvals, and disapprovals function as syntactical devices to indicate your proposals for the arts." Then, indeed, as Fry says, "it is open to anyone to prefer the elegant precision of the Greek line to the plastic power of the Chinese." Why should the critic try to dictate to another man's history?

2. Among other things the expression "context of production" serves as a metaphor [15] to convey the force of rules like the above four for the formulation of critical claims in artistically relevant discourses. Assuming that this chapter has distinguished the claims advanced in a context of consumption and a context of production, then what kind of choice is a man up against when, prepared to offer a criticism of a presented work of art, he asks whether to guide himself by the regulative principle of consumption or of production? Of course, few ever confront so explicit a choice.

A. First, a prefatory, but essential point: choosing to formulate criticism of objects normally called works of art through the rules of

[14] If the Rule of Reference has turned into a rule for "preferences" rather than "approvals," it is because no approval defined "objectively" can be differentiated except as a choice among alternatives—hence the term "preference."

[15] The point of the metaphor in the discussion of regulative principles is that the Rules of Construction and Referral, as I have labeled them, suggest how in formulating his talk the critic commits himself to a very specific sort of participation in the artistic enterprise. He takes part, a very special part, in production. Hence, "the context of production."

Alston's artistically irrelevant discourse, *or* through the rules for artistically relevant discourse elucidated above, entails no logical confusion in itself. On both alternatives, one might still reject the dogma of estheticism, since that dogma means giving that account of the criticisms of Fergusson, Fry, Blackmur, and the others which properly applies to the criticisms of Alston. Accordingly, while the dogma requires the choice of a context of consumption, the choice of a context of consumption need not require the dogma of estheticism. One *might,* quite unabashedly, work an Alstonism on *Hamlet.* One *might,* as Alston does for *The Body Beautiful,* simply make no claim to "artistically relevant controversy." To the contrary, one *might* give an account of *The Body Beautiful* through the rules that control the discourses of Blackmur, Fry, and the others, without showing how these rules are derivations of Alston's, which they are not.

B. Let us now weigh the choice between consumption and production rules when both sorts seem appropriate to the same object and when we keep in mind clearly what we are about. For while a man may in one sense consider his critical object simultaneously from the point of view of both consumption and production, mixing the viewpoints thoroughly in his mind, nevertheless when he comes to formulate his criticism in an internally consistent manner he may have to make a choice. He must not suppose that because two perfectly possible and acceptable ways of dealing with the same objects exist he can always afford both.

Hence the two sets of rules pose the critic the same choice that critics so often see facing the artist—the choice between art and the market, which circumstances may obscure but which always stands ready to dominate the stage. For all conditions of art and society the choice between the two contexts seems very much like the very familiar choice confronted in many human relations, where there are different "rule sets" available for dealing with others. So it may be necessary to decide whether to deal with others through the rules that determine one's "own interest" (whatever that may mean) or through the rules that determine theirs, or perhaps "Man's," or perhaps "God's." Such choices are hard. Perhaps most people submerge or smudge the choice, and when they can dodge the issue because the particular decision required seems substantially the same on either rule set, and differences are differences in style and manner, they are happy.[16] Yet still, of course, the choice remains; and the failure to fix a

[16] Let me emphasize that the discussion is only about cases in which a question arises whether to adopt one rule set or another. This is in no way to deny that in very many cases no such question arises.

clear and supervening course through the round of concrete decisions poisons the moral wells (to shift the metaphor for the sake of an ancient insight). For the organization of a *pattern* of behavior stands at stake, whether the pattern be as relatively simple as a pattern of moral advice and solicitation that manages before it finishes not to defeat itself, or whether it be a total life.

In criticism as in life, then, the choice of contexts is a choice of intent; hence, a choice of dispositions; hence, a choice of the long run. In criticism also, the problem for the critic of the arts is how to avoid being nothing in particular.

C. A somewhat less trite, though still obvious point follows for the logic of artistically relevant claims and reasons: it turns out that, contrary to popular assumption, (1) the choice between consumption and production rule sets, between Alston-like and artistically relevant criticism, hinges upon no claim of an intrinsically artistic nature and calls for no artistically relevant reasons to decide it; and that (2) therefore it is wrong to be *disappointed* in the possibilities of a rationale for artistically relevant controversy on discovering that you can give no good "esthetic" reason to persuade a man who doesn't "go" for a work of art, no matter what its merits, to change his mind.

If, in sum, advancing a consumer claim to value or disvalue does not properly induce the critic with his mind on artistic relevance to change (or persist) in his view, neither does advancing an artistically relevant argument properly justify another man's changing (or persisting) in his appraisal as a consumer. Moreover, even if no one "chooses" a context of production unless it seems profitable, it does not follow that the reasons which lead him to think it profitable are *or ought to be* artistically relevant, or that the claims which those reasons decide are themselves artistically relevant, or ought to be. After all, the reasons that induce men to play chess are not considered appropriate reasons for making a certain move rather than another, nor does one play chess in deciding to play chess. Philosophers who have given up expecting a moral reason for being moral ought also to give up expecting an artistically relevant reason for being artistically relevant.

Accordingly, let it be emphasized, in pushing the rules of production for the analysis of artistically relevant controversy, the present argument makes no case against using the work of art for the satisfaction it may produce. The moral is merely that no one ought to be disappointed in the possibilities of a logic of artistically relevant controversy because he prefers another sort of issue. People of intrusive candor who declare that they don't like Shakespeare and nothing anyone can say about his poetic merits will get them to like it, are wrong only in imagining that such talk is designed to change their minds. Dislike *may* be self-knowledge on their part. How could the logic of artistically relevant controversy pretend to refute anyone's self-knowledge? If the apostle of "refinement,"' on the ground of artistically relevant criticism, thinks it necessary to prove that if someone does not like *Hamlet,* he "ought" to, he merely shows that it is indeed Dr. Rorschach who worries him. He gives his case away.

Therefore, though one may be motivated to consider artistically relevant claims for consumer reasons, those claims are not reducible to those reasons; and anyone who tries to construe the context of production as a special case of the context of consumption confuses the argument for bothering with the controversy, with the controversy itself.

Chapter 8

Judgment and Artistic Merit

Judgments of artistic merit are continually made in criticism, either directly or indirectly; and, indeed, a criticism possessed of no sort of relevance for judgments of artistic merit would hardly be considered artistically relevant at all. So people who do criticism say that certain things "have" artistic or "esthetic" merit or lack it; that one object is "better" than another, or praiseworthy for some feature. They may distinguish between the charming and the "merely" beautiful; the true and the false tragedy; the humorous and the genuinely humorous. Or they may permit us to glean their views in still more complex ways, as the examples of critical discourse cited in the previous chapter illustrate. All are ways of advancing judgments of artistically relevant merit or worth. What is a proper description of such judgments in a context of production? What's at issue?

In principle, the answer is simple, at least at this stage of the game. Judgments of artistic merit express the dry, hard approvals (or disapprovals) of artistically relevant discourse, rather than the soft, wet approvals of consumption. Therefore, according to the regulative rules for dry, hard approvals, people who argue over judgments of artistic merit, in so far as they agree on the construction of the critical object, differ over the recommendations to make to the arts. Such is the line I shall have to develop if only for consistency with the previous chapter and the general account of the construction argument.

Yet to say offhand that judgments of artistic merit, pressed for their claims in the artistically relevant controversy, yield recommendations for the actual conduct of the arts seems, on the prevalent assumption of the normal version, impossible and mystifying. For always one seems to hear the skeptical doubts: you mean that I the critic, as a critic, tell the artist what to do? That I, the consumer, making my consumer judgments, give instructions to the producer, beyond the general exhortation that he pleases me or I won't buy? The answer is yes, since as a critic in an argument you are not a consumer after all. Such an answer cannot be considered merely in a derivative way.

I. The Normal Version of Artistic Merit

According to the normal version, if judgments of merit indeed affirm the discovery of values present in greater or lesser degree, then those judgments recommend nothing to anybody, although people may use them to make recommendations. I have made a mistake in principle. Legal judgments do indeed make dispositions of objects in the world; judgments of value or merit, being esthetic, do not. If they are unlike scientific judgments in their "esthetic," or subjective character, they are like them in their declarative character.

1. Critics do indeed often speak as though they applied some sort of esthetic litmus paper to distinguish the good from the bad. Some people have it and some don't. Merit, therefore, is a special quality or property perceivable by some, but not by all; reasons give the causes for the color that the good critic turns when exposed to a work of art, if any reason can be given.

Without rehashing the account already offered of the dogma of estheticism and the claims question, it should be obvious that this property theory of esthetic value won't handle actual disputes. Everybody knows that judgments of merit vary among persons otherwise supposed to possess the requisite esthetic sensibility, or litmus powers; and also that such persons themselves make different judgments of artistic merit in the course of their lives. Surely, therefore, that anyone in an argument "really" possesses the proper sensibility as a secret power seems not only implausible but also irrelevant to the argument's resolution; for whether he possesses the capacity and/or whether his capacity has functioned properly is determined in a particular instance by the outcome of the argument.

More significantly: even those *critics* who say that a critic needs a nose for value, and actually consider that a sense for value is a kind of sense, when pressed to say what they mean by the artistic merit of the critical object here before them, will hardly leave it at that. They will explain that the critical object "has" merit either "in virtue of" possessing some character or "because of" possessing some character. And if they indeed say that either you see the worthlessness of the object or not, the chances are that they thereby offer a kind of philosophical interpretation of what they are up to—the lesser probability—or that they do not think it worthwhile to talk about it. Perhaps they don't think one knows enough, or that one is sufficiently bright. The situation is quite common. On all sorts of occasions people, wisely, shrug their shoulders and walk away in despair of explaining things. Nevertheless, even on such occasions a Blackmur may insist indefinitely that Hardy's poems have "artistic merit" but the pay-off comes only on his saying that that poetry has its merit in virtue of, or because of, the way "sensibility survives violation."

Is the survival of sensibility merely evidence for the hidden fact about Hardy's poetry, that it possesses artistic merit, the way that callouses on the palms are evidences of hard work? But the hard work would have been just as hard had successful precautions been taken against callouses—the callouses are merely (fallible) signs—while the survival of sensibility in Blackmur's intent does not merely betray "merit," it specifies the merit. "Such," one says, "*is* the merit." Nothing remains to look for after *the* merit has been pointed out. The property theory of artistic merit, in which particular characteristics stand as signs or evidence to a proper consumer, slurs the distinction between "in virtue of" and "because of." While in one sense, "because of" implies *only* a causal or external relation between effect and cause, in another, second sense "because of" *does* signify a constitutive ("in virtue of") relationship between the part or "aspect" and the whole, or an entailment between premise and conclusion such that the conclusion "involves" the premise. Let the first sense slide in under cover of the second, and artistic merit becomes a property—to the obscuring of the merit arguments.

Therefore, "Do some men have a special faculty for picking up artistic merit?" ceases to be an empirical question similar to whether or not a certain animal possesses a nerve center that enables it to mimic speech.

2. An "instrumentalist theory of esthetic value" does not, of course, deal with value of any sort as a "property." Nevertheless, such a theory also commits itself to the view that at issue in the merit controversy is a kind of prediction, and must be accounted for as the most serious of the normal version views.

An esthetician writes that "X has aesthetic value means X has the capacity to produce an aesthetic experience of a fairly great magnitude (such an experience having value)."[1] "Having greater aesthetic value" then receives a definition by introducing the notion of "greater magnitude." Some experiences are more "unified" than others; in some "the dominant quality of pervasive feeling-tone," may be more "intense." Some may be more "complex." And there is proposed "a general term to

[1] Monroe C. Beardsley, *Aesthetics: Problems in the Philosophy of Criticism* (New York: Harcourt, Brace, 1958), p. 531.

cover all three characteristics"—"magnitude"—which is "a function of at least these three variables." [2] Accordingly, any argument for an esthetic object's "capacity" to evoke an esthetic experience of a certain magnitude will be an argument for its esthetic value.[3] Esthetic values are determined by a verifiable means-ends relationship. One verifies the existence of a disposition. Do critics who differ over esthetic values differ over dispositions?

Now I propose that they do indeed if they differ in what is here called "a context of consumption." Also, persons in the same critical tradition at odds over more or less familiar objects, and through no *problem* in construction, may sometimes express their actual difference as a disagreement over how persons of such and such a sensibility will eventually respond, after repeated exposures, to an object. Their issue is indeed a factual one, in whatever sense differences over dispositions are factual. But are not all differences over artistic merit now implicitly settled, and our critics employed only in settling whether they will in fact come to agree? There is a difference between agreeing on any matter and agreeing whether we shall, or will, agree on a matter.

Assuming, however, the general correctness of the normal version and that claims presented for the artistic merit of "esthetic objects" are only claims that people will reach agreement on the merit of those objects, still the instrumentalist's account will not explain the differences of opinion to which it addresses itself. The root of the difficulty lies in the concept of "magnitude," though not in the concept's vagueness, uncomfortably vague though it be.

A. "Magnitude" is said to be a function of "unity," "intensity," and "variety." [4] Perhaps a psychological account may be found for such "variables" of the "magnitude" of an "esthetic experience." But critics, in effect, worry over what *shall be* considered as a value of such a variable. The difficulty is twofold. First, while I sometimes know whether one experience is more or less intense, varied, or unified than another, often I do not. Often, that is, I don't know how to go about answering the question, which is something else than not knowing the answer. The proper "values" of such variables can be determined only within relatively fixed schema, which are precisely the issue in artistically relevant controversy. The second difficulty—and clearly both this and the first are difficulties in the application of the idea of "unity," "intensity," or "variety"—is that artists and critics both characteristically seek to get people to

[2] *Ibid.*, p. 529.
[3] *Ibid.*, p. 534.
[4] *Ibid.*, p. 529.

regard certain arrangements as unified, intense, or varied. Even if in some general way the phenomenological characteristics of unity, variety, and intensity of experience are fixed, which arrangements shall be experienced as such? "You never dreamt of such unity as this," says the painter. "Behold!" In a pertinent sense, he and the critic who supports, or affronts, him are makers or breakers of "esthetic experience," by profession. So the very question, what are the "values" of unity, variety, or intensity misstates the problem. Psychological descriptions are at best true descriptions describing states of affairs with which the critic works.

B. "Magnitude" is said to be a "function." Even, however, if we could fix upon a sense in which the "variables" determining that function themselves work as variables, how "magnitude" might be any sort of "function" at all of those variables remains unclear. Perhaps all that "function" means is, "somehow, depends upon." But that "somehow" is the issue. Reference to "an Area of Rational Undecidability" [5] will save the game only if the area does not include too sizable a portion of the domain within which the "function" allegedly holds. And the game is lost when, in those areas where a choice is indeed made among relative degrees of unity, variety, and intensity, the determining principle is a "preference" based upon some principle other than "magnitude." How *does* one "weigh"? By what principle? One would think that was the great practical question. Unsettled, it is not merely that the "Area of Undecidability," given the practical requirements of the artistically relevant controversy, has become hopelessly huge when one *applies* the concept of a greater or lesser magnitude; it is that "greater or lesser magnitude" constitutes a way of dodging the decision problem which the talk of a "function" of "variables" suggests might lie within range of solution. In sum, the concept of a "magnitude" of esthetic experience seems vacuous. If our experiences of unity, intensity, and variety enable us "somehow," by some principle of preference, to make a decision, they do, and the Area of Undecidability is closed; if they do not, it is open.

In conclusion, then, even an "instrumentalist" theory of esthetic value fails to make estheticism serve the purposes of artistically relevant controversy. Esthetic (read now "refined consumer") experience is either too general to account for the differences of opinion over artistic merit or, if specific, confounded by the capacity of art to transform the conditions of refined consumption. So the differences over judgments of artistic merit that trouble critics cannot be put as a difference over the nature and quality of the esthetic experience. Changing esthetic values from proper-

[5] *Ibid.*, p. 536.

ties to dispositions will still miss the problem, since esthetic values are not dispositions-type affairs in an artistically relevant controversy; and to call them "dispositions" blocks out the disagreements. What price a disposition theory that works only on agreement over what the relevant dispositions are?

C. The same author, not surprisingly, finds it "hard to make out a good case for saying that 'This is good' (in an aesthetic context) has a peculiar imperative component." [6] Once again, if "an aesthetic context" means a "context of consumption," by all the rules of taste and right he is correct.

Notice, however, the nature of the argument, which depends upon a distinction between "judgments of goodness in such and such a respect," now "commendations," and practical proposals ("recommendations"). "A Rational Recommendation will presumably be based upon correct Commendations, but a Commendation is not itself a proposal for action." [7] Esthetic judgments (of merit) turn out, then, to be commendations, which can only "provide relevant data for decisions"—as, presumably, the commendation of a picture as a good picture provides one reason for choosing to see it, but the judgment "the picture is good" is completely unaffected by whether or not you see the picture.

Now, it is true that recommendations cannot be put forward in an artistically relevant controversy if to make a recommendation is equivalent to making an *irrelevant* recommendation. But I have not been saying that "This is a good picture" implies, as a judgment of artistic merit, *any* recommendation which the judgment may chance to support, but only those of the sort for which the picture has received "dry, hard approvals." Recommendations are necessarily irrelevant only if practical judgments and artistically relevant judgments are different kinds of judgment because, as the thesis of estheticism has it, artistically relevant judgments are all esthetic. But if it happens, as it does, that at least some artistically relevant judgments of artistic merit make recommendations for the conduct of the arts, the dogma of estheticism must be wrong and judgments of artistic merit are not necessarily, in respect of the claims they advance, "esthetic judgments." Committed to the dogma of estheticism, it is hardly surprising that one fails to recognize that an artistically relevant recommendation could even be a possible point of "This is good." It will seem obvious that merit judgments cannot express decisions

[6] *Ibid.*, p. 475.
[7] *Ibid.*, p. 476.

as do legal judgments, that they can only express commendations for esthetic achievement or assert certain potentials of esthetic goodness.

Let us, then, glance at the matter of judgments of artistic merit afresh, so far as it is possible to do so without assuming that one account or another is closed in principle and judgments of artistic merit *must* make one kind of claim or another.

II. Disagreements over Artistic Merit

The best way to understand how "artistic merit" functions in artistically relevant criticism is through examining cases of explicit disagreement over the artistic merit of works of art. They are of two sorts: (1) cases in which whether a critical object "has" artistic merit depends, as people say, on the contestants' "definition" of artistic merit; and (2) cases in which for the question "Does X have artistic merit?" different answers turn on the analysis of "X" rather than on previously established standards of artistic merit. The first kind of disagreement, I shall say, revolves about a "formative" issue of artistic merit, the second about a "performative" issue of artistic merit, just as earlier construction arguments were found to resolve around formative and performative differences. Formative issues of artistic merit and performative issues of artistic merit, far from being independently manageable, are, of course, related in as interdependent a manner as are formative and performative construction issues.

What, then, do people differ about when they differ over artistic merit as such?

1. Consider Yeats' view of poetry in the cited exhortation to the Irish poets. He thinks not only that poets should sing to and for their people in defense of that people's national identity, but that Irish poetry, at least, gains or loses merit as poetry depending on whether it complies with his advice. Most people today, of course, think that "national" or "political" considerations are not "esthetic" ones, and that his advice is wrong. Here is a difference of opinion over a formative issue of artistic merit. What does it involve?

One might be tempted to find the difference a difference over the proper use of ordinary English. The extremity of Yeats' advice evokes such a response. "Anyone who knows English knows, or ought to know, that 'artistic merit' works as a counter in another game than 'political merit' or 'national merit.' Yeats *misunderstands.*" The only trouble is, of course, that Yeats does not misunderstand. He has merely put a certain English on his English and the resulting quasi-paradox sharpens his point: that though most of us are happy with the distinction between what concerns the nation and what concerns poetry, he wants a *change* in the rules—*despite* the fact that certain usages incorporate those rules. To pretend, therefore, that in Yeats we face a man who differs with us because of his curious weakness in logic is poor intellectual ethics.

Still, the uses and misuses of language aside, it may continue to seem that poetry is its own kind of business. Yeats' notion of poetic merit may seem quite unacceptable. *Perhaps it is.* Only, its unacceptability must constitute the conclusion of an argument, not the premise. Is not the issue between Yeats and the rest of us precisely what that business of poetry "is" to be? As Yeats very well knew, some things commonly called "poems," even by "purists," show the bardic features he enjoins. Concretely, differing with Yeats' conception of poetic value depends upon the desirability of moving more centrally toward one or another aspect of poems. The argument over "artistic merit" in the Yeats case is an instance of argument "in the conduct of the arts," of the art of poetry. That a specific poem lacks or possesses "artistic merit" means, all other things equal, that that poem accedes to an instruction: "Be it resolved that poets interfuse in their poems certain materials (e.g., Irish mythology) and certain values (the dignity of Ireland) in certain ways."

But the Yeats case is perhaps too easy. Critics don't always argue about the future, nor engage in such obvious attempts to control the arts. It is necessary to consider a formative issue of merit over the shape of things past, not the shape of things future, where Yeats' kind of overt admonition is out of the question. In writing of *Les Fleurs du mal,* Erich Auerbach said:

> Most later critics took it for granted that the book could only be considered from an aesthetic standpoint and scornfully rejected any other possibility from the outset. It seems to us that aesthetic criticism alone is unequal to the task, though Baudelaire would scarcely have shared our opinion: he was contaminated by the idolatry of art that is still with us. What a strange phenomenon: a prophet of doom who expects nothing of his readers but admiration for his artistic achievement. *Ponete mente almen com' io son bella* ("consider at least how beautiful I am")—with these words Dante concludes his *canzone* to the movers of the third heaven. But can such words be applied to poems whose meaning is so actual and urgent, whose beauty is as bitter as that of *Les Fleurs du mal?*[8]

[8] *Scenes from the Drama of European Literature* (New York: Meridian, 1959), p. 226.

Auerbach differs with "esthetic criticism" and Baudelaire himself over the poetic merit of *Les Fleurs du mal*, or, as Auerbach puts it in the title of his essay, over "The Aesthetic Dignity of the 'Fleurs du Mal.' " He refuses to dismiss the "actuality," the "urgency," the "bitterness" of the poetry as irrelevant to its artistic merit, even though he is willing to leave the definition of "the aesthetic standpoint" to those whose opinions evoke his demurral. What issues do these disagreements involve?

A. The most immediate and obvious is a construction issue. What sort of thing *is Les Fleurs du mal?* How are we to look at it, with what sort of values in mind? Auerbach has obviously illustrated an argument over which "formative rules" do apply in a specific kind of case and, indeed, which formative rules—those which bar or those which employ "life values"—shall appear in an overall strategy of criticism.

B. The other issue is, of course, where to locate the poetic *merit* or value of *Les Fleurs du mal.* The formative rules chosen in the construction argument clearly depend upon some conception of artistic merit or, given Auerbach's yielding of "esthetic" and "artistic," "relevant" merit. Patently, *Les Fleurs du mal* raises the merit question by raising the spectacle of alternative ways of doing and reading poetry. The Baudelaire faction will tell poets that it is relevantly good to seek "the beautiful" in their work, regardless of life values and whether or not there are readers to look for them; Auerbach will instruct the poets to write with such values in mind and instruct readers not to impoverish their readings by forgetting those values. Deny either set of recommendations—not just Auerbach's, the purist's as well—and the judgment of merit is in each case reversed. Moreover, that judgment is reversed as it would not be were one to deny the wisdom of some other kinds of recommendation which used the judgment of artistic merit as a base.

So, obviously, the fact that an argument occurs over the merit of a completed object no more precludes a discussion of the policies implicit therein, and their wisdom, than do discussions of the legality of past actions—which is, of course, and not surprisingly, pretty much the same conclusion reached earlier in the discussion of proper descriptions of critical objects as constructions of those objects.

2. A reminder of what performative issues of artistic merit may be like in practice is now in order. Performative issues of that sort are raised by such remarks as, "You call *that* a good novel, play, painting, etc.? What in the world do you *mean, that*'s a good novel?" All the emphasis

falls upon the particular object and its special merits; how its special merits match those of novels, plays, or paintings comes later.

Note, then, first, the significant peculiarity of the performative issue as such: "calling *that*" a good novel and "saying what you mean" in calling it that, are in practice one and the same thing, if we may omit additional formative arguments about the proper values of novels, and the subsequent matching up. With the same qualification, evidence of the novel's merit establishes "what you mean" in calling it good; "saying what you mean" in calling it good presents the evidence for doing so. Here again is that relation between "premises" and "conclusion" where the argument *builds* the conclusion (that "X" has artistic merit) by its reasons,[9] without leading the reasoner, as in the physical sciences, to another fact about the world—a fact of "esthetic value." Since actual arguments over performative issues of merit inevitably introduce great detail and require much space, I shall commit the philosopher's sin and deal with performative issues in an abstract way, hoping all the while that later discussion may make some amends.

A. To someone who questions an "esthetic judgment," then, we sometimes answer something like this: "The picture succeeds in virtue of the way in this situation the blue line complements the green patch . . . the music instead of making that obvious sort of resolution does this and that . . . the plot stops short, yet for such and such reasons it need not have done so." *There,* one says in effect, is the "esthetic" merit or demerit; and anyone who took exception would (a) have to find other characteristics which in his judgment "counterbalanced" the blue line's complementing the green patch, the music's resolving as it does, the plot's stopping short, or (b) deny that the blue line ought to complement the green patch, and so on.

a. The argument now is about what would be called the "organization" of the work of art. Is it "right" or not? Note that my illustrations aim to place only performative issues of *merit* in debate and intentionally raise no disagreement over the relevant description of the work of art, so far as a separation of merit from construction issues may be possible. Note next that by hypothesis, they are samples of judgment in an argument about the merit of a work of art, not taste. So "having it right" must mean, as in the admittedly contrived examples it seems explicitly to say, meeting instructions or recommendations made for the picture, music, novel. At the least, the concrete case entails a kind of counterfactual recommendation, or report of one: "If I'd been able I'd strongly have

[9] For further discussion of the "building" relation, see Chapter 12.

advised the artist to compensate (or refuse to compensate) in some way for the blue, the plot, the resolution." If the argument persevered, a rule would be constructed from the particular case of rightness or wrongness to hold for cases of a certain, restricted type: "Let anyone who does painting, music, novels bear in mind that under such complex circumstances he should strive for such and such."

b. For disagreement about whether an acknowledged element of a critical object is as such "right" or "proper" or "a desirable characteristic" of the work of art is at all "intrinsically right or wrong," "right or wrong in itself"—the case is even plainer. That the blue line "ought" or "ought not" complement the green patch as it does then means that the artist ought or ought not to have left out the blue line with green patch, and that any artist ought to avoid that sort of thing. There are few judgments more bluntly instructional than judgments of intrinsic *merit* or demerit, which are supposed to be most isolated from consequences, provided one sees them in their function rather than in their source. Consequently, they are the most vulnerable to the refutations of circumstance.

B. Of course, in performative issues not only does one question whether a work of art has it "right," either through its organization or through exhibiting (or avoiding) defects, but one also asks how the particular work, through its organization and defect, or defect-free status, achieves certain artistic standards established in the formative merit argument. "Does Kafka's *Trial* have the special merits of a novel?" Assuming a disagreement not based upon the need to instruct one man or another how to read novels or Kafka, performative arguments of merit will involve a reconsideration of proposals made for either and both. But the reconsideration of a proposal has ultimately the same objective as the proposal: the state of affairs, or states of affairs that the original proposal addressed.

There is no need here, however, to consider in detail the interweaving of formative and performative arguments of merit, only to suggest that after all the maneuvers are done, the justifications evaluated, and the proposals counterposed, the argument comes down to a decision about a proposal. For suppose someone insisted that in the artistically relevant controversy he took exception to the justification of an instruction or of a recommendation, not to the instruction or to the recommendation. Obviously, this is a frequent occurrence. Yet still he would employ merit judgments in the exceptions he took, which would normally constitute the crux of his point. Finally, he must say what he is proposing; and even if he puts only another justification to the initial proposal, or simply shows the initial justification mistaken, he must eventually say what difference his criticism makes for other cases. The critic may pursue the justification circuit to his heart's content and own that a further argument, and that alone, interests him in his argument. Nevertheless, however deeply and professionally he may aim but to engage another critic, the point of the engagement remains proposal and counterproposal. That is why, from the point of view of the claims question, it has made no difference whether I have put the substance of a merit judgment's recommendation as "Do this, under such and such circumstances," or "It is wise to do this under those circumstances," or "You ought to do this under those circumstances."

The choice of estheticism, then, not the consideration of the merit controversy as such—hence the choice of a context of refined consumption—makes it seem strange to assert an instruction as the cash surrender value of a judgment of merit. And I am not unreasonable in taking that instruction "in a context of production" as analogous to the instruction of a legal judgment in a court of law.

III. Judgments of Artistic Merit and Construction Judgments

The recommendations or instructions, then, which constitute the force, explicitly or implicitly, of "dry, hard" approvals or disapprovals constitute the claims of judgments of artistic merit. And even though one would not, of course, speak of any recommendation or instruction constituting a claim unless it received a certain kind of justification (of which more later), we may move on to formulate the difference between the claims at issue in the construction argument and those at issue in the merit argument. Then perhaps we shall be in a better position to comment upon the sense in which judgments "in a context of production" express decisions.

1. In the construction argument critics were seen advancing proposals for the construction of critical objects in virtue of certain regulative principles. Construction arguments, it now seems appropriate to say, put forward "construction judgments" in the manner that arguments over whether critical objects are to be approved or not put forward judgments of artistic merit. The difference is this: where judgments of artistic merit propose their instructions or recommendations upon performance and require the alteration or preservation in some pertinent way of the

conduct of the arts, construction judgments make their proposals for constructions of performance and do not themselves *directly* require a change in artistic performance. In this way the analysis of judgment in a context of production allows for the general agreement that it is one thing to say what the formal and nonformal characteristics of a critical object may "be," and still another to say what those characteristics ought to be or what worth or merit the object as a whole may possess. Of at least equal significance, however, the formulation of the difference "in a context of production" between what the characteristics of a critical object are and what they ought to be allows us also to perceive how the proposals of construction judgments, if pushed far enough, themselves also assert claims upon the practice of the arts, though not only such claims.

For the analysis of the created object, and the respect due it by all good and responsible critics, ended with a surmise that they do. The trouble was that we possessed at the time no analysis of the concept of "artistic merit" to make the surmise good. We could only say that respect for the created object required a minimum weight upon the artistic merit of a construction—the policy of respect for artistic merit. All other things equal, the proper construction would be that construction which critics could agree would possess maximum artistic value. Why construe "X" to have a characteristic "y"? Because to do so makes of "X" a "better" work of art. That is always a legitimate consideration. But though no specific discussion of "better than" has as yet been undertaken, it is now clear that "better than" as an ordering of objects in respect of artistic merit asserts a claim advanced in respect of recommendations or instructions to the arts. In order to say what the artistically relevant characteristics of a critical object might be, it becomes necessary to be able to say what they ought to be.

Construction judgments, therefore, do indeed make claims for the practice of the arts but not "directly," as do judgments of merit. And this facet of construction judgments comes nowhere so close to the surface than in those strategies of criticism which place a significantly stronger emphasis upon the rule of respect for artistic merit than they do upon the rule of appropriateness or any other of the policies of respect. Patently, they judge what the relevant characteristics of a critical object may be through an *ideal* of art, so far as they possibly may. That, precisely, is the issue in Auerbach's description of the controversy over "The Aesthetic Dignity of 'Les Fleurs du mal.' " Baudelaire's vision of poetic value leads him to a very different vision of the relevant characteristics of the poem than Auerbach will concede justified; Auerbach's conception of the relevant characteristics of the poem leads him to a radical rejection of Baudelaire's values. Press the construction argument and the merit argument immediately responds; there is no escaping the claim that in such and such a direction lies artistic merit. But, of course, in many instances the construction argument never gets down to that, either because sufficient agreement exists on the merit issue, or the policies of respect other than the policy of respect for artistic merit are dominant.

2. Leaving to the reasons question when an instruction or recommendation becomes a genuine claim, I have still not answered the question to whom that instruction or recommendation addresses itself when a work of art is judged. Obviously, nobody recommends or proposes anything to objects.

A. If the question of address means, "Of whom does the claim ask agreement?" those who have rejected the consumption-production dichotomy for artistically relevant controversy must answer that any artist will of course consider himself addressed by both merit and construction judgments and, similarly, any critic. That is why it does not follow that judgments of artistic merit, as construed here, make no difference for appreciation. Such judgments retain the function that they actually possess for appreciators: to offer a reason for reading, viewing, or hearing one thing or another, for reading or considering with particular attention one thing or another in what they read, view, or hear. Of course such judgments do not bind anyone to attend one thing rather than another if he chooses otherwise. Reasons for artistically relevant judgments are not necessarily reasons for making artistically relevant judgments; the former bind only in so far as a man has an interest in the artistically relevant practice.

B. The question, however, may mean also, "*At* whom is the recommendation or instruction aimed?" rather than the more simple question of whose agreement is required. In that event, the central point has already been made:

a. Construction judgments aim primarily at artists or critics in so far as they in their critical or artistic activities exert themselves to provide constructions of critical objects. For it is obvious that not only critics are concerned to determine the formal and nonformal characteristics of the objects presented to them; without the constructive activity creative activity would be blind, both in the determination of its overall strategy and in the step-by-step process of creation. So it is expected of artists that they "know what they are doing." Translated into the language of this study, this means that the construction judgment makes them a pertinent recommendation.

In addition, of course, artists are subject to the construction judgment to the degree that judgments of artistic merit may be entailed, in the manner described, by those judgments.

b. Judgments of artistic merit aim primarily, of course, at those engaged in the performance; but also, as has been seen, they aim at critics in so far as judgments of artistic merit enter their constructions when they apply the policy of respect for artistic merit.

c. In either event, whether construction judgment or judgment of artistic merit, the proposals that they put forward as their claims are exerted not upon individuals qua individuals but to the individual, any individual, in a certain role. Accordingly, when they come to an issue, a rule of some kind, formative or performative, becomes the issue, for the direction of individual behavior: its acceptance, rejection, or modification. Taking the sum of such rules as determining the enterprise of art we may say that construction and merit judgments aim at individuals only as participants in the enterprise of art. Hence those individuals who play the consumer game, either on their own or as members of some consuming group who do not know the rule of respect, are not addressed by the recommendations and instructions of artistically relevant claims.

In general, then, the answer proposed "in a context of production" to the address question is of the same general type as an answer to the address question would be for the law: the judgment makes a claim that asks the agreement of all members of the legal community. The judgment applies to individuals in a certain role or status. While it makes a specific disposition, the judgment aims at anyone who commits a similar act where "similar" is defined by the state of the law and the direction of its development.

3. The analogy with the law raises the question of the sense in which, in a context of production, one might want to say that judgments express decisions. The judgment of the court is the decision of the court. Is the decision of the critic like the decision of the judge? Obviously there must be further discussion of the whole notion of an enterprise of the arts and of the analogies and disanalogies with a legal system, yet certain minimal clarifications are perhaps helpful.

A. The decision of the judge of the arts, expressed both in his construction and merit judgments, obviously lacks the force of a command. Only sometimes, of course, does even the decision of a court of law issue in so strong a prescription. But normally in art there are no external sanctions; and if there were, those sanctions would have nothing to do with the artistically relevant controversy, however much they might have to do with censorship. So the decision of the judge of art can be conceived as the determination to issue a *command* only if the critic leaves the artistically relevant controversy in favor of politics.

B. Is the decision that must be reached by a judge in law or art a decision on an "instruction"? Clearly, a court might be conceived to issue instructions for the attainment of certain ends; given those ends, a legal entity might achieve a certain objective. I have used the expression "instruction" to characterize the proposals put by critics, but it is obviously much too strong. When the end itself is under consideration there is clearly something incongruous about the critic's issuing "instructions" as though it were settled. So I have not intended to suggest that the judge of the arts decides on instructions in any narrow sense.

C. I have, of course, tended to speak as though the critic's problem were to decide on an appropriate recommendation. Of course, I did not mean that his decision problem was to decide whether to recommend (as a judge may decide whether to issue any order at all) but to decide which recommendation it would be, given that in deciding to make a judgment of merit or construction he in effect decided to make a recommendation.

Obviously, a court of law does not, when it issues its judgments, whatever else it may do, make recommendations, nor is the judge's problem to decide on what to "recommend." "Recommendation" is much too weak; hence on the whole it seemed like the appropriate term to designate what the critic aimed at in making the proposals he did. And, indeed, the incongruity of "recommendation" for the substance of legal judgments would constitute a good starting place for an elaboration of disanalogies with the artistically relevant controversy, were those disanalogies now pertinent.

On the other hand, even for criticism, "recommendation" is misleading. One makes a recommendation normally to an individual or group, not to an enterprise; and, like "advice," it has a nosy quality. I do not mean to say critics decide how to be nosy in other people's business.

D. "Proposal," the obvious word for what a claim advances for the practice of the arts, lacked precisely the sense of approval and acceptance that the critic brings to his proposals. The business of artistically relevant criticism *is* the critic's business; and so therefore, and to that extent, is the conduct of the arts. Like the judge at law, the critic's decision problem is to decide what *he* will back in a matter that concerns him.

Lacking a word, then, which will express what the critic decides in a manner that will differentiate the nature of that decision from legal judgment, I shall continue, in order to express the different shades of sense that artistically relevant claims require, to use that varied vocabulary employed in the past. Obviously, the important thing is not the word, but the kind of analogy and disanalogy with the legal (or other) enterprise that one might want to point up, and the aspect of artistically relevant claims under discussion.

IV. Defining Judgments of Artistic Merit—Also, the Implications

The nature of artistically relevant claims essayed in a general way, how "define" the major *types* of judgments of artistic merit which allegedly express those claims? The "definitions" intended are, of course, explicative and in large measure summarize observations already made. Having accomplished this much, we may consider some of the consequences.

1. We may try to show, then, how in a context of production one would go about explicating (A) flat allegations of artistic merit, (B) comparative allegations, and (C) certain indefinite forms.

A. To say that " 'X' 'has' artistic merit" one asserts two things: that "X" actually has certain physically verifiable characteristics that, construed according to some set of construction rules, satisfy or do not satisfy the instructions proffered for the conduct of the arts; and, implicitly, that the satisfaction of those instructions, given those construction rules, permits the possibility of an appropriate kind of proof for all proper participants in the artistically relevant controversy.

B. When a man says, " 'X' is better than 'Y' " in the sense of drawing a comparison in respect of artistic merit, or that " 'Y' is worse" or "not as good," this is not to say that "X" possesses more of some "merit" or "esthetic value." It means that, given the physical characteristic of "X" and "Y," and some set or sets of construction rules for the construing of "X" and "Y," either that "X" satisfies some set of instructions for the conduct of the arts and "Y" does not; or that, given two satisfied instruction sets, there is some third set which, given the choice, determines that art be conducted in terms of the construction set satisfied by "X" rather than that satisfied by "Y." Anything that can be said by placing "X" and

"Y" in the same instruction set and arguing that "X" satisfies that instruction set more "adequately" than "Y" simply moves the problem of a set of instructions for choosing between sets of instructions into the problem of determining degrees of "satisfaction."

C. When a man affirms that "X" has "some merit" or "great merit," then either he issues a kind of open comparative judgment in which he contents himself with indicating that there are instruction sets he would prefer to see satisfied rather than those satisfied by "X" and instruction sets which he would not; or else, for some given instruction set, he means that at least one of the instructions in that set has been satisfied but not all.

2. In some such way as the above, then, would one proceed to formulate within a context of production the force of merit judgments as they work in criticism. But the kind of result one gets has for our purposes greater importance than any articulation of shades of meaning.

A. Central to the construction of judgments of artistic merit is the choice of an instruction or recommendation set. Judgments of artistic merit embody choices of direction, grounded on reasons so far only incidentally considered. Controversies, therefore, can be formulated as possessing for their moot point comparative judgments: that one direction is to be taken *rather* than another. That is why anyone who questions the wisdom of the prescription asserted in the normative functioning of a judgment of artistic merit will counter the implicit "Do this sort of thing!" with the question "You mean, no doubt, rather than this, that or the other thing?"

No alternatives in view, no judgment of artistic merit—though, of course, pleasure may be pre-eminently present without a consideration of alternatives. Judgments, then, as judgments terminating or introducing controversies, *not* as expressions of consumer attitudes, require, as much as in any other field of reasonable behavior, the grasp of what the judgment excludes; and that, I take it, is the force of arguing that in artistically relevant controversy only "informed" opinion counts—not elite-ism, but the logic of judgment. In a context of consumption, on the other hand, likes, dislikes, and preferences are, finally, data. Hence "informed" opinion serves as an elite determining concept, not as the necessary ground for projecting an opinion at all. (The assumption here, of course, is that only "informed" opinion knows the alternatives; the alternatives are that of which informed opinion is informed.)

B. We may now observe how the proposed way of setting up judgments of artistic merit accounts for the feeling critics often have against comparative judgments; and since even flat judgments *as judgments,* seen as controvertible if not controverted, become disjuncts in the disjunctive prescription that defines the normative force of comparative judgments, one also understands the hesitation before judgments of artistic merit of any sort.

For while in a context of consumption the mania for merit-ranking objects, no matter what their differences, always makes possible sense (as we may *always* "prefer" one object to another as an object of taste), a context of production sharply circumscribes ranking. In a context of production there may be no need to adjudicate among claims that function in different domains for different objectives and in different situations; there may be no need to say, "This is better than that," even though one *might* say, "I like this better than that."

Where it is not pertinent to "compare," it is not pertinent to judge—and the person who persists in judging lacks that which is most indispensable to the practicing critic, a sense of appropriateness and relevance. The mistake would be to conclude that, because judgment requires a principle of relevance frequently absent in situations that *look like* judging situations (in consumer situations, for example), judgments of artistic merit must prove merely a lack of sophistication in the maker.

Seeing the contingency of relevant judgment has also the considerable advantage of freeing one to enjoy things as one finds them without the fear of involvement in an unacceptable judgment of merit. The occasion for comparative judgment lacking, why not indeed enjoy something less than the best? "Good," "better," "best" in an artistically relevant sense are frequently beside the point where another sense is to the point.

C. Our method of explicating judgments of artistic merit provides for a dimension of vacuity to such judgments, as it provides for irrelevance. Consumer judgments ("This is to my taste") are never vacuous, though they may be confused or vague. They are what they are. But in a context of production we can say that a critic "knows (or does not know, or has an incomplete idea of) what he is talking about" when he proffers his judgments of artistic merit, if and to the extent that his judgments *spell out* what he *wants* of the critical object itself. To the extent that he fails in the spelling out, he fails as a judge of artistic merit in the most disturbing respect, vacuity—and this no matter how strong his feelings of acceptance or rejection, or the adequacy of their expression.

Judgment of artistic merit, therefore, can miss its mark in a context of production where it cannot in a context of consumption; and criticism as a deliberative and responsible endeavor should surely provide for the possibility of missing the mark.

D. Lastly, our method of defining judgments of artistic merit makes rather immediate the point of speaking of criticism in its controversial moments as "in a context of production." It is not merely that the critic, in doing constructions, "produces" art himself, or engages in a necessary business for achieving the ends of art. It is not even that he lays down more or less general instructions for the kind of art he wants and leaves the rest to the artist; there is a sense in which a consumer could do that much, although presumably the consumer would present final standards to be satisfied rather than general prescriptions for bringing the satisfaction about. It rather turns out that the critic, to the extent of his critical force, when he presumes to evaluate the "merit" of a work of art, establishes, so far as the impulse of the controversy pushes him, the pattern of choices that must be implemented to achieve the "merit" he talks about. Whether or not he can or should implement those choices is, of course, a very different story.

In general, then: finding fault, taking exception, justifying, when done by a "good and responsible" critic of the arts, define themselves through an assumption of a creative role as difficult to sustain as it is desirable and relevant to achieve.

V. Judgment of Critic and Judgment of Artist

Let me now suggest the upshot of this discussion of claims of artistic merit from the point of view of the distinction between critic and artist, judge and creator. If there is a distinction, what can that creative role mean? If there is such a role, as the analysis of artistic merit certainly suggests, what can the distinction amount to? Some remarks of a working artist will help resolve the puzzle:

> An artist at work upon a painting must be two people, not one. He must function and act as two people all the time and in several ways. On the one hand, the artist is the imaginer and the producer. But he is also the critic, and here is a critic of . . . inexorable standards. . . . [He is a critic] constantly objecting, constantly chiding, holding the hand back to the image alone, so that the painting remains only that, so that it does not split into two things, one the image, and another the meaning.[10]

[10] Ben Shahn, *The Shape of Content,* (Cambridge, Mass.: Harvard University Press, 1957), p. 34.

The essence of the analysis of artistically relevant judgment offered in this chapter has been to take very seriously the rather familiar notion that the artist, whatever the depth and flash of his intuition, functions in his labor as judge of both merit and of import, taker of exception and justifier—in a word, as "critic"—and *then* to add that though of course the critic qua critic never engages to carry out the kind of "instructions" discussed above, nevertheless *his* judgments constitute decisions as logically aimed at artistic activity as those of the artist himself. If in the economy of art the same person may, as Shahn puts it, "be two people, not one," so also in that economy, on other occasions with other requirements, those same two persons may function separately as two persons.

Therefore, if the preceding discussion has been correct, no paradoxes or confusions follow from our construal of the artist's and the critic's role. Difficulties follow rather from that split between consumption and production which gives one domain to the critic as consumer and another to the artist as producer. On *that* assumption, the assumption of a context of consumption for the analysis of artistically relevant claims, it is indeed correct to fear that, in the presented picture of what the judge of artistic merit claims, he exchanges his occupation with somebody else's. But in a context of production one is free to make the distinction (between critic and artist) as one finds it.

Hence, to say that criticism is "creative" means to assign no preternatural powers to the critic, nor to jack up the value of criticism over against creativity to an unconscionable degree, nor to make a busybody and a nuisance of the critic. It means rather that since there is not one criticism for the critic and one for the artist, the artistically relevant criticism of the critic is the criticism of the artist. It would be equally true to say that the process of creation is itself critical; but that is not the part of the situation which needs emphasizing in the present climate of opinion.

The following propositions, then, are *compatible* with the view that there is one and only one artistically relevant criticism.

1. *There is a distinction between the rewrite man and the critic.* To be sure, the rewrite man participates in the writing in the sense in which the critic does not. But it is, clearly, one thing to specify the sort of thing that is to be done and another thing to do it—which every artist who has ever gotten stuck knows very well. The rewrite man does it (and also knows the difference); the critic, even if he knows how, keeps hands off. But it is no more an author's business to rewrite a colleague's work than it is the professional critic's. We are under no obligation to deny that issuing recommendations and taking them up require different, if complementary, talents.

2. *A critic may judge a work of art differently from the way its creator might.* But so of course might the artist himself at other times, and so might other artists. It is not necessary, in order to judge critically, to issue a separate *kind* of judgment.

3. *The class of critics might make different judgments from those of the class of artists.* This is an empirical possibility it would be foolish to deny—but only an empirical possibility, not because there are critics and there are artists. Critics may logically differ with artists on class lines and judge in the same sense. Class lines become significant only when critics are transmogrified into reviewers.

4. *Most critics couldn't produce a work of art if they wanted to, and the incapacity in no way invalidates their criticism.* On our account a critic does not have to produce a work of art. He has to be able to discern what is significant in actual works, establish an instruction set in terms of that discernment, and leave the rest to his masters in art, the artists. The more difficult job of seeing alternative choices, when a presented work of art does not already exist to guide you, remains for the artist or, of course, for the critic in so far as he is something of an artist.

But there is no point in being proud of one's limitations.

5. *The logic of a context of production has as much to do with artistic creation as it does with artistically relevant criticism.* Shahn, of course, has made our point. Decision, careful and caring, is part of the labor of art. The rules of artistically relevant controversy, for construction and for merit, apply above all to that decision process.

In consequence, the reciprocity required by the critic's and artist's judgments within a context of production is *not* compatible with these statements (among, of course, many others):

A. *While the critic as critic of the arts pre-eminently concerns himself to construe what the artist has presented, the artist leaves the problem of construction for others and seeks merely to make his work as excellent as possible.* The first part is true; the second is false. As Shahn points out, the artist controls his productive work in order to avoid a "split" between "image," or what is sensuously available, and "meaning." Performance guides and determines his selection of actions. He produces, in our view of the principle of reciprocity, neither as a volcano of inspiration nor as a manufacturer quite happy to sell his product regardless of what you do with it. As a working critic of his own work, his aim is always and at whatever cost in energy to bridge the "interpretative" gap between himself and his appreciator. That is why many people can say that the artist aims to be understood.

B. *The artist may regard as irrelevant any judgment of merit except his own.* It may indeed under suitable circumstances be advantageous to the artist to ignore the judgments of others. But the utility of believing a proposition is no guarantee of the belief's truth. The judgments of others are, if our analysis is correct, entirely *relevant* in a context of production; and the color of truth which the proposition wears follows from the often-enough remarked split between consumption and production, which, in establishing two forms of criticism, provides the artist as producer with a romantic autonomy otherwise entirely gratuitous.

If, then, the judgment of critics and the judgment of artists are not different sorts of things, but the same thing regardless of who happens to utter them, we may summarize results so far by saying that all artistically relevant judgment is participant judgment, not spectator or "esthetic" judgment. And we may lay it down as a regulative "Rule of Participation" for the formation of judgment (of worth or merit) in a context of production, "In all your judgments, seek to do art. If no one notices, neither do they necessarily notice the artist."

Chapter 9

The Ideal of Unicity, Judgment, and the Adjudicative Process

While the last chapter examined differences over the artistic merit of particular works of art and offered to place such differences in a context of production, someone will perhaps think the placing was accomplished only by neglecting the primary end of our old friend, the "good and responsible" critic: in Matthew Arnold's phrase, "to see the object as in itself it really is," in all its particularity. And he will add that Arnold's ideal precludes, if it precludes anything at all, the notion of the critic as giver of instructions and, in general, the idea of the critic as participant.

Criticism of the dogma of the work itself has, of course, already provided part of the answer. Nevertheless, the more interesting and more fruitful portion awaits us, on this side of judgment, for understanding the artistically relevant controversy. Actual criticism, not merely a normal version interpretation of that criticism, seeks indeed the "essence" of the particular work of art confronted. Actual critics, though they may, and do discuss entities like "Classicism," "Modernism," or "Romanticism," have then either abandoned criticism for historical scholarship or are preparing and testing tools for the approach to and management of the unique object. Criticism is criticism of art; and art is, of course, as we are inarticulately assured, always "particular."

Far from wishing to pass lightly over the critic's endeavor to acknowledge the ground-floor character of this ideographic focus of artistically relevant criticism, I shall wish to urge its fundamental and far-reaching relevance in determining the nature of judgment in a context of production. For positive as well as polemical reasons, I must offer a workable interpretation of the long-standing concern of philosophers and critics to grasp what makes a work of art "unique," *this* work of art and not some other, and then gather in some of the implications for artistically relevant judgment grasped as participant judgment.

That task will lead beyond the discussion of the claims question (as conducted so far with one eye on the context of consumption) toward that broader statement of the nature and function of artistically relevant judgment required for the reasons question.

I. Uniqueness without Ontology

"Come now," one hears, "granted what none could deny, that the 'Night Watch' requires to be treated as the 'Night Watch' and not as some other painting if you want to talk about the 'Night Watch.' But surely this stray blot of ink does not require to be treated as some other inkblot, assuming one cares to bother with it at all. One thing, no matter how noble, is not more itself and less something else than any other thing, nor is any particular thing more particular than any other."

All this cannot be gainsaid. Only, it does not prove that critics talk nonsense—merely that they speak, as everybody knows, hyperbole; and the very obviousness of the objection should make us suspect that we are taking much too literally a way of referring to a usage of critical language which stands independently of that mode of reference. So, for example, everybody knows that calling one person or object "more unique" than another, whatever the ontological pathos of language, emphasizes important ways in which that object differs from others. Why not examine the language of artistically relevant controversy in a similar sense? Then the "Night Watch" becomes "unique," and the inkblot does not, because critics feel justified in dealing with them differently, while the problem of the logical analysis of "uniqueness" becomes the problem of substituting for a sheer revelation of the "essence" of a work of art, a rule of relevance and of focus for exposition and controversy.

I shall propose, therefore, that the critic who fixes, as he tells us, on the "unique" and "particular" in a work of art but relaxes his demand for such a fixing the less he considers the presented object a "work of art," accepts an implicit ideal for regulating critical activity, the "ideal of unicity." There follows now a rough description of that ideal as it would seem to function in artistically relevant criticism and differentiate an ideographic from a nomothetic inquiry: [1]

[1] Not only critics, of course, but, pre-eminently, historians as well are accustomed to emphasize that their disciplines differ in principle from science and speculative philosophy, in virtue of their concern with the "particular." The *subject matter,* some of them, notably those most connected with the movement of "historicism," will say, is different; and that is why their method must be different from the scientific method. From our point of view, in history as well as in art-relevant criticism, the attempt to fix upon a unique subject matter in order to explain a particular kind of interest would be quite gratuitous. The rules which would determine when a historian dealt with his subject matter as "unique" or "particular," are outside our province; but

1. *Scope of the Ideal:* If indeed the fundamental aim of criticism is as Arnold and others claim that it is, then the ideal of unicity will control all critical discourse in so far as that discourse proffers a *construction* of some given created object ("primary discourse") and in so far as that discourse presents a construction of some class of created objects as members of that class ("secondary discourse"). The distinction is between discourse about the "Laocoön" and discourse about Hellenistic style. All critical discourse is either primary or secondary. The ideal of unicity is specified by a rule for each.

2. *Rule for Primary Discourse:* Any construction of any created object will be considered adequate for the purposes of artistically relevant discourse only if it seeks, so far as reasonable under the circumstances, to construe a created object as a member of a class with but one member. How to specify (A) "reasonable under the circumstances" and (B) "member of a class with but one member" constitutes, of course, the heart of the "rule."

A. To seek, so far as "reasonable under the circumstances," to construe the created object in a manner that sets it forth as unique means to construe it within limits set by (1) the character of the controversy, actual or projected, with respect to which criticism occurs and (2) the character of the object, which, *with respect to conditions pertinent to the critical argument,* may not be the *sole* member of *any* class.

Being "reasonable" in matters of uniqueness, one would want to set limits to the respects in which a thing differs from all other things—limits determined not only practically, by the finitude of man, but also logically, in that without a context in virtue of which to discriminate *relevant* points of difference and similarity, no *critical* significance can be given to "going further." As a consequence of the way in which relevance varies with the shift in critical context, one would furthermore want to admit the possibility, often enough encountered in fact, that objects are *not* "unique" in relation to some of those contexts; for those objects, it would clearly be "unreasonable" to demand of criticism that it somehow find a sense in which the created object *is* "unique."

B. Given, then, that determinations of the unique nature of created objects are context-limited and limited as well by the object examined, critics seem to seek to place created objects as the sole member of one of two different kinds of classes.

---

there seems to be no a priori reason why an ideal of "unicity" would not explain all that needs to be explained in the "particularity" of history, just as it explains, according to our thesis, all that needs to be explained in the "uniqueness" of the "work of art."

Some critics press the ideal of unicity up to, but no further than, the point demanded by requirements of some specified difference of opinion (and, of course, the nature of the created object within that difference of opinion). They want to know if a created object is "unique" in this or that respect in comparison with certain other specified works of art, and in *this* manner they construct the class within which the object is in a "class by itself." They aim at a "relatively complete criticism." Relatively complete criticisms engender few philosophical arguments, taken in themselves.

Other critics, however, or perhaps the same ones in a different mood, find it desirable for works of a certain seriousness to set up in a more demanding way relevant classes in which to drop their object as the sole member. Unsatisfied with a relatively complete criticism, they use "unique" to describe an object that, with respect to a plurality of artistically relevant controversies, and perhaps all, one may call the sole member of a class; and then they seek the "exact" sense in virtue of which the object is so "unique," in some crucial characteristic or set of characteristics. Critics such as these may deny that any criticism is completely adequate unless it is an "absolutely complete" criticism in the above sense—unless, as they may say, criticism "gets to the heart of the matter," "grasps the essence of the work of art," or "appreciates its true individuality," and so on. Aiming at absolutely complete criticism, aside from asserting the "exact" sense (which may, of course, be quite vague) in which to consider the created object "absolutely" unique, critics also make a kind of wager and prescription for the course of future criticism: that for some set (maybe all) of future artistically relevant controversies of which they know nothing, as well as for those of which they are aware, or are partly aware, the sense in which the work of art has been found "unique" will continue to differentiate the object in a nontrivial way—and if it does not, it nevertheless should.

Accordingly, one may take the ideal of unicity in either a strong or a weak sense: in the strong sense, only that criticism will seem completely adequate which is an absolutely complete criticism; in the weak sense, one will rest content with a relatively complete criticism.[2] A criticism that holds the ideal of unicity in a strong sense will find few objects "absolutely" unique; these, of course, will be the extraordinary works of art, the

[2] One ought not, of course, expect sharp boundaries between a relatively complete criticism and an absolutely complete one, given the many variations in the ambition of critics and the varied prospects for interesting results that the presented object seems to offer. Strong and weak criticisms constitute directions for criticism rather than exhaustive categories.

"great successes" or the "great failures." Clearly, also, it will be this sort of criticism that will tend to promote philosophical speculation about the "nature" or "essence" of the work of art as a "thing in itself." There will seem to be some ontological power underlying the career of a work of art that takes it beyond the requirements of any particular discussion; and it will appear that one cannot talk about anything specific in the arts (proffer a relatively complete criticism) without presupposing a special power (which an absolutely complete criticism now supposedly seeks).

3. *Rule for Secondary Discourse:* No critical discourse that possesses for its object a class instead of the presented and "particular" work of art—as, for example, Renaissance architecture or Chinese calligraphy or Restoration comedy considered as classes of things with interesting traits in common—will be considered an adequate *critical* discourse (the rule does not refer to scholarship or sociology) unless it is "reducible" to primary critical discourse in the strong or weak sense. This I may perhaps have leave to call the "antiacademic rule." If secondary discourse defers to the ideal of unicity, then it is antiacademic.

What does "reducible" mean? As the significance of secondary discourse matters here only in so far as it connects with a specific critical ideal, we may skip the general problems associated with "reducing" utterances possessing dispositional concepts, the oblique use of language, and the rest. "Reducible" here means merely that disagreements over the nature or merit of all classes of works of art are to be resolved by restating those differences, so long as they persist, into a difference or differences on the primary level of discourse, where the rule for primary discourse holds sway. The rule is a rule for establishing the direction of controversy.

It is important to note that one might accept the rule for primary discourse without accepting the rule for secondary discourse, although those who think most of the "uniqueness" of the work of art mean to assert, perhaps, the rule for secondary discourse as part and parcel of the ideal of unicity. Critics, for example, frequently present for consideration certain styles as such and declare themselves in sympathy or antipathy toward a "Classic" or "Romantic" style. But whether they mean merely to summarize the kinds of conclusions reached after considering the members of the pertinent class, and then, perhaps to make a few guesses about how they will judge such objects in the future, or whether they mean to proffer a study of a kind of intension open to the discovery of more and more instances but in itself the final object of their criticism—that will depend upon the temper of the critic and how seriously he takes the ideal of unicity. For if general "common sense" in an argument instructs us to "get down to cases," the rule for secondary discourse tells us something more, which we may or may not fancy: it tells us the kind of cases to get down to. "Don't get excited about Geisten, or intoxicate yourselves with abstract styles. Avoid movements as critical objects." For the fact is that sometimes such entities seem to be taken as objects quite as genuine for whatever processes one brings to bear on "art" as the "Mona Lisa" and her allegedly induplicable smile.

4. *Some Initial Bearings of the Ideal of Unicity:* It will, perhaps, help indicate the force of the ideal of unicity to mention (A) its relation to the formative-performative distinction and then (B) to indicate the break it implies for a consumer criticism.

A. One wonders, does the ideal of unicity come to the same thing as the injunction, "Let all your criticisms be performative"? That it does not is a small point but perhaps worth making:

a. First, the formative-performative distinction requires no antiacademic rule. "Romanticism," "Classicism," "Baroque style," etc., for all this distinction cares, are perfectly legitimate objects of analysis. One may, that is to say, consider them not simply as conceptual apparatus for understanding particular objects, but as unique wholes *composed* of certain *parts,* or as essences that delight on sight. But the ideal of unicity, taken to include the secondary rule, excludes "academic" expressions as in effect names of special kinds of works of art.

b. There is, I take it, no problem in seeing that performative criticism does not require the idea of unicity in the strong form.

c. The rule for primary discourse, on the other hand, stating as it does a *condition* for settling certain performative issues (demanding that we push the specific examination to the limit relevant), provides an explanation of why it seems sensible to say that criticism is indeed concerned, *of necessity,* with the work of art as "unique." If one is going to talk about presented works of art, as a working critic, performative issues will always demand to be settled. The rule for primary discourse tells how to handle them.

d. Nevertheless, all this means is that if one wants to start with the specific work of art, one will face performative issues, which can be taken as "defining" the possibilities for what the created object might be. It does not in any sense tell us to start with the specific work of art in the convergent activity of formative and performative analyses, as the ideal of unicity does.

B. Certain consequences follow from the rule of unicity for differentiating artistically relevant criticism from consumer criticism, for which we may stop.

a. The aim of Mr. Alston's criticism was precisely to show that *The Body Beautiful* belonged to a class that, happily, *did* have more than one member: the class of "fun shows." But the other critics, the less serious critics, upon whom the fate of show business and the leisure hours of millions did *not* depend, although they might begin with their primary object as members of a class, reached toward the "uniqueness" or special character of that object. In general: entertainment criticism tries to place its objects under some rubric and to evaluate them according to the degree they meet specifications; but for artistically relevant criticism, where the ideal of unicity serves the critic for a conscience, such considerations are *post factum.*

b. If an antiacademic rule holds for entertainment, or, more broadly, commodity criticism—and, conceivably, one would want to insist on such a rule for "serious" commodity criticism—nevertheless, secondary discourse about commodities does not reduce to primary discourse of the sort that concerns artistically relevant criticism.

c. If the ideal of unicity holds for artistically relevant discourse, that discourse ought not be expected to exhibit the kind of ordering function of a consumer criticism, which displays itself so characteristically in fixing "The Ten Best Plays of 1961" or in awarding first, place, and show to the pictures at an exhibition. The priority business ought to fill the "true" critic, in so far as he makes use of the ideal of unicity, with embarrassment; and so it does. For if indeed what is "unique" in the created object chiefly concerns him, how shall he know how to order the candidates? Ordering them, he feels himself parading under false colors—performing, perhaps, some sort of social function but vaguely wishing all along that he needn't.

II. How Criticism Particularizes: Paradox and Explications

Broadly speaking, the problem now is to see how the ideal of unicity applies to an artistically relevant criticism, how actual criticism might particularize, understanding that the process of particularizing constitutes a rule-bound procedure. For, to begin with, we face the difficulty reflected just above in the alleged position of the consumer critic: it seems that either one judges or one particularizes, since in judging one considers objects as members of a class and, particularizing, one strives to talk about them in the respect in which they are like nothing else. First, then, for the resolution of the difficulty:

1. For construction judgments the resolution is fairly obvious: the question being how to construe an object presented for criticism, the object will be differentiated and understood as such in virtue of the complex of relationships which that object sustains in the matrix of art and of society. A series of performative rules will then tell all and sundry what to make of the work of art. These rules will define the object's uniqueness, since the ideal of unicity will demand those performative rules that differentiate the "meaning" or "import" of the critical object, in a nontrivial way, from the meaning or import of any relevant other. ("Nontrivial," of course, means relevant to an artistically relevant controversy.) One will now have deferred to Matthew Arnold's recipe for criticism, and, obviously, without making discourse mystical. Judgments will still recommend to other critics; and they may accept or reject those recommendations, as they think best.

Now we can approach the more significant difficulty, the apparent paradox of that unique artistic merit which critics forever protest to seek out, and which seems so much like a contradiction in terms. The resolution consists in recognizing an alternative to a standard of merit fixed in advance of criticism and functioning like God on the Day of Judgment, who, with the scroll of history rolled up, judges the past by immutable values. For the work of art makes a difference, profound or shallow as the case may be, in the movement of art to come and in the construction of the art that has been; and that difference constitutes its uniqueness. Why, therefore, should we not approve or disapprove just *that* difference, just that uniqueness *qua unique* difference, for the sake *not* of keeping things in their proper holes, but for the sake of art as a present activity?

Remembering that created objects are from the point of view of artistically relevant controversy not tight little isolates in an esthetic vacuum, but objects-in-proper-relation, we can say that the critic's quest for the "unique merit" of a work of art ceases to resemble the hunt for square circles and becomes instead the attempt to reach a decision on some turning point, large or small, in what I have called "the conduct of the arts." If, then, the critical object constitutes no such pivotal point, explicates no previously considered possibility, then arguments about the merit of that created object are not arguments about its *unique* merit. They are instead arguments about a "derivative" merit, about how the critical object resembles objects that *have* made differences in the conduct of the arts. So the notion of a unique artistic merit remains as meaningful as the notion of the unique significance of a certain experience or the unique legal import of a certain court decision.

2. There follows the radical importance in assessing any artistically relevant criticism of the ideal of unicity. It had been thought that the "uniqueness" of a work of art necessarily made judgment special, "esthetic." But now one sees instead that in a context of production the ideal of unicity actually gives content to the recommendations of the critic and renders those recommendations pertinent to actual states of affairs in the arts. One sees that without the ideal of unicity criticism might never quite mesh with the conduct of the arts; instead it might become a quasi-relevant commentary, forever missing the point and engendering critiques for which the artist could not have the slightest use. The final and, as I should like to call it again, the "radical" importance of the ideal of unicity is, quite simply, to heal the breach between consumption and production in the arts; and the name currently given to the criticism that specifically fails to heal that breach through the industrious pursuit of the ideal is "square."

It must be emphasized, however, that not only does the ideal of unicity possess a central procedural significance for criticism (judging within a matrix of art and of society upon the uniqueness of a work of art, the critic necessarily takes his stand on at least one pivotal occasion in the procession of the arts), but objects satisfying the rule, objects that are determined as "unique," are then said to possess a special value. Uniqueness in a critical object is considered all to the good even though no a priori reason exists why a critic might not push the ideal of unicity in order to *disdain* the objects that met its requirements. But such a critic of course would have turned his back on the movement of the arts. He would have opted for a perpetually familiar art, in effect, have made the proposal that art stop short on some celebrated day. Not a context of production, then, would determine his critical world, but a context of consumption, in which art would have ceased to be something *to be* made, and all judgments of artistic merit would have become appreciations.

We may lay it down, therefore, as a further explication of the ideal of unicity, that uniqueness, all other things being equal, is a value; and that people make use of the ideal of unicity, when they are "good and responsible critics," not through fear of the future but because they wish to signalize themselves part of a growing enterprise.

3. A glance now at criticism particularizing: for direct arguments arise over the particularizing functions of criticism, arguments that exhibit specific differences of opinion over whether the job has been done

correctly. In the following manner, then, would one go about explicating the sense of the more familiar issues concerning "uniqueness," and the claims lying more or less at the center of the particularizing argument would be such as these:

A. People raise the question "Is this critical object 'unique' or not?" I have, of course, formulated the ideal of unicity directly in terms of that question. But dependent on the uniqueness decision is the issue whether or not the object will be admitted among the objects that are "works of art" and/or proper subjects for artistically relevant controversy. For only those objects that possess the value of uniqueness in one way or another are normally held to be "genuine" works of art or worth talking about. Everything here depends upon the justification of constructions.

B. "Is this object really as 'unique' as it seems to be?" Agreement now exists that in certain respects at least the object under inspection falls into a class by itself. The issue is whether or not the traits in virtue of which the created object claims uniqueness place the object in interesting and relevant classes; and the answer to this will clearly depend not only on one's constructions, but very directly on one's judgments of artistic merit.

C. "Is this fellow just trying to be different?" Anything is in some respect a member of a unique class. The question remains whether the class is artistically significant. As in the paragraph above, the questioner is talking not about motives but about accomplishment as it bears on an artistically relevant controversy.

D. "Which of these affairs is the most unique?" "Original" would of course do just as well. An entire complex of questions is involved: which object makes the more interesting difference for the art in which it occurs (a question of comparative judgments of artistic merit), which is more fairly described as unique (agreement over merit, perhaps, but disagreement over the proper constructions of the compared created objects), which if either succeeds in the sense of absolute uniqueness, and which if either in the sense of relative uniqueness, and so on.

E. "Agreeing that the object deserves the appellation of 'unique,' is it a masterpiece then, and in what way?" This fuzzy and familiar inquiry still constitutes a question of sorts if a "masterpiece" is an absolutely unique rather than a relatively unique object. How in any instance can one settle a difference of opinion? One tries to measure the height of the "achievement" and sustains the estimate by making comparative judgments of "achievement," that is, of differences made in the business of the arts. Argument now tests the entire spectrum of construction rules and merit claims that the protagonists bring to bear; and that is why arguments whether the "masterpiece" is indeed a masterpiece are so often unresolved. For they may turn, in the end, around basic tools and positions in criticism rather than any particular difference over the particular work of art. So the masterpiece status of *Hamlet* becomes the occasion for critics to pronounce their final views on the matrix of society, the matrix of art, criticism, and life itself—the occasion, in effect, for a formative argument of maximum complexity.

It would seem, then, that concrete "uniqueness" controversies are intelligible, as the general analysis required they should be, in terms of construction issues or issues of artistic merit, formative or performative. Of course, further instances of uniqueness criticism might conceivably resist the analysis; but one would be hard put to know what they would be like, if they were not instances of the way "uniqueness" functions in critical discourse for purposes *other* than the purposes of artistically relevant controversy.

III. Practical Judgment and the Practice of Judgment

What kind of thing, then, is artistically relevant judgment? What is it like? It is time to assess in what direction the attempt to offer an alternative to a normal version account of artistically relevant judgment may have led and to assess the force of the specific analyses presented. For upon that force depends the treatment of the reasons question.

I must, then, in the light of the discussions of constructions, artistic merit, and the ideal of unicity, suggest as the truth about artistically relevant judgment, at least for its function within controversy, what must seem like a major heresy or a major misunderstanding: If judgment in its normative force recommends and, in recommending particularizes, and recommends moreover, not in a one-shot sense (like "Close the door!") but in a sense (a "participant" sense) making for one kind of conduct toward situations rather than another, then there seem to be good grounds to consider artistically relevant judgments as *practical* judgments rather than (whatever it might mean) "esthetic judgments." Inevitably, the problem of rationality in criticism now becomes the identifiable, if difficult, problem of justifying decisions in a particular practice.

I should like first to recall the requirements ordinarily laid upon "practical judgment" and then to remark on some of the more obvious analogies and disanologies with the practice of judgment in courts of law:

1. Regardless of the interpretative function of the classic distinction between "knowing," "making," and "doing," which lays down a difference in principle between reason in action and in production, certain ground-floor expectations exist of any judgment deserving to be called "practical." Artistically relevant judgment, as hitherto described, meets those expectations.

A. For, first, only that judgment is normally considered "practical" judgment which concerns particular cases; and a person is said to "show" judgment only when he examines cases in virtue of their individual requirements. Hence anyone who deals in an abstract manner with the individual cases that generate his problem will be said, depending on the circumstances, to behave "impractically" or to lack "judgment." And so it is for criticism in the arts. The ideal of unicity formulates the operating conditions for dealing with objects in respect of their particular characteristics, in the sense that a man of judgment, sensitive to unexpected conditions, approaches them—not as so many hard data to be subsumed under one rubric or another but in complex relation, within a matrix of art and of society.

B. Moreover, it is always said that judgment is "practical" when aimed at directing action, but not otherwise. Above all, the practical man supposedly decides on courses of action, while the "impractical" man concerns himself "merely" with observing or appreciating. But the entire focus of analysis to date has been to exhibit the prescriptive force for managing the arts, of artistically relevant judgment. In a context of production, the critic defines his relevance precisely in the sense that he is not a "mere" observer or a "mere" appreciator. Of course, "practical" people do not ordinarily consider the conduct of the arts a "practical" activity.

Nevertheless, practical judgment is participant judgment; and so is artistically relevant judgment.

C. Though the practical man in his practice constructs the practice in which he participates, he is never thought to construct it from the ground up, as it were. Practical judgment is judgment *in* a practice. People are normally reluctant to say that the creation of a practice itself constitutes the exercise of "practical judgment," even though they never clearly indicate the point at which "reconstruction" becomes "recreation." But this again is a point made all along: that the artistically relevant judgment that comes to terminate a controversy, or even to enter a controversy as a candidate for acceptance, determines its force and legitimacy in an already existing art with an envisaged real future. That an artistically relevant criticism does not create the world from nothing has been the point of insisting on criticism in a context of production.

It would seem, therefore, that there is nothing paradoxical in thinking of artistically relevant judgment as a form of practical judgment provided, of course, that one eliminate the prejudice against certain ends that common attitudes toward "practicality" entail.

2. Far more important, however, than the matter of common expectation is the question of the analogy between the practice of judgment in criticism and the practice of judgment in morals, politics, business, law, and so on. If the analogy is strong enough we will be inclined to admit artistically relevant judgment as a kind of "practical" judgment—if not, not; and the *sense* of calling judgment "practical" will be specified by the strength of analogy (and disanalogy) in a nontrivial way. Since I cannot here compare judgment in artistically relevant criticism with judgment in all the various practices to which "practical reason" admittedly has some relevance, I shall again make the comparison with that "practical" activity that most overtly and professionally "judges"—the business, of course, of passing judgment in courts of law.

A. Previous discussion has already made amply clear that in criticism one advances proposals for the construction of critical objects and the establishment of a proper conduct in the arts, *and in much the same sense* (omitting the matter of sanctions) *in which legal judgment extends to its object.* For the judge in any court of law faces also the double problem of placing a construction upon the case presented in council to him and, in the light of his construction, deciding on its legal merits. The tendency, therefore, to dismiss the judgment of critics as "interpretative" rather than "practical" misses the point. Judgment in courts of law places the same kind of priority upon construction processes, upon saying "what sort of thing the case is," or "what's actually involved," that artistically relevant judgment does; and in the process, instead of lapsing into "subjectivity," it performs a most essential function in organizing social behavior. It is a mistake to assume that judgment, to be practical, must always assume that the construction function is minor—the drudge's mistake.

B. For judgmental functions of both construction and merit, judgment has the force of precedent—in artistically relevant controversy, as we have seen, as in law. We were even led to formulate a "rule of law" in the discussion of constructions, a rule the appropriateness of which was confirmed in the consideration of artistically relevant discourse and extended to judgment of artistic merit. For we found that, in the very nature of the claim advanced and argued in artistically relevant controversy, the configuration of circumstances remarked in the particular work of art under consideration, being approved or disapproved, was taken as having a bearing upon future action and the construction of past actions—the bearing of precedent. The very "uniqueness" of the object under examination then became the vital respect in which *other* objects could be appraised, now that "uniqueness" was taken "without ontology."

Therefore, it seems fair to say, *both* criticism and the processes of legal decision employ themselves in the process of "making the law," establish the instruction sets in virtue of which judgment and action are to proceed. And it no more follows that because in the arts one "makes" one's law that judgment is of necessity special and nonpractical—"creative" in some special sense—than it follows for courts of law.

It was, of course, the systematic neglect of the precedent dimension of artistically relevant judgment—the insistence on regarding such judgment as a one-shot affair—that made possible conceiving such judgment as different in kind from judgment in any other practice, this, and, of course, the underlying confusion between enjoyment and judgment.

C. But perhaps the most suggestive way in which artistically relevant criticism functions in the sense of judicial decision appears on considering the "adjudicative" process of judgment in law. For, plainly, judicial decision, in pronouncing its judgments, "adjudicates" among the claims presented by counsel—deciding which claims are genuine, what force such genuine claims possess, and in its final dispensation rendering the conclusion for the issue at stake.

Similarly, however, the complex decisions of criticism dispose of the various elements of a critical situation. The critic too must rule out of consideration, by a "rule of inclusion and exclusion"—as incompetent, irrelevant, or immaterial, so to speak—certain facts such as (to take extreme cases) the physical location of the painting or who performs the music, and he must rule other facts germane. Then, also, in order to decide what the work of art might "be" or what "merit" it might conceivably have, the critic must seek to "weigh" the significance of those facts about the critical object that he has, implicitly, declared competent, material, and relevant. He will consider, for example, the relation of line to color, of one character to another in a certain sort of plot development, of theme to harmony, and so on. This much accomplished, then, he will expound his best judgment of the nature of the object before him and of its merit. And if asked to explicate his judgment he will refer to the exclusions, inclusions, and weighings he has presented for consideration, just as, if the lawyer seeks to ascertain the content and significance of the judge's decision, he too will refer to the complex conditions under which the judge has disposed of the particular case one way or the other.

In ways such as these (discriminating within a matrix of art and of society which claims are mere demands and which demands have some claim to legitimacy, through weighing legitimate facts, through drawing the implications of his weighings for the field of art) the critic exhibits his "good judgment" and makes good the claim to act as a "judge" of the arts in more than an outrageously metaphorical sense.

Observe, then, that what seems to make the adjudicative process qualitatively different in the arts and in law is actually the consequence of the way in which the legal process makes explicit and formalizes the logic of adjudication in the light of certain social purposes; but the logic is not therefore different. Here in court stands the contending counsel calling for the construction and judgment of merit upon contending claims presented not only as claims *on* an estate, for example, but as claims deriving legitimacy from the whole body of common law and statute: as *claims to* the estate. There stands or sits, the judge, referring to what is in principle, if not in practice, the same body of law that counsel does, to determine the legitimacy and strength of claims to the estate and finally, by his judgment, to dispose *of* that estate. And so it goes also with artistically relevant judgment except, of course, that, in what must seem from the outside like a ferocious display of energy, the same man, internalizing the entire logic of criticism, may bring the action, argue the claims of all parties (of whom, to boot, there may now be an indefinite number), and in the end find his way to the bench to deliver his finding: "Let such and such be our understanding of the play. Let so and so under these circumstances constitute a principle of dramatic construction, not this and that."

In general, then, although the elaborate institutionalization of the adjudicative process in the law rests upon a different appraisal of the consequences and temptations of adjudicative distortion and variation than it does in the arts, nevertheless we speak appropriately of "justice" in criticism, as of "justice" in law, for we testify thereby to the product of an adjudicative process.

Those who would pressure criticism into a context of consumption fail to see that the objective of the "good and responsible" taker of exceptions is justice, not his own way.

3. But also the real and apparent *disanalogies* between law and an artistically relevant adjudication are required to illuminate judgment in the arts.

A. Consider first that while the "findings" and "verdicts" of critics of the arts make at most a hypothetical difference, the constructions and merit judgments of courts bind actual persons. But whom does the critic "bind" except himself? The logic of adjudication aims at different conclusions in law and in criticism.

Once again we must consider what it means for a judgment to "bind," and remark the truistic distinction that people may be *compelled* and *not* feel "bound," or feel "bound" without being compelled. That is, they may, as in the latter case, simply acknowledge the "justice" of a proposal, and it is in the sense of such acknowledgment that the findings and verdicts of art and law have been compared. Hence we ought not to be put off by the discovery of what is at best an ideal of the law and not an actuality: that the law adjudicates what a citizen "ought" to do or has "right" to do only in so far as he may be *compelled* to meet his obligation *or* have his "right" enforced.

Moreover, the fact that legal judgment may also be said to bind because, for a certain class of cases, the citizen has no recourse but to go to the law for judgment also fails to establish a significant disanalogy between the adjudicative processes. For either, the notion of binding introduces again the previously noted confusion between the compulsions of justice and the compulsions of the police, or it serves merely to *extend* the scope of judicial process so far considered. Such an extension is no doubt justified. An adjudicative procedure of some sort is necessary to *indict* for a crime, not merely to convict for one. But then, so far as artistically relevant criticism goes, it also may be quite appropriate and under certain circumstances even necessary to justify the consideration of an object's suitability for criticism.

Next, in so far as the objection to comparing legal and critical adjudications rests on a concern for simple effectuality, it ought to be noted that, while legal decisions are in fact frequently unsuccessful in getting themselves implemented, the recommendations of even those critics who are not artists evaluating and controlling their own work may often get their judgments acted upon. We do, after all, speak of "influential critics." People *are* taught art. But the common acceptance of the normal version makes criticism's irrelevance to the processes of artistic activity seem so plausible the obvious facts get hidden.

On the other hand, of course, a significant disanalogy between law and criticism lies in the rule of *stare decisis:* Courts are "bound" under certain difficult-to-state conditions to consider the decisions of other courts as law. Critics and artists are not bound to take the judgments of other critics and artists as law in any analogous way. They lack any official authority.

B. People very often think the task of criticism is hopeless because criticism lacks anything like a body of law to justify decisions. If there were anything like a body of law, then, they feel, artistically relevant decision would constitute a genuine adjudication, but not otherwise. Attempts to save the rationality of critical judgment thereupon set up a kind of constitution of art to guide a "judicial criticism."

The difficulty, however, is not merely that a judicial criticism mistakes the processes of artistically relevant decision, which it does; the difficulty is also that in a similar manner such an ideal of criticism mistakes the processes of legal decision.

For, of course, pertinent and nontrivial precedents and rules, given a legal controversy, do *not* stand immediately available for the judge to employ; and this holds for constitutional and administrative law quite as much as for the so-called "common law." Precedents are endless and conflicting, circumstances novel, and the force and pertinence of precedents and circumstances in perpetual dispute. The objection against the analogy between judicial judgment and artistically relevant judgment, therefore, makes the false assumption that a body of law exists ready to be "applied" without the intervention of precisely that "judgment" upon which the analogy rests.

Moreover, be it observed, legal law is surely not supposed to bind everywhere at all times and all places. What is marriage in one state is incest in another; what is usury at one time is interest at another. These are obvious enough observations, but the notion that the analogy between legal and artistically relevant judgment requires the assumption of a more or less fixed "body of law" certainly seems to require them. For *both* law and criticism the problem of decision consists precisely of what "body" of traditions, habits, expectations, to choose and to interpret. "Under *which* king, Bezonian? Speak or die!" The question holds for magistrate as for critic; and, to put it mildly, it is far from clear for whom the proliferation of traditions is more confusing, their pertinence more problematic, and the difficulty of answering Pistol's question the more subtle.

But perhaps the real reason for dislikening artistic and legal judgment on the ground that "law" exists in one but not the other lies simply in that the accumulated judgments of past and present law are official whereas the judgments of critics are not. The former carry at least the pretense of power and enforcement. Nevertheless, it does not follow that official decisions have a higher logic in them, or even a different sort of logic, than unofficial ones.

C. Given such legal materials as are available to the judge for constructing his decisions and such artistically relevant materials as are available to the critic, someone may claim that nevertheless in a specific courtroom attorneys and magistrate in conducting their arguments appeal to the "same" law, but that an attempt to subject the artist to standards that he may very well refuse to acknowledge—to a "different" law—marks the critic as judge. A "duality" of judgment exists in the latter case which does not in the former, and it distinguishes the adjudicatory processes.

Once again qualifications are necessary on both sides.

On the side of the law, the primary fact to remember is the presence of contending counsels and of a judge, who may dismiss the arguments of one or the other contender or of both. The "same" law is the *product* of judicial decision, not its condition, as the judge rules on counsel's claims. Counsel, perforce, *yields* (although even here reserving right of appeal) as the subject of criticism need not. Nevertheless, the existence of legal argument makes inevitable a working duality in their relations to the law, of judge and counsel. That is why the judge is judge. Once again the objection pictures law as a process, this time shared among judges and attorneys, of cranking out logical conclusions.

On the side of criticism, discussion has already tried to show that in a context of production the existential situation to which the critic appeals—the bodies of precedent, the directions of artistic activity, the possibilities opened and foreclosed, the very movement of human life—is not different in function from the situation to which the artist appeals. The objector to the adjudicatory analogy ought not mistake it for its opposite. The duality of judgment is indeed a fact for the consumer critic with his rule of taste. But judgment, in artistically relevant controversy, is participant judgment and criticism, determined by principles of respect and referral, no mere game like parchesi; nor are the judgments of merit, which project favorably or unfavorably the constructions of created objects, logically independent of the action of the arts.

Hence the judiciousness of the critic does not divide the decision situation, any more than the judiciousness of the court divides the legal situation. For the judiciousness of the critic of the arts rests upon the same fact as the judiciousness of the judge in the law: the fact that, among the contending claims of artists and other critics, he seeks to examine what has been made of the common situation, and in the process he perhaps makes something different from what those others have. So in law and in criticism the duality of judge and judged holds as a *practical* fact; there is no theoretical reason for it to hold in one instance and not in the other.

In general, then, in a context of production, artistically relevant judgment on its cutting edge is "practical" in a serious sense. A "judgment," of construction or of merit, states or "renders" a decision come by. Hence any endeavor to work out in a systematic manner the justification for artistically relevant judgment—the logic in virtue of which artistically relevant controversies are open to rational settlement—must consider how the factors entering into the establishment and sustenance of an artistically relevant decision are differentiated from the factors determining the controversies of other practical domains.

At the same time, of course, the difficulties to which practical judgment in general falls heir become also difficulties for the philosophy of criticism.

IV. The Factors of Judgment

Hence we must go beyond considering what people demand of critical objects given a variance in artistically relevant judgment, or even the "practicality" of judgment of this sort. The next move toward understanding the nature and limits of artistically relevant controversy must be to ascertain the structure of that adjudicative process within which judgment in the arts appears and in which different sorts of judgment are differentiated.[3]

For guidance we may recall that, with greater or lesser efficiency, legal processes formally institutionalize the adjudicative process. Such as the following, then, are those "factors of judgment" in virtue of which decision in the law secures its characteristic legitimacy and justification. They are discernible in other "practices" as well. In the way they operate, they serve to define a "practice."

1. In the law, as elsewhere, every judgment requires its "proper occasion." To understand the nature of the judgment rendered requires understanding also the nature of that occasion. So also for criticism, judgment is rendered *on* a proper occasion.

Generally, then, one says that one occasion "calls for" judgment and not another—and that those who go about judging, regardless of the occasion (on "improper occasions"), "lack judgment." But in doing so one does not thereby intend to commit oneself to any *interpretation* of judgment in general and of its general reference to concrete occasions, such as Dewey's analysis of the "problematic situation." One merely

[3] To take up Holmes' gambit, so far we have for the most part, although by no means exclusively, been considering artistically relevant criticism from a perspective analogous to "the bad man's point of view" in the law. For the bad man wanted to know what *difference* the law made in the world; and so did we, for critical judgment. Now we begin to turn our attention to judgment "from the judge's point of view," as the product of an adjudication.

acknowledges the existence of specific requirements for approaching any situation, regardless of what it may mean to be a "situation," with judgment of a certain kind as the end in view.

So, for example, the United States Supreme Court will normally refuse to render an advisory opinion even though such an opinion may bear very directly on the making of some political decision; and in general some courts will "hear" certain cases and some courts others, while some cases will never find a hearing in the law and, hence, never actually achieve the status of "cases."

As for the processes of artistically relevant criticism, the attempt to differentiate the business of appreciation and the business of pedagogy from the business of controversy, and, in general, to differentiate the occasions of "consumer controversy" from the occasions of "artistically relevant controversy" disclose that a distinction between proper and improper occasion exists there too. We have, for example, deprecated differences of opinion in the "ranking" of critical objects according to some pre-established standard, as improper occasions for artistically relevant controversy. We will never make sense of the logic of artistically relevant controversy if we ignore the proper occasion of critical judgment or systematically attempt to justify such judgment by a reference to an improper occasion.

2. In a court of law, patently, anyone may have an opinion but only a judge renders a judgment. In determining the nature of any adjudicative process, and hence the force of "judgment" in that process, there is always the question of who is the proper judge. Judgment is rendered *by* a proper judge, or not rendered at all. It is in respect of the requirement of a "proper judge" that artistically relevant criticism sometimes seems to fall from the condition of a genuine judgment. Who *is* the proper judge?

Now, of course, in most organizations of law no real question exists of the qualifications of a proper judge. He is a formally designated individual; he has an office; how well equipped he comes makes no difference. The mistake is to imagine that, once the rules of taste has been appropriately rejected, a proper judge can still be determined only through the kind of qualifications required in the legal order—and, hence, that because there are no formally designated judges in criticism there are no proper judges.

For, in fact, while people frequently say that everybody *can* be a judge of the arts (has a "right" to judge the arts as he does not have a right to sit in court), not everyone says that anybody *is;* and the requirement for "being a judge" in the arts, as normal version philosophers have seen (and misconstrued), is a knowledge of the matrix of art and of society in which the work of art takes form as a critical object, and also, of course, a capacity to bring that knowledge to bear. Unlike the judge in the law, then, the proper judge in the arts is the *good* judge—but the normal version conclusion that he is a good judge in virtue of being a proper judge does not follow.

What does it signify, then, to be a proper judge of the arts, lacking formal rank and title, and assuming possession of the qualifications that make for justifiable decisions? What it is found to signify is that one becomes the person with whom those actively engaged in art and criticism will actively *dispute* to make their judgments good—the person who, in his criticism, participates to the best of his ability in the general conduct of the arts for the interest of the arts, as he understands that interest. Status comes from peer group, on possession of proper qualification, and in this the practice of criticism is less like the practice of law, a bit more like the practice of medicine, and considerably more like the practice of science.

3. Every legal judgment has a very specifically designated "proper recipient." A judgment is issued *to* a proper recipient or recipients. In a civil action the proper recipients will be the litigants in the action; in a criminal trial, the defendant. Although the lack of institutional structuring may make for considerable confusion in art, it is always pertinent to ascertain the proper recipient of judgments in other domains, if one wishes to grasp the force of the judgment. For the proper recipient is he who faces the difficulty, the conflict of claims, which the judgment comes to adjudicate. Others may say, "If I were in that predicament the judgment would apply to me." But if they are not, the fact that they understand the judgment does not of itself imply that they are its proper recipients. Judgment applies to the man who has the headache, in the light of the headache-producing situation.

Who has the headache in art? Once again, as in dealing with proper judges, the answer must be that *anybody* may, but that, obviously, not anyone does; and that he who feels the headache is he who participates in the conduct of the arts, in the sense that he does. For such are the individuals who will confront the problems germane to the practice—the person who deals with art in a context of production rather than consumption.

To say, therefore, that the requirement of a proper recipient holds for judgment in the arts means finally that the force of a judgment can be determined only by first assessing the specific construction or merit problem to which the judgment refers. Anyone "may" assume that cross.

4. Lastly, and perhaps most worthy of note, judgment in the law, though obviously not only in the law, does not seek the reasoned accord of anyone who understands the difference that judgment makes, but appeals for its justification to some individuals and only to some. Judgment is not only rendered *by* a proper judge, *on* a proper occasion, and *to* a proper recipient, but *for* a "relevant public," nor does it matter in the least that those who are not members of a relevant public *cannot* be convinced by the reasons extended for the judgment in question, that, in effect, they do not find those reasons to be "reasons for them." The beginning of practical wisdom lies perhaps in the perception that in action or the recommendation for action we are not called upon to convince everybody.

Those persons constitute a relevant public whose reasoned participation (not subjugation) in the enterprise in which I am involved constitutes the condition for the achievement of my ends in the enterprise. My relevant publics are my actual or potential collaborators. This is, of course, fearfully vague, but in fact it is characteristic of "practical" reason that there may exist considerable difficulty in determining for all instances who my collaborators are, and for the reason that difficult cases require decision rather than reference to a table of rules. Hence, in fact, only experience and the nature of my intent can disclose more exactly the nature and degree of the "reasoned participation" I require, and how seriously I shall take the "potentiality" of such collaboration.

In the law we may see *both* the way in which the determination of a relevant public is bound up in decision and how difficult even under the most favorable circumstances the determination may be. Accordingly, a court of lower jurisdiction assumes as its relevant public the higher courts and courts of equal jurisdiction, but not either lower courts, the recipients of judgment, or the public at large. The positions adopted in the higher court alone require consideration in the framing of judgment—for the simple reason that otherwise judgment may be vitiated, either through direct reversal or through neglect of the decision as precedent. And in very consequence for the court of final appeals, all the usual difficulties of determining relevant publics come immediately to view. When such a court strives to discover by whom its reasoning must be upheld, indecision emerges; and the court appeals perhaps to future members of the court, or to the membership of previous courts and their inferred positions, or perhaps to those considered good judges of their country's welfare, or to a constitution. Far from proving the vacuity of a relevant public, the testings and explorations that ensue upon an openness and indecision in the matter of the relevant public demonstrate its importance.

So, in the arts as in law and all other fields of decision, if nothing less will satisfy me than to exact the agreement of *anyone* I can induce to listen—if, in effect, I demand the support of God himself and his divine ideas before painting a stroke, or the approval of the entire city before marrying the girl—then I do not necessarily fail because of the irrelevance of good reasons in matters of art or matrimony, but because I have neglected a prime factor in the nature of judgment: that judgment be formulated *for* a relevant public. In both art and law there exists an entire, complex society of relevant publics, the relations among which are in a constant state of flux and reorganization, a society taken for granted at one's peril. That peril is the peril of confusion, bigotry, and pretension, as one suppresses the obligation to choose one's end in all consciousness and hence misses one's relevant public or mistakes it for another.

In sum, then: artistically relevant judgment advances the recommendations *of* a proper judge, *on* a proper occasion, *to* a proper recipient, and *for* a relevant public. Unless the instruction sets advanced in respect of the objects of criticism by proper judges, on proper occasions, and the rest, are indeed advanced in such a "complex of decision," they function as mere demands and lack the full status of "claims"—for they then lie outside the possibility of justification and an artistically relevant controversy. Just how criticism of the arts establishes the conditions for propriety and relevance in its complex, and so differentiates itself as a practice, has been intimated, to be sure, only in the most oblique and partial manner. Nevertheless, it should be clear that the question of reasons can never be handled in matters of art without taking into full cognizance the existence of a special complex within which reason comes into existence in accordance with the nature of that complex. That is the final upshot of the position advanced in these pages, to consider judgment "practical": judgment participates in a certain practice, which is no less a practice because it is not some other; and, like any other, it has its own special subject matter and rules.

Chapter 10

How Artistically Relevant Controversy Is Possible: The Structure of Proper Occasions

How, this essay began, does artistically relevant controversy, as "genuine" controversy about artistically relevant matters, actually work? There was no doubt but that it did. Every endeavor aimed only to dispel the doubts raised by the normal version; and to that end I sought to show that critical controversy revolved around the construction of a construction, and that the claims advanced in argument involved recommendation sets for the doing of art. Now I must finally bring the discussion into focus by making peace with artistically relevant controversy from the explicit vantage point of the reasons question, which asked us to interpret in a suitable manner the process of justification in that controversy.

Peace for the reasons question means answering three questions sufficiently to dispel the skeptical doubts engendered by the normal version and to establish what justification would be like "in a context of production"—which amounts to making manifest the consequences and requirements of the positions already assumed in this essay. First comes the task of showing how the *problems* to which critics proffer solutions in their artistically relevant controversies are generated by the structure of the concrete occasions that proper judges of the arts hold proper for their controversies. Secondly, it is necessary to consider what the reasons are through which people compose their differences and what sorts of rules decide that one critic has indeed come one-up upon another. For these are the reasons and rules through which proper occasions are handled properly, the reasons and rules that determine how one functions in making artistically relevant decisions and, therefore, what it means to "practice" criticism on its proper occasion. Lastly, and throughout, there arises the problem of proper expectations, which is to show what sort of thing might properly be expected of reason in the arts and how proper expectations here differ from proper expectations elsewhere.

Therefore, the reasons question exists as the question of the nature of reason within the practice or conduct of the arts, not the question of whether that reason is in some higher sense reasonable. The end is to grasp how a certain kind of proper judge justifies a certain sort of claim to a relevant public where that claim is levied on a proper recipient. Hence there is a difference from that normal version inquiry which systematically identifies the problem of justification in the arts with the problem of justifying the employment of such justification.[1]

What, then, are the occasions like that generate the problems of criticism, in so far as they do? In a general way, of course, those occasions will be the ones, as remarked at the start, in which a difference of opinion occurs over the evaluation, explication, appreciation, etc. of a work of art. But what sort of situation provokes such differences in evaluation, appreciation, explication, and the rest—how is the problem actually set *for* the participants in the disagreement? And, given a problem set in such a way, under what conditions is issue joined and disagreement "real"? These questions comprise the question of the structure of "proper occasions." Answering them ought to show how controversy is possible in the first place.

I. What Makes Proper Occasions Proper?

Critics, of course, say very explicitly what makes an occasion a proper one for joining issue: the confrontation of a "work of art," rather than some other sort of work, the occurrence of problems of "form" and "content," the need to distinguish the better from the worse and so on. Lest such dicta be interpreted to preclude the very possibility of significant controversy, it may perhaps help to ask generally what sort of "structure" do reference and claims questions, as they have been answered here, impose upon the proper occasions of artistically relevant controversy.

1. Unless nearly everything said has been mis-said, patently the occurrence of "the work of art itself," hard, impervious, and finished, will not make a proper occasion for such a controversy. For the occurrence of "the work of art itself" signalizes that the artistically relevant controversy has already done its work, and when the job is done is surely no occasion to begin arguing. So, if one wants to formulate the propriety of occasions

[1] For a similar, though hardly equivalent, attempt to draw the consequences of the distinction between "justifying a practice and justifying a particular action falling under it," see John B. Rawls' "Two Concepts of Rules," *Philosophical Review,* LXIV (1955), 3–32.

in terms of the occurrence of works of art, it must be emphasized that the work of art needs to be taken as a created object upon which it is at least permissible to place a construction. Set before the critic on any proper occasion are always created objects partly unfamiliar or to be treated as though they were.[2]

Also, of course, what will make an occasion proper will be the fact that art has not stopped dead. A conduct or practice of the arts continues to exist to which instructions may be logically pertinent; the functions of criticism and creation are interinvolved. Why otherwise try to make it good that in some respect or respects one thing is better than another? Art of course *might* sometimes stop dead. The collections in the museums might never be changed. But then criticism would have become a cluster of games, each game with its own rules. Criticism—the criticism of the "good and responsible" critic—would have lost its cutting edge and, in the process, its identity.

Clearly, the general conditions for construction judgments and judgments of merit "in a context of production" must determine the occurrence of proper occasions; but the chance for a more particular account of the structure of artistic occasions depends upon recalling the critical traditions for some chapters gone uncalled upon.[3] Obviously, no proper occasion for controversy exists if critics approach their critical object empty-headed; and if they are not empty-headed, "critical traditions" stuff their heads.

Expanding slightly on the earlier discussion, a "critical tradition" refers to the set of relevant or partially relevant hypotheses with which critics who are responsive to the regulative rules of respect and referral approach the created object. Accordingly, a critical tradition comprises the constructions that the critic or his colleagues may already have placed upon the critical object, many another construction of many another critical object, formative rules of all sorts reached on other occasions and maintained with greater or lesser firmness, the merit judgments which, generally, the critic may have attained, and the strategies through which he allocates weight among the policies of respect. Critical traditions are, obviously, shared or sharable (when so considered they are sometimes called "schools") and stand in complex relations to philosophical, politi-

[2] A totally unfamiliar object would be immune to artistically relevant criticism and controversy, which, when such objects occur, no more proves the emptiness of such criticism and controversy in themselves than the totally unique case would prove the impossibility of law or the totally unprecedented the impossibility of science. One looks for connections. One tries to devise handles. In the meanwhile no one thinks of arguing, or ought to.

[3] See above, Chapter 4, Section III.

cal, and generally social positions, from which it is neither possible nor useful to distinguish them sharply.

Given, then, the critical tradition or traditions within which the critic functions—given, in effect, his "mind," though his "shared" rather than his "personal" mind, and remembering that anyone may be "of two minds" about something—he must on a proper occasion decide the formal and nonformal characteristics of critical objects in their appropriate matrices. He must, that is, in order to reach a judgment of "the work of art" decide both what those characteristics "are" and "ought to be," construction judgments and merit judgments, at those points at which his traditions intersect the critical object in its matrices of art and society. While, for one critical tradition, some characterization of a critical object seems quite unobjectionable, for another tradition it is indeed objectionable, either that the object is or that it should be that way. So the critic must "make up his mind" at the "intersection," which may mean either altering a critical tradition, or reconsidering his assessment of the matrices of art and of society, or reformulating his hypothetical instructions to the present conduct of the arts.

The proper occasion for artistically relevant controversy is set by the intersection of critical tradition with the matrix of art and the matrix of society at the point of the presented object. Once again, recourse to the customary analogy will prove helpful.

2. Normal version preconceptions of artistically relevant judgment set aside, the predicament of the proper judge in the criticism of the arts looks very much like the predicament of the judge in his court; no one questions but that the judge has himself not created the legal issue, and that his views of the law enter in an essential way into the grasp and solution of that issue. To see what it means for problems to occur "at the intersection" in artistically relevant controversy, let us therefore see how problems occur "at the intersection" in the courtroom.

A. First, then, the legal suit which the proper magistrate must adjudicate comes to him with significance originating outside the law as such. The case has a relevant existence in the analogue to the critic's "matrix of society"; and the magistrate ignores *his* social matrix at the price of that abstraction and false relevance which goes by the name of legalism, the way a similar ignoring for the critic goes by the name of "formalism." Certainly, the nonformal characteristics with which the proper judge at law deals in a case of negligence do not normally involve the "celebrant" characters of human existence, though some sort of plea might be entered for the celebrant and "expressive" functions of at least some legal decisions. In any event, the magistrate faces a genuine, externally given conflict either between individuals, among communal interests, or between individuals and communal interests. There is aggrievement, perhaps, and a claim to innocence, a cry for "justice," and an opportunity to secure an end that both overrides and underlies considerations of law. Not for nothing do legal theorists attempt to find the "basis" of legal adjudication in natural law, or consider the precise relevance of morals. For law, like criticism in the old metaphor, is not like parchesi; and the judge who seeks to determine his problem without considering the substantive human interests involved, who does not seek to unite legality and "justice," has missed the point of his vocation. He has failed to appreciate the "occasion" for his judgment, which is the delicate task of administering "*justice* under law."

Nonformal considerations enter into the critic's predicament, I shall want to say, as they do in the judge's. Critical objects "intersect" with a critical tradition and a matrix of society in artistically relevant criticism just as cases "intersect" with a judicial tradition and a social matrix in legal decision.

B. Next, consider the manner of the pleading. Advocate as he is for one interest or another, counsel knows very well that, given the resources of the law, his case might be presented in a variety of ways and that his adversary will construe the features of the case in a very different way. If one and only one construction and decision were possible in the law, why would they have come to court? In order to have the material interests that are represented considered at all, counsel on each side seeks that "intersection" between the matrix of the law in its great complexity and extent on the one hand and those empirically given features of the case on the other which seems most propitious for those interests. Any legal point that counsel seeks to make will secure the most extensive justification in precedent and statute which counsel can discover. The last thing a decent lawyer will do is present the legal aspects of his case as a free invention; almost the first thing he will do is show, if he can, that his adversary's presentation amounts to just that.

Hence the counsels' claims, among which the judge must decide with respect to the case being heard, represent in "difficult" cases (but, of course, the discussion of artistically relevant controversy among proper judges is concerned only with difficult cases) "genuine" alternatives, and so generate the judge's decision problem. In judgment he must decide. But *he* never made the case.

Formal characteristics of critical objects, I shall want to urge, in accordance with the analogy, enter into the critic's predicament not as simple, set ingredients but as real possibilities not all of which are compatible. Critical objects "intersect" with a critical tradition and a matrix of art in artistically relevant criticism just as cases "intersect" with a matrix of law, given certain ends. Critics must decide, in the process of construing formal values, how the physical object *shall* intersect with the matrix of art.

C. Consider the judge again as he confronts the problem of choice among a plurality of legal characterizations and a plurality of constructions of "justice." His problem can be put quite conventionally: if he is supposed to give equal *justice* under law, plainly, also, he seeks that justice *under law.* As a judge he must consider, given the plural possibilities for decisions concerning the formal and nonformal characteristics of the presented case, what are the nonformal characteristics of his formal decisions (do the characterizations he decides upon make for justice?) and what are the formal characteristics of his nonformal decisions (is his justice legal?). His task, if he can manage it, is to achieve a coalescence between the legal "image" of the case and its human and social significance. Any "split" shows the poverty of his construction, and he may curse the problem that discloses its limits.

Critical objects, then, "intersect" with a matrix of art and a matrix of society as the case in law "intersects" the legal and the social matrix both, each intersection having consequences for the other. In virtue of that intersection, they generate analogous problems, as the critic makes and remakes his critical tradition in the light of compatibilities and incompatibilities discovered at the intersection of the matrix of law and of society.

In sum, then: like the judge in the law the critic is no voyeur. He faces, like that other judge, on his proper occasion, a problem posed by careers and histories he never made though he may affect them. Therefore, he no more than the magistrate turns the problem any way he chooses so long as he merely keeps his eyes on the empirically given aspects of the presented case. Rather, he participates in an artistic action in virtue of an occasion that exhibits requirements satisfiable in different ways with different consequences.

But now we must leave the general answer and the analogy and try to assess the structure of the proper occasion specifically in artistically relevant criticism. The remainder of this chapter, therefore, will outline a possible account of the intersection of the matrices of art and of society ("Intersection 1"), of the critical tradition and the matrix of society ("Intersection 2"), and of the critical tradition and the matrix of art ("Intersection 3").

II. The Intersection of Art and of Society

Consider now the judgment which finds a proper occasion for artistically relevant controversy only when considering critical objects as "works of art." This side of tautology, what does the judgment signify? At least this much: an acknowledgment that proper judges construe their critical objects at the intersection of the matrices of art and of society. Under appropriate circumstances therefore we may expect to find a proper occasion for artistically relevant controversy at Intersection 1. Those circumstances grasped, at least in principle, we may undertake to say how those proper judges, the "good and responsible critics of the arts," *in practice* "agree" and "disagree" at Intersection 1.

1. That "works of art" are actually held in practice to occur only under the conditions of an intersection of the matrices of art and of society, appears in this: that when critical objects are taken otherwise they provide occasion for *other* kinds of controversy than artistically relevant controversy.

A. For, to begin with, restricting the consideration of a critical object solely within a matrix of society so that controversy ends on locating the critical object within that matrix, means construing that object merely as the occasion for philosophical, sociological, psychological, etc. controversy. Such controversies, of course, do occur over presented objects. They are artistically irrelevant not because they introduce the critical object into a matrix of society but because their conduct has not been ordered by the problems of Intersection 1. They concern themselves, as it is sometimes said, not with "the saying of something" but with "what is said"; and the falling away of controversy from the significance *of* a work of art to the truth or falsity, importance or triviality, of the point *as such* is a common enough phenomenon to make critics wary of nontechnical criticism. Nonformal considerations of meaning and truth, then, are part of the structure of artistically relevant occasions only in so far as they occur in conjunction with or through some set of formal characteristics. The occasions for artistically relevant controversy occur "at the intersection." [4]

[4] Be it noted that Yeats' advice to the poets, that they become Irish bards, did not therefore commit the error of substituting politically relevant controversy for poetic—not when he wanted, rightly or wrongly, to say the kind of thing poetry ought to be doing. He merely made a recommendation *for poetry.* He was, therefore, in our language, considering poetry "at the intersection" of the two matrices—not arguing politics. Of course his reason might or might not be political.

B. On the other hand, neither does the structure of the proper occasion properly include the critical object merely as it comes within the matrix of art. *Purely* formal occasions are not artistically relevant occasions. And thinking otherwise sterilizes and distorts the character of the matrix of art itself—the domain, as has been pointed out before, not of arbitrary forms, of curiosities, but of forms that in their relationships to one another "mean" something, become "significant," for celebrant communities. Accordingly, the endeavor, as a matter of purist principle to ward off the presence of the world in which the matrix of art exists, turns forms into technical products and criticism into the relatively mechanical business of deciding whether critical objects in specified respects belong within one technique or classification or another; and, thereupon, strictures of the introduction of a purely "technical" criticism as positively harmful to the appreciation of art become justified. For the serious critic's headaches are never purely technical, and to take works of art as raising purely technical problems means ceasing to deal with critical objects as "works of art."

The alternative, then, to finding the proper occasion for controversy at Intersection 1 consists in neglecting what people often call "the interests of art" in favor of either an "ulterior" criticism or a technological discussion. Yet it does not necessarily follow that if one were only to take critical objects at the intersection, one would thereby take them as "works of art." One use of "work of art," the use that employs the expression most sweepingly, might justify drawing that conclusion. One *might* want to say that art exists wherever "significant form" does. On the other hand, of course, people sometimes impose restrictions on what "significant forms" they will consider "art," hence on "works of art."

2. What problems have been provoked at the intersection of the matrices of art and of society to turn the occurrence of a work of art into an occasion for criticism? Those problems which the critic "recognizes without creating" must be the problems of what Shahn calls "the shape of content," of "form and content." With them emerges a proper occasion for artistically relevant controversy. When there *can* be no question of such a problem, there can be no artistically relevant controversy; and to handle "the problem of form and content" is perhaps the primary task of critical analysis, the potential if not the immediate presence of which defines the artistically relevant occasion. Hence, only that occasion constitutes an occasion for artistically relevant controversy which might require a *decision* on the relationships between formal and nonformal characteristics of a created object. Which of a variety of possible things is one to

look for in the picture, sonata, poem, novel, etc., given a range of possible variations in the meaning or significance of the work of art? Which of a range of such meanings or significance is one to look for, given a variety of possible discriminable formal characteristics in the work of art? If this and this is what a story means, read the events in relation to that particular incident; otherwise, to this other incident. If such and such is the moving quality of the music, then observe how the structure of the music requires such an unfolding; but if, on the other hand, you take this passage largo, you ruin the effect. (Part of the reason for the difficulty in ascribing nonformal characteristics to music at all may lie in the real possibility of *choice* of nonformal characteristics, given some set of formal characteristics. Most estheticians feel it somehow wrong to have such choices. But performers, or advisers to performers, know better, which is why musical criticism may excite them. Consumers do not, which is why they think it perfectly reasonable to say *anything* one likes about music or, equivalently, to say that music is "pure form.")

"At the intersection," then, in the attempt to organize formal and informal characteristics with one another, one encounters the key problem of "form and content." A few further comments on the subject may now be in order.

First, it is necessary to remember that the problem is a genuine one even though "content" as such be irrelevant to the work of art and "form" as such purely trivial, and even though in a "successful work" of art there is no "separating" "what" is said from "how" it is said. For, on the one hand, finding the occasion for criticism at the intersection precludes disposing of the problem through some kind of purism at one extreme or Tolstoyism at the other; and, on the other hand, the famous "inseparability" of form and content is not a natural fact at all (why one *natural* fact any more than another should have their "form" and "content" inseparable constitutes a mystery very much like the mystery of why one natural object should be more "unique" than another). Rather, inseparability is at once an *ideal* for an artist working within a matrix of art and of society and a condition the critic has imposed upon himself for the resolution of his decision problem. The artist is supposed to make his forms significant and his significance formal. The proper judge is supposed to be able to see how and whether this has been done. In this sense it is perfectly true that in a work of art nothing has been left unsaid and whatever has been said has been expressed: for a good judge will always seek a complete solution for the formal-nonformal problem and demand that artists not make the solution impossible. But should any portion of the "meaning" be "split" from the "image" or any portion of the "image" from the "meaning," then either the critic's power of perception has proven inadequate or the artist has bungled.

Next, it seems only fair to note, saving the traditional form-content problem has made a certain, by this time familiar, change in the notion of "content." "Content," as traditionally used, refers indiscriminately to the nonformal characteristics of works of art qua formal *and* to that which lies "outside" the work of art—to the work of art as a "representation" *of* something else, as the presentation of some point, and so on. But we are required to distinguish. For characteristics of representation in painting, or characteristics of point making or reporting in literature, are not the sort of thing equivalent to nonformal characteristics, given our account of the characteristics of art in a matrix of society. On that account, works of art must indeed possess nonformal characteristics but representational or didactic characteristics they may or may not possess, and these latter become *relevant* "content" only when and as they perform celebratory functions with respect to some community. Hence, no philosophical problem exists of making the admittedly irrelevant ("content") relevant, merely the task of discriminating different uses of materials. And the serious question about imitation and "external" reference for works of art consists in determining whether the nature of the relevant celebration requires an imitation or a moral or a realistic setting or the sound of cannons to secure its nonformal characteristics of seriousness, truth, importance, humor, or whatever they might be. In practice, of course, everybody knows this—it is only the thought that some sort of a dogma must settle all questions of celebrant requirements in advance which makes people feel that the "subject" of the critical object necessarily makes no artistic difference *or* that if they cannot find a "subject" the object must be mere decoration, if that much.

Hence, music and abstract art become on this account neither more, nor less, "pure" forms of art than realistic drama or naturalistic painting. Both kinds of art become artistically relevant at the intersection of the matrices of art and society, an intersection that establishes in one instance no more than in the other the characteristic problem of critical construction: to show the nonformal characteristics of characteristics of form, and the formal characteristics of nonformal characteristics. Since such characteristics do not exist as simple data but must themselves be constructed in their appropriate matrix, the resulting decision problem becomes the highly complex one that in fact it is found to be.

A moment's further consideration of the "problem of music" may perhaps be interpolated here. Music has puzzled people terribly because it is thought to exhibit "pure" form, lack "content," and possess deep significance if any art does. How can that which lacks content be important? The point would be that one need not deny music nonformal characteristics because one denies it characteristics that for any particular occasion have nothing to do with the music. If there is nothing odd about the *identifying* characteristics of a portrait having nothing to do with its artistically relevant content, one ought not to think music particularly *difficult* because music normally identifies no one—merely, *less* confusing. Furthermore, the whole question of the significant "purity" of music is in a sense gratuitous. "Music" as an art need not even object to "content" in some quasi-representational or didactic sense, *provided,* of course, artistically relevant use is made of such content and one has not defined repugnance for certain things into the structure of "music," allowing only a "pure" music as "music itself." Sound patterns have been used in "imitative" ways before; nor is it logically necessary that the only uses made of those patterns continue to be the uses of the Army drill sergeant, that last surviving Platonist.[5]

In general, then, if the need to resolve the "form-content" question makes the occasion proper for artistically relevant controversy, "Intersection 1" accounts for that occasion without raising false issues of the sort which plague people who talk about "content" in the arts.

III. The Force of Disagreement

In a context of production, then, where the created object is held in a proper respect and "form" and "content" do not simply intersect or fail to intersect as a matter of consumer's choice, Intersection 1 sets problems defining proper occasions for the agreement or disagreement of good and responsible critics—proper judges—in two primary ways:

1. First, since not all critical objects adequately approximate the ideal of "inseparability of form and content" achieved by the "successful" work of art, Intersection 1 generates occasions for disagreement over whether a critical object "be" propaganda, decoration, philosophy, fetish, etc., or rather (perhaps simultaneously) a "work of art." "Don't waste your time," a critic might conceivably say as a proper judge; "That's just a

[5] Let me explicitly say it, then: "program music" is quite as pure as "nonprogram" music; and it is notable that while "formalists" will point to the horrors of Tchaikovsky's "War of 1812" overture to show the contaminating influence of a program, one never finds them doing as much for the "St. Matthew Passion." Obviously, it is the "total effect" which counts. Purity is for fixed tastes, for school teachers fixedly faithful. An artist or a critic who gives a hang about the arts plays fast and loose with the categories.

piece of dressed up propaganda. Or philosophy in verse. Or a national symbol." Someone may often be found to disagree.[6]

Disagreement, of course, centers around the construction of the critical object with respect to some set of general rules for including critical objects within a going criticism. But the roots of the disagreement penetrate beneath the rules for the critical game and suggestions for the amendment of those rules, to the structure of the created object itself and the relationship exhibited by formal and nonformal characteristics. For it must be decided to what degree and with what seriousness nonformal characteristics are conveyed independently of some set of formal characteristics—upon whether or not it pays to seek to organize the great body of available knowledge concerning the object "at the intersection" of art and society.

2. The second, and more significant, variety of decision problem generated by Intersection 1 after agreement has been reached on the critical object as a "work of art" is, of course, the characteristic question of the relationships between formal and nonformal characteristics. What in any instance are they like? How can one agree or disagree about them? No one is claiming that form-content relationships, even as determined by the intersection of the matrices of art and of society, always present occasions for agreement and disagreement. The state of the arts at any time may indeed allow for no differences of opinion among proper judges, and may present merely the task of *showing* persons not themselves proper judges what every proper judge knows very well. In order, therefore, to make as clear as possible the nature of disagreement in Intersection 1 we ought not choose for our paradigm case a familiar work of art where the factual model might seem appropriate, but as unfamiliar a critical object as possible, and at the same time the most simple one.

Imagine again, then, a cathedral made entirely of cardboard presented to a group of architects for their judgment. The problem is to see something of the ways matrices of art and of society may be made to intersect and hence to see something of the nature of the disagreement to be expected. What, if anything, is it worth? What values does the cardboard cathedral have?

"Formed content," explains the builder, "contented form. What else would you expect from an artist? Notice that the cathedral avoids splitting into two things, one the 'image,' the other the 'meaning.' "

[6] The artist's intention to do or not to do a "work of art" may or may not enter into the decision how to treat whatever he has come up with—just as the intention of the defendant to commit an illegal act may or may not enter into the construction the court will place upon that act.

"Yes," says Critic A, "I see the gaiety, the sensitivity of the conception, all brought about through a deliberate parody of the cathedral form. Gay irony in architecture! The direct result of a tension between the forms of architecture and the materials chosen!"

"What tension?" says Critic B. "The architect has simply ignored the discrepancy between the meaning of a cathedral and a cathedral worked in cardboard. The collapse of tension presents the disjointedness of the means-end relationship in contemporary life. Gay irony indeed! This is Kafka in architecture, 'Guernica' in three dimensions!"

"Wrong!" says Critic C. "The whole point of the peculiar form, cathedral-in-papier-maché, is given away by the fact that this *is* a cathedral. Presented here is irony neither gay nor sad, but, simply—religion. The builder has expressed metaphysical convictions, whether he knows it or not, whether you care for his metaphysics or not. His is the religion of Transience. Here you have the iconic sign of commitment to the flux."

"How strange," says Critic D, "that everyone should have overlooked the sheer engineering achievement in constructing an oscillating Chartres out of papier-maché. All of you see the whole thing too abstractly and miss the accomplishment. Standing there, as clear as such things can be, is an incarnated act—a *dare* flung at improbability, a dare made good; hence the proper monument to the eternal nature of human aspiration."

"All of which," says Critic E, "shows what can happen when architects forget that they are architects and fancy themselves sculptors. Call that thing sculpture!—or, if not, admit it a bungle executed by a man who couldn't keep sculpture and architecture separate! For if, perversely, you do consider it a building, you ought to find the sharpest division of form and function, form and content. A priest would be lucky to get *one* mass said."

"What do you mean, 'sculpture'?" retorts any one of the others. "How many times does a building have to be used before it's a 'building'? There's no necessity to make scarcity values define the nature of things."

And so it goes.[7] A decision problem exists because it is possible to

[7] In our examples I have, of course, been contrasting formal characteristics as the characteristics of the presented physical object which possess certain possible significances in the context of the matrix of art, with "characteristics of meaning and truth" (nonformal characteristics) in the most obvious sense possible—for every critic has seen fit to affirm or deny certain attitudes or messages which clearly transcend the limits of the cathedral itself. We ought also to note, however, that all nonformal characteristics are by no means as obvious or as easily distinguished from the formal characteristics of a critical object.

construct innumerable sets of formal to nonformal relationships by establishing the critical object differently in the matrices of art and of society. Each critic above speaks for one such set of relationships. We shall understand the nature of the disagreement as disagreement at Intersection 1 when we understand that (A) neither is the internal organization of alternative sets completely random nor (B) are all alternative sets compatible, though some are.

A. Surveying the list of constructions possible at Intersection 1 and recalling, perhaps, his own experience with the interpretative imagination, the reader may feel his opinion confirmed: a critic may say absolutely anything so long as it is pretentious enough. All combinations of formal and nonformal characteristics are possible and, where anything constitutes a possible alternative, it is foolish to speak of alternatives *or* decisions. *Does* anything constitute a possible alternative, however?

Observe, first, that the proffered constructions, wild as they are, are so, partly at least, in proportion to the actual strangeness of the critical object. We ought to expect, rather than to be put off by, a certain failure to distinguish the plausible from the implausible on first sight of the pretty much unprecedented. *Initial* explorations *have* to be fantastic. Hence, the common structure even among fantasies is all the more suggestive. We notice, for example, that every presented construction of significance and form solves the problem of making sense of the odd cathedral by restricting consideration to composition, shape, and structural characteristics even though no a priori reason exists against expanding consideration to include, say, the property of distance from Rome. And if a newcomer appeared on the scene claiming to find a part of the "meaning" of the cathedral in its distance from Rome, the others surely would not deal with him as they did with one another. They would neither say to him, "You're mistaken," nor accuse him of superficiality. Before joining issue, if they decided to join issue at all, they would rather seek to ascertain from what distant and alien artistic planet he might have descended. Distance from Rome, making no difference in the matrix of art as it historically exists, while a characteristic of the cardboard cathedral, counts neither as a formal *nor* a nonformal characteristic.

Not *everything* then, is possible in the way of discriminating formal and nonformal properties. A distinction exists between the multitude of alternatives that may exist within an art, game, science, or practice, as that activity has been structured, and the different alternatives which exist when that structure has been swept away.

Next, it is important to observe, equi-possibility among different sets of formal and nonformal properties (where *this* structure "carries" *this* meaning, *this* meaning is "expressed" by *that* structure for each set) constitutes an occasion for seeking further, in a context of production. In practice, one takes the plurality of possible interpretations as setting a problem to be worked at. Hence Critic E raised the question of the pertinence of all the other positions advanced, and the others thought his question deserving of an answer; nor would Critic E for a moment doubt the artistic relevance of the ensuing argument. Working critics, then, have it as their job to *hone down* the alternatives worth considering, rather than to assume them to begin with. The fact that considerable argument may arise over just what is relevant shows only that artistically relevant criticism bears within itself the possibilities of its own reconstruction, not that it is a deteriorating kind of set and formal game.

Lastly, fantastic though our examples were, even they did not warrant the assumption of any relationship as a possible one. It is clear that some formal properties "go" with certain nonformal ones and *some do not.* Gaiety and parody both "go" with an incompatibility between cathedral and cardboard; they do not go with a "flat ignoring of the relationships"—rather does something like "disjointedness." Further, it is obvious that the fixing of one nonformal property will serve as evidence to suggest that one formal property but not another obtains for the critical object; and, of course, determining that the critical object has one formal property and not another will restrict the range of possible nonformal properties.

It is simply false, therefore, that *any* intersection of formal and nonformal properties is possible. If imagination may range far indeed, it may not do so without observing limitations. Nor is there any puzzle in principle hidden in the complex but quite familiar sense of "go." Why, indeed, should a cathedral shivering in the breeze serve as an "iconic sign" of "transience" rather than "permanence"? Why, for the most part, if not because of the nature of the world and human expectations? In this world, things simply do not, after standing fixed and motionless under pressure, suddenly collapse and disappear, nor when they sway and shake do they continue in their state indefinitely.

But there might be such a world. The possibility of challenge marks all "goings with" and "goings against" in the relationships among formal and nonformal properties; they are grounded, whatever the mechanism, upon "the association of ideas."

B. It is of at least equal significance, however, for understanding how disagreement is possible at Intersection 1, that not all sets of intersection proposals are compatible as sets, though some are. For example, one cannot hold the constructions of Critics A, B, and C simultaneously. But one *might* add to any of them Critic D's proposals, while if one accepts E's picture of the cardboard cathedral, one must reject the conclusions of all the others.

a. Why "must" one choose, then, in those cases where one must? Since construction judgment at Intersection 1, like judgments of artistic merit, still function as prescriptions, it will be useful to consider a truism holding for prescriptions in general. While we cannot logically, in some sense of "logically," simultaneously obey the commands "Shut the door!" and "Leave the door open!" we might very well manage to satisfy the commands "Shut the door!" and "Open the window!"; while it is entirely possible that every time we shut the door we jammed the window. Some prescriptions, then, are "necessarily" incompatible and some of them incompatible (or compatible) in the nature of a situation.

Consider, then, the relationship between formal and nonformal sets of characteristics as analogous to those obtaining between shutting doors and opening windows. Clearly, those sets will be incompatible in which each set attributes formal characteristics that are incompatible or nonformal characteristics that are incompatible. But that is not the incompatibility which matters at Intersection 1. The sort of incompatibility that occurs at Intersection 1 as such I shall call "cross-incompatibility." If someone says, as he considers the cardboard castle in its delicate balance of form and "content," that no tension exists between shape and material, then he must find against certain nonformal characteristics, "irony," perhaps, gay or otherwise, and, obviously, in no "logical" sense. If he says the cathedral expresses Kafka in architecture, then he must deny once again for "factual" reasons the existence of "tension" and declare for the felt presence of disjointedness. Formal characteristics impose restrictions on nonformal characteristics, and vice versa. Because formal and nonformal characteristics may be "cross incompatible" we are entitled to speak of works of art as "inseparable" unions of form and "content" (nonformal characteristics), and to differ with one another over those "unions."

b. But in seeking to understand differences of opinion at Intersection 1 we may look a little further. Critic E, in breaking with the others, pointed out not merely that the cardboard cathedral would not stand. Everybody knew that. His point was that to make the kind of building that would not stand constituted a bungle, and a bungle relevant to the status of architecture as an art. The reply blamed his view on a gratuitous assumption: that a building ought to stand as long as you can make it stand. Apparently, then, not only does the evaluation of an object's merit depend on the construction proposed for it but, conversely, the construction (what the things "is," a mere "imitation" of a building, a piece of sculpture, or a cathedral erected to the passing moment) depends upon agreement over what ought to be the case. Therefore, since merit judgments function in a context of production as commitments for movement within a going practice, for that reason also not all apparent alternatives for construction in Intersection 1 are worth considering, while those that enable us to discern artistic merit will, barring other disabilities, appear as true candidates.

c. Nevertheless, of course, it is not enough to show that disagreement over the critical object at Intersection 1 depends upon differences in judgment of artistic merit and the fact of cross-incompatibility. For what awakens the doubt about the possibility of genuine disagreement over form-content constructions is not really the thought that *anything* will do as well as anything else. What causes the trouble is rather the thought that anything that proper judges offer will be likely to do; and one does not understand how the disagreements that nevertheless ensue can be attributed to anything else but a kind of cultural imperialism. But I should like to suggest that such skepticism overlooks the most interesting occasion of all for artistically relevant differences in critical constructions.

For observation suggests that, in the actual operation of criticism, a plurality of apparently acceptable constructions may itself sometimes become the ground and source of a critical engagement far more in the center of the critical stage that the simpler sort where people merely push their constructions at one another. Each and every construction of that plurality may legitimately be turned into the materials or data for a further, a more penetrating construction. Are not, indeed, the works of art thought best which are most "suggestive," the most "rich"? The proper judge finds his best occasion in the chance to account for the critical object so that various compatible constructions in its double matrix occur as parts or consequences of what he may perhaps call the "true nature" or "essence" of the work of art, or even, perhaps, "the work of art itself." And even constructions that in isolation appear to demand an either-or choice may in such a later synthesis seem like aspects of the same remarkable complexity.

Be that as it may, construction in a context of production makes positive use of the proliferation of diverse opinions and their rivalry in order to go "deeper" still. The existence of a plurality of acceptable alternatives among which one sees no clear way of choosing, either because one doesn't know whether one ought to or because even if one ought to one doesn't know if one can, far from eliminating rational differences among proper judges, raises such differences to a new and more interesting level. The last thing the intellectually active critic (as distinguished from the individual who makes his judgments without concern for differences of opinion) may be expected willingly to accept is just that plurality of constructions (one for Harry, one for Dick) that appears most natural in a context of consumption. Seeking the "uniqueness" of the work of art, he seeks a ground and reason for the variety of things seen and things imagined, and he does so no less than the physical scientist searching for the principle that unifies highly diverse phenomena. Failing in his integrative or higher level construction, the good critic will conclude not the impossibility of rational constructions of works of art but rather the poverty of the work of art "itself," of the created object he judges. The logical possibility of disagreement at Intersection 1, then, is ensured not merely by the direct confrontation of incompatible constructions but by the possibility of integrating a variety of lower level constructions to a higher level, and then by the possibility of confronting one higher level construction with another of the same sort.[8]

Hence the business of criticism is to find and finesse its own inadequacies. In that process criticism accepts the opportunity to connect the apparently unconnected, the chance to show how apparently incompatible positions misunderstand or badly put their own points—points that, clarified, become consequences of a supervening position. In some such way, one suspects, would the argument presented over the cardboard cathedral grow were the disagreement real; through some such dialectic, a complex and fine-spun controversy would develop where previously there had been only a welter of allegations more or less thinly supported. It takes the assumptions of the normal version, which makes people (as consumers) look only for the final results of critical analysis ("Is it a fun show or what?") to make a variety seem like final data and an obstacle to reason.

IV. Further Intersections

Recognizing that artistically relevant criticism occurs only on a proper occasion requires also a minimal insight into the special problems created

[8] Theoretically, of course, nothing stops an indefinite series of constructions as Critic A seeks to get one-up on Critic B by showing how he can integrate B's higher level construction into one of his own which will take care of B's higher level difference with C.

by the intersection at the critical object of a critical tradition with a matrix of society (Intersection 2) and with a matrix of art (Intersection 3). For sometimes in an expanding art and an evolving community, agreement on formal characteristics may be inadequate for choice among nonformal characteristics inadequate to settle differences over formal considerations. Then we are compelled to settle the decision problem at Intersections 2 and 3, taken in relative and temporary isolation; we are compelled to ask, agreeing on the "meaning," how the "meaning" has been expressed when different possibilities exist for the answer, or, given provisional agreement on the nature of the forms employed, just what those forms "mean" when a plurality of answers seems possible. Such are the problems when the critical object represents either a novelty (such as our cardboard cathedral) or an object established in the canon or art that, given changes in art and in society, suddenly seems unappreciated and misunderstood.

1. *Intersection 2:* Most familiar, perhaps, of all questions raised in criticism are such questions as "But what does it mean?," "What's the artist saying?," "Just what's the content?"—where "content" means the *relevant* nonformal, as distinguished from the irrelevant nonformal, characteristics. Not only does the effort to place the critical object in the matrix of art not settle the matter, but we may have to answer those questions *before* being able actually to establish the formal characteristics of the critical object with any conviction. And this means recreating the critical tradition in virtue of which we are accustomed to attribute nonformal characteristics. We must reach agreement over differences of critical tradition where the critical object exists in a matrix of society.

Concretely, then, is the point of the cardboard cathedral—*assuming formal considerations neutral among alternative answers*—to make manifest the transience of human life, a means-end distortion in the modern world, the human capacity to fling a dare at change, or what? We shall face not one, but two, kinds of disagreement, two kinds of problems in the resolution of the disagreement at Intersection 2.

A. Most tangentially to the artistically relevant discussion, agreement may require some minimal prior agreement upon the relative significance and worth of the alternatives. When formal considerations are *not* determinative, a man who thinks that the more things change the more they remain the same is far more likely to believe that the cathedral's point is to fling a dare at change than it is to serve the celebrations of a religion of transience. In consequence, critics are not by accident great debators of "philosophical" issues, as they trace an opponent's "wrong" nonformal characterizations to superficiality or triviality or downright ignorance. For the attempt to construct a critical object sometimes forces the critic (at Intersection 2) into the kind of "disagreement" he tends to call "philosophical." It is not surprising that works of art are understood to "test" a man for his net worth as a civilized human being and, failing to make such a test, are judged "trivial" and perhaps not even "really" a work of art.

Sometimes, of course, critics cannot resolve their general differences of attitude and belief, though it is by no means true that no one ever gets the whip-hand over another even here. However that may be, where a settlement becomes out of the question on "philosophical" grounds, a second kind of disagreement occurs, a second kind of decision problem, characterizing artistically relevant controversy at Intersection 2.

B. For philosophical debate collapsed, philosophical positions now serve to define criteria for membership in one human group or another, and discussion, with the alternatives at least partly clarified, goes on to ask which group, which public, the critical object is "properly" said to serve. Disagreement over the nonformal characteristics of the critical object—whether it exhibits "transience," "eternity," etc.—now mirrors disagreement about the precise location of the critical object in the complex matrix of society. We are staking out the relevant publics for the work of art. How does one handle disagreements over which publics are relevant? For, plainly, sometimes critical objects receive a "meaning" in some communities but not in others and even gain and lose significances in the "same" communities, and not because sometimes people are brighter than at other times.

We must once more begin with the indeterminacy situation. There is no a priori reason why the critical object might not simultaneously provide the point of intersection for a plurality of critical traditions and a plurality of relevant publics *all* of which constitute parts of that broader "matrix of society" in which the critical object occurs. Why should it be strange that the same token might acquire different "meanings" in different games? Once again the point is that such "indeterminacy" ceases to seem like a block in the way of rational discussion of the arts when one sees how it functions in controversy:

For, first, the "good and responsible" critic, caught up in a clash of opinion over nonformal characteristics, may apply a kind of rule of charity that enterprises like law preclude. Where at first a characterization seems incomprehensible, the very progress of the controversy, in disclosing the grounds on which that view rests—the view of "man and the world" in virtue of which the characteristic has been attributed—may make that view intelligible and valuable. Far from maintaining his own against every other view, the mark of the proper judge then becomes precisely that he seek out, articulate, develop, make more consistent and sensitive the range of possible views engendered by the diversity of human interests.

One of the businesses of criticism, then, is to compose differences, in charity, on the ground that a charitable composition remains a composition. "Indeterminacy" in the choice of relevant publics has now become an objective to be achieved as far as scholarship and sympathy make the achievement feasible. Therefore, as such, it constitutes no hindrance to reason in the arts at Intersection 2; and to the question "How does one handle disagreements at Intersection 2?" part of the answer, at least, must be that one explores them, that one seeks to understand the publics that inspire them, and how and why they do.

But, of course, there is more to it. Criticism is tolerance mitigated by acerbity; in actual criticism we do not merely seek to proliferate different senses for different relevant publics. The proper judge of the arts may employ at least two kinds of finesse that make argument pointed in a more unyielding way and entitles reference to "disagreement" in a non-Pickwickian sense.

Arguments over nonformal characteristics, first, may occur because under certain circumstances we indeed try to foreclose the critical object as a work of *this* time and *that* place—and the question arises, *which* time and *which* place? The job of inventing an imaginary community that will do anything interesting with a critical object is far from easy. Critics like other people are in part fact-bound in their actual controversy [9]—which redeems the labors of scholarship from antiquarianism and sends people searching for such affairs as "intentions." Rather than attempting to place the critical object directly within the matrix of society that the critic himself inhabits, the proper judge may seek to explicate the force and sense of the critical object within its historically given environment, in that way fixing on the "real" meaning of the critical object. *Then,* having construed the nonformal properties of critical objects with respect to relevant publics other than those to which he himself belongs, he proceeds to seek significance and force in the spectacle of that different

[9] Like lawyers and judges, among others. What, for example, makes the case of the Speluncean Explorers irrelevant as evidence for a construction in a court of law? Merely that the case did not happen to occur. "It is not law," says the lawyer. "Consider the historically pertinent construction," says the critic. Another way to make the point is to say that the critic is bound by the policy of appropriateness for respecting critical objects.

universe celebrating itself—seeks, as it were, significance and force in significance and force. The consequence is a great narrowing down as those nonformal characteristics are rejected which fail to take into account, when possible and desirable, what the critical object may have meant, historically.

Such, then, is the first finesse of an alert criticism: following a ruling principle of all good critics—so construct as to maximize artistic merit!—when critics get nowhere arguing over the critical object as a performance of their own society, they may go on to take it as the *performance* of some other real and significant one and see how that performance performs.

The next finesse follows hard after. Differences in human commitment, suitably interpreted, and with allowance for divergences in manner and occasion, are not always as radical as they first seem. In essential respects men *may* belong to the same relevant community without knowing it, put off by differences that *for the purposes at hand* are superficial—and this commonly recognized fact obtains for the arts as elsewhere. Hence a possibility exists for establishing the relevant public for any work of art in a manner paralleling the expansion of controversy noted in the discussion of Intersection 1: one may seek the formulation of a still more inclusive community to provide a place for the plurality of public already noted and spoken for in the controversy. And one does this not simply through the discovery that, after all, each of these publics, too, is composed of "men" but in the specific sense that particular commitments are themselves accepted for what they are and rendered comprehensible as significant parts of the total community.

There exists a drive, then, I am suggesting, in the doing of the arts and in the attempt to construe them, toward "the universal" (is not the work of art supposed to show its true character by appealing, as people say, "to all men" who have reached a certain level of education?), not in the dull and literal sense of the minimal "common" but in the sense of a general and articulated society of man that illuminates and gives purpose to its parts. There are, of course no a priori grounds to believe that for all works of art there must necessarily be a universal public. But the person who can present a picture of such a society ("relevant public") for purposes of referring to the construction problem of the arts for any critical object will have done that object the best of all possible favors and gained one-up on the critics whose proffered constructions have now become intelligible in a way never expected.

Available, then, is the "finesse of universality" at Intersection 2, which itself provides for *controversy*. For, of course, critics can and do disagree whether "justice" in the total picture of the celebrant society has actually been done, on any presentation, to the many voices that proper judges may rightfully think to enter the chorus. Still, the presentation of that public most adequately satisfying the various claimant voices in the growing controversy will be accepted as the best, the most "relevant."

2. *Intersection 3:* Nevertheless, there remain problems in which the *formal* characteristics of critical objects are in question *and* in which such agreement as exists about the *nonformal* characteristics of the critical object will not settle the arguments of critics equipped with different critical traditions for determining formal characteristics. Such problems occur at Intersection 3; in virtue of them Intersection 3 constitutes a source of proper occasions for artistically relevant controversy. First we may remind ourselves how in a context of production "genuine" alternatives are generated in regard to the formal characteristics of an object, and then see how, given those alternatives, argument proceeds.

What, then, does it mean "in a context of production" to view the critical object from the vantage point of the matrix of art? Above all, it means a restriction on the critical tradition: in a context of production there may exist no difference "in principle" between the way criticism functions in artistic production and the way criticism functions for people who come to the work of art to appreciate, analyze, evaluate, and so on. Critical traditions, therefore, pose schema for the doing of art, where those schema constitute no self-sustaining rules but representations and proposed revisions of the rules determining artistic creation. Those alternatives are "genuine," then—become the alternatives of proper judges—which are formulated in consonance with the tradition(s) of artistic construction, or as *departures* from such traditions for which good reason can be presented, whatever good reason might be found to be in artistically relevant controversy. Though Polonius never required of Hamlet a good reason or, indeed, a poor one, for shifting his cloud interpretations from one interpretation to another, in art we want to know *why* we should see things differently.

The critic says it for us: he sets up no independent practice for himself, but " serves the cause of art." If so, at any given time the possibilities of criticism are the possibilities of a given matrix of art and must be grounded therein. Through the humility which enables the proper judge to accept that condition (which is the real point of his "respect" for the created object) his service follows: to explore (and weigh) the possibilities *of* a living art and establish the formal characteristics of critical objects in different kinds of relation. If, therefore, on the one hand he takes it upon himself to *decide* what the artist, knowingly or not, has accomplished, on the other he summons all his sensibility and all his judiciousness to block himself out of the picture, to stand as the voice of an impersonal judgment. If he weighs the construction of his critical object, he does so not for the devil of it, but because he must—because the presented object has set him real puzzlements *in a given matrix of art.* He does not *create* his questions; they follow, as people say, from his knowledge of art.

Hence, finally, it is the artist who makes the questions, his own and the critic's, by what he has *done* to the matrix of art in which he works. "Shall the painter, then—I foresee the question—decide upon painting? Shall he be the critic and sole authority? Aggressive as is this supposition, I fear that, in the length of time, his assertion alone has established what even the gentlemen of the quill accept as the canons of art, and recognize as the masterpiece." [10] So wrote Whistler. To be sure, it is not the work of the particular artist but the work of artists in the matrix of art that does the trick. To be sure also, the question is not a question of the relative "influence" of one sort of individual in affecting the course of art and taste. The point is the logic of criticism, in which the performance and possibilities of artists determine the scope and possibilities of the critical tradition. The artists, finally, teach what to look for, what to see, what to subordinate, what to project—and in the process make trouble for themselves and their colleagues the critics.

But, of course, if a distinction exists between genuine and spurious alternatives in constructing formal characteristics (as, of course, it did for nonformal characteristics) it still remains to say how to decide among such "genuine" possibilities where the "cross-incompatibility" for formal and nonformal characteristics leaves *more* than one candidate solution. The details need not concern us, merely what "disagreement" and "agreement" among "genuine possibilities" (which, of course, will be those recognized by "proper judges") might mean. And the pattern for disagreement over formal characteristics is the pattern already exhibited for disagreements over nonformal characteristics.

For, on the one hand, critics may be tempted by a relatively simple additive procedure: "It's true that if you look at the thing in this light, you get such and such results; and that if you look at it in this other light you get this and that. Let's do both!" Anyone who can show *how* to do both will have won the trick; his formal hypothesis will be the deeper and better one. And if "perceiving" the critical object in one way

[10] James McNeill Whistler in *Artists on Art,* ed. Robert Goldwater and Marco Treves (New York: Pantheon, 1958), p. 349.

"works against" some other, resolution will once again depend at least in part upon a judgment of artistic merit, either to decide between different ways of perceiving the object or perhaps to justify new habits in the perception of what "works with" and what "works against."

But I need present here no more of the shifting patterns of controversy over formal characteristics than will suffice to show that disagreement, and agreement, being played according to some set of principles, are real enough, and not mere confrontation of quarreling attitude with quarreling attitude.

V. Proper Occasions for Judgments of Artistic Merit

Since judgments of artistic merit often seem the ones most lacking propriety in a situation that does not call for the critic's personal taste, a few explicit remarks on what makes occasions proper for judgments of artistic merit appear warranted.

1. Judgments of artistic merit find proper occasions when in the construction argument judgment depends upon the resolution of a difference concerning artistic merit. We have seen that construction judgments often enough rotate finally upon a difference in the appraisal of "genuine" merit, and the principle of respect for artistic merit as a regulative principle of the construction argument indicates that we ought not be surprised to find ourselves forced by the logic of the argument to a judgment of merit. Judgments so forced upon the parties to a construction argument are forced upon a proper occasion.

2. Still, experience of the differences among critics suggests that differences over artistic merit are not all forced in this manner. Sometimes critics find occasion to differ in their judgments of merit even though they agree on their construction judgments. Very likely, differences of merit are often intimately tied in with differences in construction. But they need not be, not always, at every point. What, then, would those proper occasions be like which are "free" for judgment rather than forced?

Since the hypothesis of a pure difference in taste has been precluded by the attempt to place criticism in a context of production, the proper occasion in question must lie in the condition of the arts. Remembering that judgments of merit stake claims (for the purposes of controversy) beyond the particular case, the occasion for "free" judgments of artistic merit must lie in the state of the practice of the arts at a given point in their history. Some specific work of art indicates something fundamental which the critic proposes to support or to reject or to modify in the way art or the arts in general may be going. So judgments of merit become the product of a discrepancy between a critical tradition, which always incorporates judgments of merit, in covert if not in overt manners, and the matrix of art and the matrix of society. Proper occasions for artistic merit, like the proper occasions of construction judgments, also occur, then, at the intersection, but at the intersection of a larger practice considered as such. All of which, of course, is in substance if not in jargon, old hat.

The question whether to accept only those proper occasions which are forced takes advantage of the opening a critical object may offer for a larger appraisal. That old criticism still known as the New Criticism may perhaps be distinguished as the style of criticism that preferred to make merit judgments only when those judgments were forced. More recently, reputable critics seem to prefer the larger opening and, not surprisingly, find themselves involved in basic questions of art and life.

This essay is not concerned to take sides in such differences.

Chapter 11

The Structure of the Evidence

As an aid toward grasping the reasons that artistically relevant controversy proffers to support rival claims and adjudicate among them, the preceeding chapter considered the occasions and problems in reference to which considerations of one sort or another act as reasons. The process made it evident that the very "relativity" and "indeterminacy" which normal version philosophers encounter in justifying resolutions of artistically relevant controversy, far from constituting intrinsic obstacles to giving good reasons, typically comprise the actual means for developing the controversy in a progressive way.

Now, in order to establish the reasons question more firmly within a context of production, it is necessary to consider directly rather than in relation to other problems the nature of the evidence through which proper judges of the arts maintain or fail to maintain their positions. Assuming that regulative principles hold very like those already considered for the conduct of the artistically relevant controversy, I must in the present chapter ask the following questions: (I) What kinds of consideration enter into the resolution of artistically relevant issues in artistically relevant controversy? (II) How do such considerations "bear" upon the wisdom of artistically relevant judgments, so that they sustain or inhibit one conclusion rather than another? (III) Are those "bearings" such that the models normally projected to explicate the reasoning of artistically relevant controversy do so fairly?

I. The Considerations That Comprise Reasons

Which considerations does the practice of artistically relevant criticism characteristically bring forward to support its points? What serves as evidence here? Anything *may* be relevant, though on any specific occasion *everything* never is, for the considerations relevant to artistically relevant criticism are those relevant to the production of the critical object, which means, ultimately, to the historically encountered critical tradition and the matrices of art and of society. For that reason, and because determining on any proper occasion the relevance of a consideration demands fixing the *stage* in the decision process at which the questionable consideration has been or is to be introduced, the selection of proper considerations cannot be made a priori. Without a gratuitous distortion of the artistically relevant controversy, there are no grounds on which to generate a problem "in principle."

Such is the general answer, and the answer sets the present task. For while the earlier discussion of the claims question chiefly denied that the *claims* advanced in artistically relevant controversy were, as such, "esthetic," claims, if artistically relevant at all, may "ultimately" rest upon *reasons* that are esthetic. If they do, as estheticians commonly hold, then the proffered general answer will have confused the variety of considerations or circumstances to which esthetic values might accrue with the characteristic of those considerations that render them reasons in an artistically relevant controversy.

To avoid the charge of triviality, then, we must consider the attempt at esthetic reductionism in direct relation to the reasons question and evaluate the normal version claims that (1) there exists one and only one class of considerations (tastes, immediate data, esthetic experiences, etc.), which in the last analysis a proper judge will take as a proper reason in an artistically relevant controversy; and that, in consequence (2) the variety of reasons offered by critics in sustaining their views are subject to a philosophical analysis (of the sort exemplified earlier in the discussion of intention), which will classify them as covert members of the one relevant class of considerations or mistakes in principle.

1. In appraising the normal version claims that proper reasons for construction or merit judgments are esthetic (factual statements as such being taken, presumably, as prior to the artistically relevant controversy and setting the stage for it), it is important that, literally, at least, the normal version cannot be correct as a description of critical practice. Proper judges of the arts do *not* take their own esthetic perceptions or anyone else's as the sole proper considerations sustaining judgments—nor do they take those perceptions to possess *in themselves* the status of reasons. Moreover, esthetic perceptions cannot constitute the sole proper considerations for proper judges, if construction and merit judgments themselves function in the manner presented here. Nor can esthetic considerations in themselves amount to reasons if critics need to compose differences over the appropriateness or rightness of their immediate experiences of the arts and hold their experience corrigible. Obviously, if

esthetic perception functions evidentially, as experience-sustaining judgments, still on any proper occasion such particular perception will bear no intrinsic claim to authority on its visiting card, let alone comprise the only consideration come calling. (A) Why then press a view that, taken literally, at least, seems quite mistaken? and (B) How *do* esthetic appearances function as reasons for claims on proper occasions?

A. First and primarily, people want to press the view that we ought only to consider esthetic considerations in evaluating artistically relevant judgments (or, alternately, that all proper reasons are finally esthetic) because it seems self-evident to them, for reasons sufficiently discussed, that the objects of criticism are esthetic objects and the claims addressed against critical objects are in some sense esthetic claims. "Esthetic objects" being intrinsically observed objects (unlike nonesthetic objects, which may be observed but are not taken to exist in observation or as possible sets of observations), it would seem that any relevant judgment concerning them must find *complete* justification in the observings that exhaust that "object," and in nothing else but such observings. The tests for judgments become tastings without the intervention of any process of inference, while that which is not a tasting is not a proper test of the "esthetic" judgment at all. As an "esthetic reduction" for an "esthetic object" will always, and uniquely, be complete, so will an esthetic reduction for esthetic judgment into the tastings that at once constitute and sustain it.

A network of mistakes of some importance, therefore, helps make credible that artistically relevant reasons are simply esthetic reasons, which is the claim of estheticism on the side of the reasons question. They are the characteristic mistakes of the normal version: a failure to perceive that "esthetic objects," the outcomes of appreciation, are the upshots of the construction argument, not its initial reference; that a necessary characteristic of the construction argument, that the parties to the argument have required perceptual capacities, constitutes a reason *for* constructing a critical object in one way or another; that the findings offered for reasons are finds, discoveries of a special order. In brief, the normal version mistakes the structure of the proper occasion of artistically relevant controversy. It takes that occasion as a discovery occasion of a peculiar sort rather than as a decision occasion for the making or building of a critical object and submerges the problem of choice. Hence it fails to distinguish the reasons or evidence *for* a policy from the reasons (or evidence) *that* a situation obtains, and a new and special type of reason emerges, the "esthetic reason." Esthetic reasons are those unique "reasons-for," which are simply "reasons-that," or those unique "reasons-that," which are "reasons-for."

Under the circumstances, the notion that in art more than anywhere else one constructs a *case* upon statements of appearance, raised now to the dignity of esthetic reasons, turns into one of the more interesting ironies of the normal version. For, of course, it is in the sciences, not in the arts, that reductionism has in fact even a prima facie case. Clearly, somewhere in the normal version a misapprehension exists concerning the sense in which a position rests "upon" its evidence—most particularly "upon" reports of appearances or, more specifically, of appreciations. Since such reports are in *some* way pertinent to artistically relevant controversy we must consider, or reconsider, their use.

B. How, then, *do* esthetic considerations function as reason for claims on proper occasions? More concretely, in what sense does a man give a "reason" when he says, for example, that a critical object is or ought to be taken in a certain way because doing so bestows a certain "esthetic value" upon the object? [1] Regarded without the normal version commitment, the appearances of things have no weight or relevance as such but depend for weight and relevance upon the infinitely complex organization of a large number of decisions. All of which, of course, is not to deny that whether an object actually "presents" a certain appearance may indeed occur as an *issue,* or that that issue, settled, may function as a kind of premise in subsequent discussion.

Perhaps someone will object that, in appraising a construction or merit judgment, a man must nevertheless ask himself how the thing *really* looks to *him,* and that this has nothing to do with normal version preconceptions. Everyone who values art will insist that no one ought to allow himself to be talked into a position he does not feel. So it seems that in accepting or rejecting judgments appearances do have an authority, even if not an absolute authority, "in themselves."

The difficulty is: authority *for what*? It is one thing to say that it is better to be honest and wrong than dishonest and right—or even more strongly, that there's no *point* here being right and dishonest. It is another to say that to the extent one is honest one cannot be wrong. Accordingly, our intuitions are authoritative for determining the truth *of our alleged convictions,* which here, as anywhere that a difference of opinion has arisen, cuts no ice regarding the merit of those convictions. That differ-

[1] It is supposed now, of course, that such "values" can be talked about, as indeed they are, with a fair degree of understanding among the participants in an artistically relevant practice.

ences in the judgment of the arts characteristically involve at one point or another differences over proper appreciations ought not to lead us to identify the genuineness of the appreciation (or "telling") with its propriety.

Of course, it is the implicit assumption that the honest appreciator or noticer is the proper judge, which tempts us to identify sincerity and evidence. The proper judge will always have presented a proper consideration to the extent that as a proper judge he is honest with himself. But honesty only mediates. A certain sort of relationship to the matrices of art and of society gives a judge his status, not the bare facts of his taste.

Still, if any consideration becomes proper only on an occasion of decision, how do considerations of esthetic experience, having become proper, function on that occasion? In a context of production, just because it is a context of production, whatever the complexities of detail the general answer is clear: esthetic experiences work as reasons in decision questions where they appear in the role of subject matter of the argument and material of the construction. For now the overriding question is, if the previous analysis has been correct: what is to be done? And certainly the possibilities of the esthetic experiences of proper judges are genuine enough considerations determining, *with respect to some end* and never in themselves, what can be done. The artist and the critic, therefore, work in esthetic experiences as their ultimate media. It is of the essence that response is manageable for certain ends, though those ends be themselves responses. It is of the essence that, while those responses are not infinitely malleable, they are not natural but formed in the long histories of art and of society. Accordingly, if the statements that describe esthetic experience function as evidence for or evidence against judgments of the arts, they do so as statements about the properties of materials are often supposed to do: by bringing artists and critics hard up against what will "work" (the metaphor is revealing) and what will not "work" for certain kinds of ends in some practice.

Hence the normal version, which grasps the qualities of experience as the evidential ground or base "upon" which artistically relevant judgments rest, will not serve, even though at certain stages and moments of the artistically relevant argument prior agreement may establish them as data. Their existence is the condition of art, not its proof; and there is a serious ambiguity in the metaphor of "ground" or "base." Protocol statements, statements of appearance, and the like are in the first instance, if anything at all, never reasons-for, but descriptions. Media characterizations, on the other hand, are never, in the first instance, descriptions; they are opportunities *for*. Opportunities spelled out comprise, of course, indispensable considerations justifying any right decision. In this sense, so does esthetic experience; but "esthetic experience" evidential in itself constitutes a logical confusion.

As to the priority of esthetic experience in furnishing (not constituting) reasons in artistically relevant controversy, I do not in one appropriate and essential sense need to argue against it. The normal version was, of course, quite correct in holding that esthetic experience had something particular to do with an artistically relevant criticism: artistically relevant criticism distinguishes itself from all others in the central consideration it gives to the possibilities of esthetic experience. Not all practices are so concerned.

2. The general position I have sought to put forward is that anything may be a reason in a context of production, depending on its place in a process of decision. Therefore, having defended against the charge that there are privileged considerations, reasons in themselves ("esthetic reasons"), I am obliged to defend against the claim that there are intrinsic *nonreasons.* Even though it were true that there were no reasons in themselves outside the complex of decision, it might still turn out that in the complex of decision certain considerations were excluded. In effect, therefore, I am about to ask the reader once again to recall the considerations that entered into the analysis of the reference question by considering the more or less characteristic normal version effort to organize the reasons actually advanced in the arts into those which are intrinsically good and those which are not. It will be of particular interest to notice how the normal version feels free to adjudicate *within* the practice of criticism, correcting or supporting that practice where its thesis so requires.

The first group of considerations, then, that in the normal version view (for the sake of concreteness I shall once again refer specifically to the excellent normal version formulation of Professor Monroe Beardsley) fail to qualify as reasons for critical evaluations are "cognitive" considerations: judgments that such and such is "profound," "important," "insightful," etc. The second group that fails to qualify are, broadly, "moral" reasons: the object to be evaluated is judged "inspiring," "edifying," "evil," etc. Both groups are irrelevant because, while they ascribe worth to the object, they do not ascribe artistic worth. The last group consists of reasons that are "peculiarly esthetic," which divide into "objective reasons" that "refer to features of the esthetic object itself"; "affective reasons" that "refer to effects of the object upon the recipient"; and "genetic reasons" that "refer to the causes and conditions of the object." [2] Only the first of this last group does Beardsley hold unequivocally relevant.

A. Surely no one can deny that " 'X' is artistically good" cannot be equivalent to " 'X' is morally true" or " 'X' is plain true." "Moral value" is not the same as "esthetic value," nor is "truth value." Hence showing that an object has one such characteristic will not show that it has another. Why then should there be any doubt but that moral and cognitive reasons are not artistically relevant as such? Why should critics be so stupid as forever to introduce patently irrelevant considerations, so that the normal version correction is required? Why not, if not because there is a question of what "artistically relevant as such" means "as such" and because specific issues in the tactics and strategy of criticism lie below the easy, verbal ones?

Disabused of the prior necessity of a context of consumption, it is not hard to say what those issues are or why the problem of artistically relevant reasons "as such" is something of a problem. If moral or scientific "truths" are used for moral or scientific purposes then, in so far as they are so used, of course they cut no ice for a debate over artistic purposes. Only, of course, they need not be so used. They *might* be used to construct artistically relevant decisions that would settle differences over proper appreciations, expectations, teachings, and the like. They are then "irrelevant" *as such* only on the assumption of a prior agreement on the business of the artistic enterprise to provide a previously specified artistic value of which cognitive and moral values would in no way be constitutive. Either that, or moral and cognitive values would have relevance because, and in the limited sense that, for various extrinsic reasons, people could simply not "appreciate" certain critical objects unless those objects possessed some of those values.

Yet caricatures are what they are because they are in one sense true (to) and in another sense false (to) and any attempt to exhibit the artistic merit or demerit of a caricature would proceed in part by making those senses explicit. Baudelaire's *Les Fleurs du mal* does have a certain cognitive-moral value, a "truth" derived from bitterness, a "bitterness" from truth, which makes it at least an option whether to construct for moral and cognitive values or simply for "esthetic" ones (unless on pseudo-logical principle one eliminates the choice). To be sure, it is not

[2] Monroe C. Beardsley, *Aesthetics: Problems in the Philosophy of Criticism* (New York: Harcourt, Brace, 1958), Chapter 10, pp. 456–457.

clear to us how cognitive or moral considerations might function in an essential way in music, although it seems to have been fairly clear to Plato. Yet the "esthetic" value of a group of *sentences* might "be" one thing if those sentences were true and another thing if false. Such conditions are capable of making a major difference in the presence or absence of the quality of a joke. We might not want to bother about the truth value of the *Divine Comedy*'s theology and therefore find the truth value of the *Divine Comedy* no good reason for one critical evaluation or another. On the other hand, to take the *Divine Comedy* as true or to take it as false, *does* make an artistic difference—unless "an artistic difference" excludes by definition any consequence in construction which follows from construing the statements of the *Divine Comedy* as true or false.

So, moral and cognitive considerations can constitute reasons for critical evaluations. If we remember that created objects possess nonformal characteristics, that conclusion comes as no great surprise. Nevertheless, it is independently supportable. The normal version error is to think that, because nonformal values of works of art are logically irrelevant to artistically relevant controversy when not seen as values *of* works of art, the demonstration of nonformal values of truth or falsity, good or evil, is therefore logically irrelevant to artistically relevant controversy when those values are seen as the values of works of art. The mistake is to assume that because assertions of moral and cognitive values are not sufficient, without further considerations entering the matter, to establish judgments of merit, those assertions are not considerations at all.[3]

B. Are "genetic" and "affective" considerations, with some qualifications for the latter, perhaps intrinsically nonreasons? Neither from statements like " 'X' is new and original," " 'X' is skillfully done," " 'X' is an example of successful expression," nor, on the other hand, from statements like "I like it" or "This interests me" or "This sends cold shivers up and down my spine" does an allegation follow of the form " 'X' is good."

Once again, the question is one of artistically relevant bearing, not of proof, conclusive or inconclusive. From the proposition that an object is new and original or that someone finds it interesting, one is not necessar-

[3] Beardsley recognizes explicitly, of course, that reasons do not need to be conclusive to be genuine (*ibid.*, p. 456). Yet he denies that some reasons have any bearing on critical evaluations because those reasons attribute or deny moral values or truth values (see pp. 456–57) not because those reasons are inconclusive. Relevant considerations in his view might also be inconclusive. So, obviously, there are two kinds of inconclusiveness: the inconclusiveness of the inconclusive but relevant argument and the inconclusiveness of the inconclusive and irrelevant argument.

ily *supposed* to deduce the artistic merit of the object or even the probability of the object's worth. But without such an obligation the genetic or affective fact may very well remain to be considered as a factor in the decision that an artistically relevant judgment advances. So, as was in effect indicated in the discussion of "esthetic" reasons, artists and critics know that audience effect constitutes a significant consideration in justifying a decision to do a play one way or another or to judge it one way or another. "Does it work for an audience?" is surely relevant, whatever doubts one may have about affective reasons "as such." And it is only when one takes affective reasons in a context of consumption that they won't do as reasons in artistically relevant controversy—which Beardsley senses when he finds affective reasons "weaker" than objective reasons, though vastly more relevant than "genetic" ones.

Since, then, affective reasons in his view fail only partially as reasons for critical evaluations, while "genetic" reasons are unequivocally bad reasons, the question of whether there are any intrinsic nonreasons for critical evaluation may best be served by considering some of the supposed clinchers for the badness of genetic reasons. So Beardsley asserts that:

a. For those genetic considerations (skill, success, etc.) that depend directly upon the intention of the author "we can seldom know the intention with sufficient exactness, independently of the work itself, to compare the work with it and measure its success or failure." [4]

But is it not enough that on *some* occasions intentions are sufficiently determinable? Surely no one, not even an "intentionalist," holds genetic considerations to be reasons in an evaluation when they cannot be established, but only when they can be; nor is it necessary for a kind of thing to be a reason that we always know it. That is why we *look for* reasons. Indeed, sometimes the best reasons are the hardest to find.

b. "Even when we can do so [that is, compare the work with the intention and measure its success or failure] the resulting judgment is not a judgment of the work, but only of the worker, which is quite a different thing." [5]

That Bach successfully achieved his intention in the "St. Matthew Passion" is "quite a different thing" from the judgment that a given performance is indeed an excellent performance of the "St. Matthew Passion," depends of course on a lack of interest in whether or not the performance conforms to Bach's intention. On the other hand, many musicians and critics, and those not the worst, think that the "St. Matthew

[4] *Ibid.*, p. 458.
[5] *Ibid.*

Passion" ought to be performed so far as possible as Bach intended it to be performed; and in evaluating a performance they regard the score *and* whatever musicologists can glean about the way which in his time Bach would have wanted the score to be performed. So the quoted statement is true only on adding a missing assumption, which turns out to be precisely the matter at issue: that judgments of intention, even when they occur in the form of judgments of expressive success, are irrelevant for the evaluation of works of art, including performances.

But perhaps it will be admitted that judgments of the conformity of a performance to the intention of the artist are indeed judgments of the performance. The same thing does not hold of the nonperforming arts. Still, once again, a specific decision has been smuggled in under the camouflage of the difference between performing and nonperforming arts. Suppose there were a custom that every painting must be destroyed as soon as it was viewed and the custom were enforced. Then painting would become a performing art, with directives for producing paintings well or poorly "according to the intent of the artist," as composers produce directives for producing music. Indeed, painting would become a performing art in rather the sense that some parts of music which work with tapes show signs of becoming nonperforming arts. The difference exists, in this custom, that every painting must be destroyed as soon as it is viewed. It will be agreed that such a custom, while undesirable, is a possible option we have not chosen. It ought also to be agreed that nothing prevents the much weaker custom of regarding every painting as though it fell under the custom. So the view that, however it may be in music or theater, in painting and sculpture judgment of the work and judgment of the worker are "quite different things," cannot be true without the adoption of a specific choice within the artistically relevant controversy.

c. Even if the artist realizes his intentions, exhibits considerable skill in doing so, and leaves no doubt of his sincerity, "the question immediately arises whether [the work under consideration] was worth intending." Accordingly, even originality "has no bearing upon worth; it might be original and fine, or original and terrible." [6]

Of course, the apparent truism that a man might deliberately manage to achieve an original work of art, which was also terrible, assumes that "originality" means simply different. Any object, however, is different from any other and, indeed, *all* others. "Originality" in criticism means, however, as the discussion of the Ideal of Unicity suggested, different in

[6] *Ibid.*, p. 460.

artistically relevant ways; so, although other considerations might override, originality has in actual criticism enough positive value to make us hesitate to call a piece of original work "terrible." Does not the perception of originality induce an added excitement even in the moment of consummation? Why such purism? The real trouble is that Beardsley believes it wrong to consider works of art in relation. He wants us to consider the "work of art itself" for which, of course, originality is indeed no consideration—a consequence that ought, but does not, generate unease with the normal version.

But the principal argument has already been made. While few, if any, consider evidence of originality *conclusive* for their artistically relevant praise or dis-praise, only that extreme view is disproven by observed conjunctions of originality and dis-value. In experience, originality, success, skill, and the "genetic" rest are considerations pertinent in conjunction with others at certain points in an artistically relevant controversy. And, after all, propositions may have a "bearing" upon the truth of other propositions even though they may be irrelevant without still other propositions.

Perhaps, then, it will be granted that when the critic's problem is making, not proving, the following circumstances obtain: that (a) there are no considerations to which the critical controversy appeals that are in themselves irrelevant; that (b) indeed, no considerations whatsoever can be excluded a priori from the decision process; that (c) there are no considerations, "objective" or otherwise, which travel with their authority precertified; and that (d) considerations of truth, morality, genesis, effect, and the like actually do relate to artistically relevant decisions under appropriate circumstances.

Given, then, that any consideration might serve the artistically relevant controversy as a "reason" for taking one stand or another, though, doubtless, not all possible considerations ever have or ever will, the crucial problem for the reasons question is not the problem of classifying the different types of considerations which have in fact entered the controversy and which might be expected to do so, much less the task of settling criteria for prior eligibility. The crucial problem is to understand how what allegedly are reasons "bear upon" some artistically relevant judgment of construction or merit.

II. Differences over Reasons

On the whole, in science, one knows how to do inductive inference, or seems on the way to finding out. But in the criticism of the arts how and whether a "reason" for accepting a view "actually" has any bearing upon that view seems indeed a much more questionable thing and an almost constant issue. Are good reasons in art even possible, then, when the very reasonings of critics are open to question? I must at least provide some illustrations to show that resolvable arguments about the binding force of the reasons for judgment do occur and, roughly, what those arguments are like "in a context of production." Moreover, it is of some importance that such illustrations center about the most distinctive activity of critics—the criticism of particular works of art rather than the discussion of formative rules as such or of the general concepts of critical theory. Then there will be time to consider the general "logical" problem of an appropriate characterization of reasons in artistically relevant controversy.

1. Plainly, then, construction judgments articulating the structure of some critical object are advanced by critics to sustain or inhibit their judgments of merits, nor is it trivial to see how this works in practice.

In one sense, of course, the relevance, at least of the construction judgments advanced as reasons, cannot be disputed. To the question "Why do you think your evaluation of the particular critical object "S" correct?" any adequate answer must include a series of construction judgments "P" such that it is ridiculous to say that a judgment "Q" does not "follow." If "P" is what the man has in mind by his judgment of merit "Q," that is what he has in mind. Nevertheless, having acknowledged in the first stage of a controversy that one now understands what the other fellow wants to say, there still may exist in the next stage a fair question whether "Q" actually holds. Very likely, it is the possibility of such a turn of events (in which one asserts the "truth" of a construction judgment along with the "falsity" of the merit judgment allegedly sustained by it) that induces some philosophers to analyze "merit" as a special property adhering to some formal and nonformal values, but detachable, "subjective," "private," in a word, "esthetic value."

A. So, to the allegation "This play is bad because of what goes on in Act I," I may answer, "You understand rightly Act I. Nevertheless, you are too severe. All in all, the play's a good one anyway."

To understand the contradiction, and hence the implication denied, in this kind of inference to an "all in all" or summary conclusion, one must distinguish. We might be agreeing, for example, that the evening would have been pleasanter without the difficulty in Act I, but one of us has a pleasant evening anyway and the other does not. Each of us speaks for his evening; and the argument, if it comes to that, is an argument "in a context of consumption." Then, indeed, the judgment of what goes on in Act I actually constrains a merit judgment neither one way nor another and justifies a certain skepticism of the genuineness of reasons in criticism.

Yet perhaps a bearings issue was joined for the artistically relevant controversy after all. Denying that the play was "all in all" a bad one, though agreeing to the account of what went on in Act I, I might have wanted to point to the relation of the agreed upon reading of Act I to some other, relatively inclusive set of constructions pertinent to the play, to call attention to some other set of characteristics of the play that mediate between the reason and the conclusion. Perhaps those characteristics are inevitably linked to Act I, perhaps not. But how they are dealt with determines indeed the binding force of the inference from the construction judgment to the "all and all" judgment "in a context of production." "P" and "not-Q" are together false because of some set of reasons "R," "S," "T" . . . which are also true. Pushing the argument further would no doubt raise differences concerning other judgments of artistic merit. Still, at this stage of the argument, there remains a procedure for adjudicating bearings.

B. I might, however, have answered the man who thinks the play poor because of what happened in Act I by the rhetorical question "What's wrong with Act I?" I still agree with his account of Act I. But now the difficulty is with the evaluation of *Act I,* not of the play "all in all." The same kind of issue is involved in an agreement about *The Skin of Our Teeth,* taken all in all, that it constitutes "the marriage of Plato and Groucho Marx," followed by a disagreement whether in consequence the play's any good.

The bearings argument is again, as in the case of inference to summary judgments, quite different in a context of production and in a context of consumption. In a context of production the "value" difference is characteristically consequent to the artistically relevant controversy, not initial. The application of a prior standard may constitute a fair enough procedure in a context of consumption to determine whether or not the formal or informal value in question has a certain merit or not. But at the moment when the disagreement over the implication of the play's constituting "the marriage of Plato and Groucho Marx" resolves itself into a disagreement over the "values" of which *The Skin of Our Teeth* now represents an instance, the artistically relevant controversy has ceased. For in such a controversy nobody wants to prove or deny the "value" of marrying Groucho and Plato as such, but only on the specific occasion of the play. Instances serve for tastes already formed; but "in a context of production" what are "instances" in a context of consumption serve as *materials* for the preparation of merit judgments.

Hence the significant tactic generated by the question "What's *wrong* with the critical object 'S' in respect of some construction judgment 'P'?" will consist in showing "P" part of another broader construction such that "P" sustains that construction, that construction is correct and there is no further pertinent merit disagreement. If the tactic succeeds, the exception is sustained. As Fergusson himself says of the marriage of Plato and Groucho Marx when he approves it, "Now that the work is done we can see what a brilliant notion it was to translate Joyce's dream-like and ironic meditation on the eternal recurrence of human history into the ancient jokes, irrational horseplay and shameless sentimentality of burlesque." [7] In effect, he now shows how the apparent incongruity works, how it doesn't "follow" that because the *Skin* consists in the marriage of Plato and Groucho there "must be" something wrong with the play. The same incongruity that previously ruined the enterprise has been built into a new construction that "saves" the value of the play and possesses therefore, in the artistically relevant construction, a prima facie superiority, to the extent that it succeeds.

In general, then, disagreements whether judgments of merit "follow" or "tend" to follow from constructions are not *supposed* to be resolved by an inspection of the premises and the conclusion, but from the continuous interposition of further constructions conceived as having value and justification in the artistically relevant controversy. When no one can think of a rival construction that will hold water within the artistically relevant controversy as so far developed, then the terms for further cooperation and discussion of the development of the arts have been set. But refusal to consider expanding the context of the argument because doing so indeed leads to another opinion concerning the "bearing" of "P" upon "Q" does not constitute in the artistically relevant controversy a legitimate defense of the controverted bearing. It terminates the controversy. Not here any more than in science does the method of tenacity constitute a defense.

2. Obviously, critics use estimates of value to sustain or inhibit other estimates of value. Yet, in the artistically relevant controversy, one merit judgment cannot "follow" directly upon another, or any set of others—not where each judgment proffers an instruction set and the end is

[7] *The Human Image in Dramatic Literature* (Garden City, N.Y.: Doubleday, 1957), p. 57.

not to demonstrate "standards" but to generate them in the concrete. How, then, does one judgment of merit sustain or inhibit another?

Obviously, sometimes, merit judgments will be sustained or inhibited by other merit judgments in so far as they possess the character of precedent. "If you can approve of characteristic 'P' of critical object 'S,' how can you disapprove of characteristic 'P' of critical object 'R'?"[8] Such considerations are vital for sustaining merit judgments in particular cases. They are handled partly by considering general policies as considerations. But also they are handled by considering the merit of the characteristic as that merit works out in a particular structure; and that is the kind of case which concerns us here primarily.

For such cases, the construction approved or disapproved in the merit judgment supports or inhibits the construction that constitutes the content of the merit judgment supported or inhibited. If I have approved a characteristic "S," the approval of which I justify by the approval I have given to some other characteristic "T," it is because that characteristic "S" is required by the approved characteristic "T." The "logical" connection between merit judgments becomes *in the analysis of the texture of the specific critical object* a connection among constructions. So it is possible for an object to have the defects of its virtues—he who says "a" must say "b" if he is to say anything at all, and Lord knows where saying "b" will get you. Or sometimes a merit will seem so overwhelming in a work that certain virtues can hardly not follow. Such possibilities must be examined; and anyone who wants to contradict the sustaining or inhibiting import of one merit judgment upon another would do so by exhibiting a different relation than that first laid down between construction judgments or by proposing, implicitly, some shift in the overall theory of the critical object.

Ought I distinguish between the reasons for flat attributions of merit and comparative judgments? But since in a context of production comparative judgments (of merit) become ways of formulating specific choices concerning how art is to be done or not to be done in this particular critical object ("Do 'X' sort of thing here rather than 'Y' ") the defense and attack of comparative judgment reduces to the rivalry between distinct judgments, which is what I have in effect been discussing. " 'X' is better than 'Y' " seems to require some special sort of "reason" because

[8] So also, for construction judgments in their bearing upon critical evaluations, one might raise the question whether if you approve a merit judgment because of such and such a construction here, why in the case of some other critical object did you not approve given a like construction judgment there?

implicitly we think of "X" and "Y" as satisfying some pre-set standard in greater or lesser degree, and we forget that in the endeavor to construe the "unique" work of art we seek to make such standards, not to apply them.

3. Having glimpsed the interconnexity of decisions in artistically relevant controversy from the perspective of merit judgments, consider now how *construction* judgments "follow" or "tend to follow." The question, of course, has already and inevitably been considered in subsections 1 and 2, but I wish now to take the matter up more directly. In what way or ways, then, baldly, does one attack the inference from, say, Hamlet's berating of his mother in the bedroom scene to the conclusion that he Oedipally loved her?

A. One might say, "It doesn't follow at all. Everyone who berates his mother is not in love with her." The bearing of one construction upon another that such a rejoinder puts is evidently psychological in character. Generally, construction arguments will always involve at one phase or another cognitive judgments. The justification of making one decision or another in any art will always include a technological consideration; and the critic, or the artist functioning as critic, seeking to understand what has happened, will always seek to touch that consideration as home base.

But, of course, home base does not even count for home base except on the diamond. Affirming a construction antecedent and denying a construction consequence on empirical grounds must be part of a further process if it is to be taken seriously among critics of the arts. That process opens up more interesting and characteristic senses in which the "bearing" of reasons might be questioned.

B. "Regardless of the prevalence of the Oedipus complex," one might want to say, "there are in the play dramatically more interesting consequences of the berating scene which do *not* require that Hamlet love his mother in an Oedipal sense." In effect, contradictions of inferences from construction to construction seem to become fully relevant to proper judges of the arts only on pointing to some further class of connections to which an allegedly proper construction of the play ought to attend: Oedipus is fine, *but not in Hamlet.* For, otherwise, critical discussion remains on the artistically dead level of fact.

Technological considerations aside, then, what "follows" from a construction decision for another such decision depends upon a network of other such decisions. Such networks aside, *no* construction sustains or inhibits another in itself, and I would repeat what is in effect, if not in formulation, a truism: that one construction decision in the artistically relevant controversy stands to another not as scaffolding to edifice, rather as brick to parts of building and parts of buildings to the whole. They stand in the relation of decisions over means to decisions over ends, in a "means-ends continuum." Hence either the construction antecedent discriminates characteristics implicit in the construction consequent, so that accepting the antecedent *demands* accepting the consequent, or a more inclusive characterization demands a more restricted one.

It follows that contradicting the "bearing" of one construction upon another means finally proposing another construction or constructions to mediate between one construction and another, unless it can be shown that the one being contradicted would, if induced to look again, on his own terms reject his first conclusion. With that proviso, then, disagreements over whether constructions inhibit or sustain or do neither become disagreements over what is to be done with materials, over the sense in which they are to be handled; hence they are intelligible only "in a context of production" where the critical object, no longer "the work of art itself," stands in relation.

C. Accordingly, one might say, "I don't question that the bedroom scene supports your notion that Hamlet loves his mother, that is, if I grant your terms. It is true that on those terms a mutually sustaining network of constructions can be provided to make the connection serve. But so does Thurber's lady detective story aficionado turn *Macbeth* into the wildest tissue of mutually sustaining improbabilities. What could be done with *Macbeth* could be done with *Hamlet.* For whether or not the bedroom scene really sustains the notion that Hamlet was in love with his mother depends on what you choose to make of Hamlet (whether you choose to do an Ernest Jones, Dover Wilson, or perhaps Goethe again); *and also* what you choose to make of Hamlet will depend on what you choose to make of the bedroom scene (Oedipus complex, the brim of sanity, moral crisis, some combination, etc.)."

To affirm the antecedent (Hamlet berates his mother) while denying the consequent (Hamlet loves his mother) now means forcing the principles on which one does criticism, though not necessarily arbitrarily. For, in any practice, effective decisions concerning critical objects other than the one in question "determine" (with the help of judgments of artistic merit) the "rightness" of one set of part-whole (means-end) relations and the "wrongness" of another. What shall we make of such and such a product of the avant-garde theater? To exhibit Swift-like characteristics helps. It helps further to show "Absurdist" techniques to make Swift-like points. A critic characteristically *uses* decisions concerning other critical objects—the one thing he cannot do, and fairly ask for the assent of a rival, is to ignore the shared file of decisions for the proper construction of other objects along with the policy decisions made by carefully sifting those decisions.

The implication is plain: behind every assertion that one construction "bears" upon another, waiting to be tested and reconstructed in every "bearing" argument, is the totality of construction judgments determining the "field" of the relevant art. Nor is it in virtue of any ontological characteristic of "fields" that this is so but in virtue only of the observable rules of a competition that pushes the question of who wins always one step *ahead* and assigns no final victory. When one man contradicts what another alleges of how one feature of a work of art "bears" upon some other, no mere difference in miniature threatens, no restricted difference of opinion of the critical object as such, but rather an entire capacity, training, and judgment.

D. The most obvious retort to anyone who wants to reason from Hamlet's berating of his mother to Hamlet's Oedipus complex is, clearly, that to take that inference seriously makes a rotten play. Construction judgments sustain or inhibit other construction judgments also in virtue of judgments of artistic merit. Such judgments, finally, guide the construction of critical objects, determine the "proper" use of previous constructions of other critical objects, lead to establishing in the long run one set of formative rules or another. For the game of art is incomplete. Given this incompleteness, differences over whether or not one characteristic "follows" from another depend not only on differences concerning the "field" of decisions in which the critical object has been placed, but on what one wants from the arts.

Accordingly, let me conclude this discussion of the interconnexity of construction and merit decisions by making the obvious remarks about what it means to deny that on the basis of a certain judgment of artistic merit a certain construction rather than another "follows." Assuming that a judgment of artistic merit proposes some instruction set for doing art one way or another, the argument, of course, becomes whether a given construction satisfies that instruction set. "What the artist does here does *so* make for lucidity, humor, depth, etc." How is the difference resolved? Obviously, if the analysis has been correct, it is resolved not by some "mechanical" reading off of an instruction set and some direct and unquestionable finding that the set has been satisfied or not, but rather by an elucidation of the formal and nonformal characteristics of the controversial object in such a way that the standards, the proposals for the arts, are themselves reconstructed. It is resolved, in sum, by generating further judgments of artistic merit on which agreement is requested, by pressing forward the concrete discussion of artistic merit at specific points.

Therefore, properly, the question of whether or not a judgment of artistic merit "bears" in one way or another upon a construction is among proper judges never finally "answered." It is passed *through,* seen as the wrong difference, as a misunderstanding, or the right difference seen in the wrong light—a light which never was until later on.

4. At the same price of redundancy paid for judgments of construction and of artistic merit I must now remark how judgments normally not considered artistically relevant bear upon those which are. And, obviously, the basic point will be that considerations sometimes considered artistically irrelevant *in themselves* are so considered because the bearing problem has been systematically submerged as a problem at crucial points.

A. I must hearken back to remarks previously made about such values as "truth" and "falsity." If it is true that a novel presents a true picture of nineteenth-century Russia, then, assuming judgments of merit held constant, that fact makes a great difference in what one makes of the novel; since if the judgment were false, the entire construction of the novel would shift. Perhaps, for example, the novel might become a political novel, in which part of the very point was the clash between the reality and the presentation. So it is simply not the case that in a context of production differences over the bearings of "truth" judgments, "moral" judgments, "political," or "religious" judgments are simply differences in the imposition of external standards. Differences over the bearings of such judgments are resolved by a choice among constructions.

B. Similar considerations hold for the bearing of such judgments upon judgments of merit. Obviously, in the justification of merit judgments, the construction judgments imposed upon criticism by morals, science, or politics bear upon judgments of merit. Does it follow, however, that for certain kinds of critical objects, a judgment of "truth" constrains directly to a favorable (or unfavorable) judgment of merit? It seems clear that the answer must depend upon a choice of formative rules; nor does it seem at all impossible that a set of such rules includes the rule "Let all critical objects of a certain sort be set up to secure, in the ways appropriate to them, representations maximally adequate," in some appropriate sense of "adequate." Given such a rule, the conclusion follows for that particular art-game. Only, it is to be observed, in that case a "bearing" has been described in relation to a formative rather than a performative issue of merit; and the fundamental issue of construction remains, which is the endeavor to construct a concept of art. (So, even for the formative argument, "standards" in a context of production function differently from the way they do in a context of consumption, being themselves considered for their use in a wider enterprise.

In sum, "deducing" the worth of a critical object from its "truth," "morality," "religiosity," or the like, or its lack of worth from their opposites, critics commit no "fallacy" at all, if one understands what they are doing—that they are considering the "bearing" of an artistically relevant decision that invokes such values upon some other artistically relevant decision.

Assuming, then, that the rules of right and taste, let alone Rorschach's old principle, do not hold for artistically relevant inference, and if such inference is the kind of thing described, what shall we make of it? Four historically given models for interpreting the logical force of artistically relevant bearings, all of them based on projections from other "rational" activities, now require consideration. Perceiving the respects in which these models [9] go wrong may afford a more adequate grasp of what artistically relevant reasoning might be like in its distinctive characteristics, even if it should be the case, as it undoubtedly is, that all those models for inference are pertinent at appropriate points in the artistically relevant controversy.

Sometimes, then, it is said that understanding how a consideration "bears" upon a judgment requires "weighing" or "balancing" that consideration against others. At other times people seem to think that reaching a judgment on the nature or worth of a critical object means deducing that judgment from others. Still others find the relation of reason to judgment "dialectical," while some oppose the deductive model by arguing that only dogmatism and the dead hand of custom prevent perceiving that the evidence for evidentially grounded judgments of the arts is inductive in character. Of course, there are always some who say that nothing functions as a reason except as one chooses to take it so; but this last, or Protagorean position, deserves no consideration here. It fails even to attempt to take into account the specific character of artistically rele-

[9] These "models" are not proposed to represent distinct "schools" of metacritical analysis for criticism but rather constructions of artistically relevant reasoning which may be traced in many or most efforts to account for the force of reasons in criticism.

vant bearings in order to comment on the force reasons have to buyers attentive to the salesman's pitch.

III. The Weighing Model

Because anyone reasoning about the arts needs to take a great variety of considerations into account, it comes easy to say that considerations bear upon a judgment in that they possess a certain weight that contributes to a judgment or subtracts from it. Considerations "weigh" heavily or lightly; and it is almost as though one put objects possessing an odd kind of weight—"esthetic" weight—into the scales of a balance and waited to see which way the balance went. Perhaps a large part of the metaphor's appeal stems from the secret conviction that there is one and only one kind of intrinsically relevant consideration in artistically relevant controversy. Be that as it may, since in evaluating the worth of a critical object nobody can state prior to the evaluation the rule by which one set of particular considerations weighs more heavily than another, the conclusion *seems* to follow either that effective reasoning in matters of art must wait for the coming of a greater human wisdom or that reason here is, somehow, inherently weak in the very grain, or, of course, impossible.

1. All that prevents such shoddy skepticism is the existence of an important sense in which one does not *want* to weigh considerations in the arts as one would in those domains in which the weighing metaphor indeed holds up (as, for example, in fixing certain kinds of business or political policy). For, suppose a critic finds that a novel has "sacrificed" plot for character exploration, or thematic development for orchestral effect. Then in the critical process, however it may be when the critic tries to summarize his findings and present his credo, he plainly does not "weigh" character exploration and plot or orchestration against thematic development in order to determine the sum value of the critical object before him. He points out a flaw. Perhaps he condemns the artist for lacking the imagination, given his materials, to avoid the "sacrifice." Perhaps he observed that an unflawed object could have been constructed by modifying the materials appropriately. In any event, relevant considerations do not weigh *against* each other at all. They are to be "controlled," "adjusted," "integrated," etc. *Nothing is to be sacrificed. The critic chooses the optimum.*

Or, supposing the critic were concerned primarily to construct a critical object rather than to evaluate its worth; it may be thought that he seeks to determine the weight to give to various considerations. And, indeed, some critics do place greater emphasis upon one sort of thing rather than another. Yet now the critic's relative utilities are determined *after* the fact of criticism, on the inspection of the criticism and its comparison with another's. He does not weigh the demands of color, texture, line *against* one another and appraise the picture described as the peculiar object that satisfies those demands in the precise ways it does. For it is obvious that while color, texture, and line are separably discriminable, their *demands* are not, in the criticism of this particular picture; they constitute linked traits. Hence the problem of the critic in this critical phase of his activity may once again more properly be described as organizing or even exploring considerations, rather than weighing or balancing (in the economic sense). How could anyone formulate a utility scale on which to place color, texture, and line in order to determine an optimal payoff? The procedure is perhaps appropriate for a context of consumption. For artistically relevant criticism ("in a context of production"), it is absurd.

Such observations suggest that if a weighing procedure will not justify drawing certain conclusions from some set of considerations about the arts, the failure is not a relevant failure, hence no failure at all either for the model or the subject matter. It is not as though utility scales were, somehow, impossible here. We do not want one. There is no "work of art itself" for which to fix the effects of the characteristics discriminated within it, fixing so much responsibility here, so much there. The alleged impossibility of quantifying the arts or the taste that judges them has nothing to do with the matter. Indices are irrelevant at crucial points in the arguments over bearings.

I emphasize the qualification "at crucial points" because it is obvious that weighings in the ordinary sense in which one says that one set of advantages or disadvantages "outweighs" another will be appropriate from time to time in artistically relevant controversy. But then they will be brought to bear in the sense that agreement *exists* on some index so that one can speak of greater or less approximation of an end. Accordingly, for the purposes of live discussion, such agreements constitute materials and elements of the discussion, not "critical points"; and we may meaningfully ask to make good the bearing of a "weighing" upon a conclusion.[10]

2. Nevertheless, the more instructive question asks what precisely in the condition of choosing in the arts renders the weighing model directly irrelevant for construing bearings in artistically relevant controversy; and

[10] Further discussion of the positive role of the weighing model will occur in the next chapter (see Chapter 12, section II). It is only at one phase of the artistically relevant controversy that the weighing model is inappropriate.

by way of a partial answer I should like to make two very familiar points of some importance for understanding reasons in the arts.

A. First, choice of the *right* construction of the critical object or of the *proper* action in its production is free, as choice is not always free elsewhere. The proper judge of the arts does not need to choose between one work of art and another, one construction of a work of art and another, as a man of good judgment needs to choose between one wife and another, one business and another, or even one legal judgment and another. Choice in matters of the arts is free first of the need to compromise in judgment. Far from being required to make allowances, the proper judge of the arts may in so far as he takes an exception—indeed *must*—demand "perfection" of the critical object. Why then should the critic weigh one merit against another demerit as though he were concerned whether the artist made the best of a practical bargain? He may, of course; sometimes he does. But the critic's taste is supposed to be an "exacting" one because it refuses on principle to weigh one consideration against another. Secondly, choice is free in the sense that no one expects the critic to marry one among the many sorts of perfections, one among the infinite variety of works of art, to the exclusion of all others for all time and eternity. Therefore, he does not need to weigh one work of art *against* another as he formulates his vision of art, any more than he needed to weigh one consideration against another as he formulated his vision of the particular critical object. And proper judges of the arts regard "catholicity of taste" as among the necessary virtues of the professional critic.

The idea is simply to describe a practice, the practice of criticism. This is the way it is, the critic announces. This is wrong, this is right, don't blame him. He is very sorry if the artist's materials proved intractable and the artist had to compromise. The critic will leave the question of whether for him one consideration has "greater weight" than another to people attempting to summarize his views or predict which way he will in all likelihood judge. *For him* to add here, subtract there, to render the completed account on some scale of value holding for all artistically relevant considerations and all works of art would be germane only on the condition that he were not, by profession, free.

Someone will of course reply that even a proper judge has limited time and energy, so he is not free and must choose *between.* Still, that reply holds water only on the normal version assumption that critics of the arts as exception-takers decide which critical object to watch or read or listen to. Such concerns are real enough. But they are not the concerns of an artistically relevant controversy working through one of the considerations (the artistically relevant one, of course) relevant to deciding how a man might allocate his time.

B. If, however, the justification of an artistically relevant exception stands exempt from the limitations of a finite economy, then to understand *why* it does and hence *why* the weighing model fails requires another look at what we already know. For, after all, we know very well that the "freedom" of criticism does not depend upon the artist's and critic's attainment of Eden all over again, everything provided for, everything possible. *That* freedom is appropriate to dreamland, not to art; it is the freedom to which the consumer aspires as he dreams of escape from "choice between." The freedom of artist and critic described here exists within the conditions of what has been called here the "context of production." In the practice of criticism, if the problem does not consist in what to *settle* for, choice nevertheless arises in all its concreteness when the critic asks what he will choose to have. The view advocated all along on the nature and function of artistically relevant judgment makes the point: the critic in so far as he takes exception and seeks to substantiate his position must decide, bearing in mind the rules for artistically relevant controversy, among which there is *not* a rule for choice *between,* what he will require of critic and of artist in the employment of certain materials. That is the force of his judgment; and it defines the nature of his freedom, which is, given what he has, to make the future.

Everything depends upon the notion of deciding what one will have "in a context of production." Not only does the problem of deciding what one will have not consist in selecting among an indefinite range of goods rather than among a finite range, it does not even consist in choosing among an infinite series of given blueprints for such goods. Instead, the problem is the problem of *making* the blueprints, in which all previous goods, including the blueprints for those goods and the blueprints nobody ever used, serve as grist for the mill to generate another plan. This is the kind of "choice" the critic faces: producer's choice, inventor's choice, participant's choice, subject only to the rules of artistically relevant controversy—rules which, as the last chapter in effect exhibited, drive the creative process further and further.

So, if a man should be asked to state, leaving aside his particular resources or the skill of any particular architect, what sort of house he would choose to have, he would not necessarily limit himself to available plans nor would he, in devising his own plans, "weigh" one consideration against another like a man on a budget. He would rather seek to discover what he really wanted. Assuming he ever did, as soon as he found himself "weighing" one advantage against another he would recognize that something had gone wrong with the blueprint before him and either devise another or explain where the fault was so that another might be devised for him.

So also the working artist, when "weighing" line *against* color, style *against* plot, proves not his critical mind but his desire to leave off artistically relevant creation at the point at which his imagination fails him. For his business is to go for broke—which, concretely, means reworking until there is no question of "weighing" one consideration against another, until all considerations "reinforce." That, finally, is why decisions do not "bear" upon one another in the sense of having greater or lesser "weight" in the performative argument.

IV Some Other Models

I have dealt first with the weighing model for determining the force and relevance of reasons because in many ways that model seems prima facie closest to what the exercise of judgment, in art or in science, requires; and hence it ought to inspire the greatest caution. Nevertheless, historically, other models have tended to receive at least an equal play and deserve their share of attention. For, though elements in the analysis and criticism of these other models have been picked off from time to time, they have not been generalized.

1. Conclusions in criticism are sometimes represented as proved. But even though formal (and informal) fallacies are as assiduously to be avoided in the discourse of critics as of other people, we ought not to be deceived: the "proof" represents a rhetorical formulation of positions already agreed upon; and the discovery of a "fallacy" would normally justify "working up" a different formulation rather than changing considerations or conclusions. The reason is that "the deductive model" radically mistakes the kind of support people ask of reasons in the artistically relevant controversy, mistaking reasons in the sense of "evidence-*that*" for reasons in the sense of "evidence-*for*."

No one, then, ever "deduces" his decision concerning any critical object from any set of established considerations (perhaps the basic reason for the credibility of the weighing model)—and, alternatively, the confusion of "evidence-for" with "evidence-that" constitutes a serious mistake—for the following reasons.

A. All relevant considerations in artistically relevant judgments bear upon judgments in the sense in which decisions bear upon judgments. That is why the discussion of the ways in which bearing arguments were specifically conducted could sometimes use "decision" and "relevant consideration" (or "reason") interchangeably. So much is what normal version accounts actually notice when they find the reasons of criticism special affairs—"esthetic" affairs—unlike reasons anywhere else.

Suppose that I get somebody to notice a blue color he had not previously distinguished in the painting. "Right there," I say, pointing, "the painting is blue." In Beardsley's language, I have "referred to features of the esthetic object itself,"[11] and provided an "objective reason" for a judgment. Yet why is the reference a "reason," leaving aside "the esthetic object itself"? "The painting is blue right there" is either true or false—it is not therefore at all clear what is "esthetic" about it if "esthetic" now includes "artistically relevant." The statement constitutes a relevant consideration, "bears upon" an artistically relevant judgment only in virtue of the acceptance of a recommended choice: to construe the painting in a manner that includes the blue fact. That fact, like the gathering of dust or the cracking of canvas, *might* be neutral for discussions of certain kinds of art; and, even after one has decided on the kinds of things one ought to look for in pictures of a certain sort, the fact of blueness located "there" *might* have no relevance to the controversy. Then the sheer blue fact would become a garden variety fact. So if the sheer blue fact bears upon a judgment of the nature or worth of a judgment in criticism, it bears as the decision to take up and consider that sheer blue fact bears upon judgment. The controversy is about the decision to do so.

B. No decision is deduced from any other, although, obviously, some decisions under appropriate circumstances sustain or inhibit others. Even if some uniform way existed of fixing upon the principle or ratio *decidendi* of every case, the decision to apply that ratio to some other case, the ratio of which that ratio was held to "subsume," would itself constitute a decision.

It is instructive to recall how as a consequence of the relationship between judgment and decision one now rejects an alleged deduction. To review the case discussed above: someone says he thinks the *Skin* a poor play for marrying Groucho and Plato and we decide to help him make his judgment *follow* by supplying the missing premise. "I take it," we offer, "that you think any play marrying the two must be a poor one, whatever the play's other virtues or vices." Then, as we saw before, our help has placed the critic in the false position either of surrendering his judgment or of admitting as a premise in his argument a standard to which he

[11] *Aesthetics: Problems in the Philosophy of Criticism,* p. 534.

cannot agree. "Obviously," he may be presumed to answer, "I don't mean anything so silly as the generalization you ascribe to me. Of course, the marriage *might* sometimes be successful. I meant merely that it doesn't work in this play. The other virtues and vices not only matter, they are the heart of the problem."

In general, then, the applicability of the deductive model signifies the close of controversy and the occasion for an appropriate formulation of the results. All of which is not to deny that that formulation may have heuristic value for forcing to the surface just what decisions have been made. But (as in the law) cases are *built* up by analogy, projection, precedent, experiment, and waiting for an antagonist to top one—either to do better, according to the rules of a complex controversy, or to admit that, provisionally, at least, the judgment stands. It is hardly surprising that anyone who conceives a deductive ideal for the bearing of reasons in criticism and the arts despairs of good reason to the degree he is sensitive to the arts and familiar with the practices of critics. Nobody *wants* to deduce anything.

2. If, however, critics do not "demonstrate" their judgments, nor want to, neither do they make their judgments in virtue of some purely dialectical process. To be sure, in the dialectical process one does not begin by knowing the definitions or standards, but seeks them when in particular cases the question arises of just *how* one has managed to reach the judgment one has: one may be forced to eat crow. So the obvious trouble with the deductive model does not arise here. Yet the basic difficulty remains: that taking "evidence-for" on the dialectical model, definitions and standards remain objects of *discovery.* We want to find out, if only we can, what we "really" believe. Yet, if the preceding discussions are correct, critics do not search for hidden values through logical any more than through any other means, but seek decisions not already "implicit" in previous decisions, no matter how those previous decisions may "bear" upon this one. Judgment proposes a course of action, it does not record a listening-in; and the careful feeling over of one's opinions in the quest for standards, in missing that point, is pretty well guaranteed to end in a conventional response or in confusion. So that once again a model projected from other domains for the interpretation of artistically relevant bearing fails through neglecting the productive or constructive aspects of criticism.

3. Consider now for one last time the inductive-empirical model of artistically relevant justification, even though it should be apparent by now that that model cannot work any better than the deductive one.

Though neither empirical science nor artistically relevant criticism ascribes conclusive relationships between ground and conclusion, nevertheless it does not follow that science and criticism must *both* assert inconclusive relations as though the only alternative to rejecting the deductive model was to accept the inductive-empirical one. For in artistically relevant criticism we do *not* try to ascribe a probability to a judgment relative to a certain ground. *Any* probability is always a probability *that* a certain event or set of events will occur. Such criticism rather considers the evidence *for* introducing one state of affairs or another. Hence, while the "inconclusiveness" of inductive reasoning amounts to ascribing a probability, the inconclusiveness of artistically relevant reasoning amounts to this: that it is always *open* to us to deal with sets of considerations in different ways, so long as one remains within the guiding rules of the artistically relevant controversy.

But the incongruity of the inductive-empirical model becomes most manifest if one should try to raise the question of the probability of an artistically relevant judgment. What's the probability of "Suppose we construe a critical object in such and such a manner!"? The question's absurd. Only propositions have probabilities, hence sustain inductive evidence. As for artistically relevant judgments, those are "probable" only in the sense that someone might pass judgment upon the likelihood of their being made—which hardly constitutes a good reason *for* the judgment. Therefore, empirical or "naturalistic" interpretations of the evidence *for* an artistically relevant judgment (such as those implicit in the effort to make a "science" of criticism, replete with generalization, prediction, experiment, and deduction) systematically miss the point. What they "prove," however "tentatively," has nothing to do with what they need to justify.

Underlying the nest of confusions generated by the inductive-empirical model is the normal version blindness to the fact that criticism decides rather than simply records. Indeed, the skeptical position that either denies reasoning in the art or finds it congenitally weak—or, for that matter, the optimistic view that looks to remedy that weakness in the future—rests equally for all three models upon a wrong expectation of the nature of artistically relevant reasoning: that one ought, somehow, for the sake of rationality, superimpose one of the familiar models upon a reasoning that occurs "in a context of production."

Chapter 12

Reason in the Arts: A Concluding Portrait

Having fixed the kind of thing people do when they reason in an artistically relevant way from ground to judgment, having seen the considerations appropriate to that reasoning and the issues and situations encountered by the reasoner, and also having examined what went wrong with the traditional ways of construing the logic of reasons, we seek now at the end a glimpse of the kind of rationality to which a proper judge of the arts might properly aspire "within a context of production." At the very edge of the inquiry, in order to formulate the terms under which, if the discussion amounts to very much, further and specific inquiries into the logic of the arts must be conducted, the problem becomes one of presenting a last portrait of reason in the arts that is recognizable, and different from the normal version's, in this: that it will exhibit the particular rationality of the arts as just itself and nothing else, neither absolutely unique and unintelligible nor entirely equivalent to the conduct of reason in other domains if only one reduced and translated hard enough.

I. Reason as Creative

It has been recognized for a long time that an alternative exists for justifying judgments in the arts, or, for that matter, elsewhere, other than by deducing those judgments from principles, providing inductive evidence for them, searching them out in our presuppositions, or weighing their advantages against their disadvantages. Ever since Hegel, critics and philosophers of a certain type have felt that the development of the arts, like the development of history in general, exhibited a special connexity that at any stage rendered them intelligible and justifiable. If the Platonic dialogue exhibited reason in process (a process in which every position was forced to yield its own "contradiction," every negation moved the argument further to a new synthesis which at once included and transcended whatever might be "rational" in the proposal it negated), so did the progress of the arts. There would be a special "logic" to the arts, therefore, as there would be a special "logic" to history in general, which the "static" logic of a merely analytical philosophy would miss. Novelty would arise "of necessity," "spontaneity" would enter human affairs, and reason would become not merely critical but "creative."

In this section I want to speak of the Hegel-like characteristics of a model of justification appropriate to the arts in their development without assuming either that everything is related to everything else—the absolute unity of the story, so to speak—or that any antithesis exists between a "merely" formal and a dynamic logic. For reasons which will become clear I shall call that model a "creative model." A practice exhibits a "creative rationality" or manifests a "creative reason" as it is organized to employ a "creative model" or employs it. The distinctive features of the creative reason in the practice of the arts are, of course, "Hegel-like" characteristics:

1. First comes what is in effect a class of such characteristics. Reasoning in matters of art, if I am correct about the artistically relevant controversy, does indeed exhibit a general rhythm and development not entirely unlike that which Hegel in his famous metaphors ascribed to history. Such reasoning is properly called "creative," and its model of justification the "creative model," in virtue of the expansive and finessing movement of artistically relevant controversy built into that controversy. Showing what follows from some decision entails showing a moving pattern of relations within a matrix of art and of society in process of transformation. Clashing opinions (where the argument is serious, rather than where the critic's peculiar cranks and specialities are at issue) tend themselves to be reconstituted not because of the critic's personal predilection for change but because that is the name of the game, that is how one comes one-up. Controversy visibly acts, in fact, rather with the cunning of Hegel's history, making of differences of opinion, differences in perception, differences in relevant publics, the ground and opportunity for further development, sources of the motion. Tradition and media constitute neither rules to dictate judgment and action nor affairs to be dealt with according to a private taste, but opportunities precisely in that they are what they are. Critics and artists reason and judge "creatively"—which is to say, not mysteriously, through some higher power, but through the nature of the practice, to the best of their abilities.

Accordingly, the regulative principles in virtue of which a critic may lay claim to victory or an artist to achievement assign a role to distinctiveness. "Novelty"—as has been noted—does matter. "Brilliance," "originality," "resourcefulness," "imaginativeness" are prima facie values either of the critic's argument or of the created object. So if to do something new is at least one mark of creativity, that is a further reason to speak of the "creative model" for justification in the arts and of the arts as exhibiting a "creative rationality." The ideal of unicity builds a demand for novelty into the process of criticism itself. If the ideal is frustrated, then it is said that the critical object, whether created object or criticism, is "of no importance."

2. Next, the logic of the artistically relevant controversy, conceived in relationship to an on-going practice, binds the parties thereto to seek at least part of their justification for any judgment in the future course of controversy, either their own or in controversies to come in the relevant art. Not that the parties to the controversy aim to say merely, "I told you so. Now that we've had it out you will agree with me," or "Wait and see. Others will agree with me." There is a Hegel-like point involved. The reason for the reference to the future is, again, the name of the game. The disputants do not appeal to the future because they are so very clever no one yet can understand them, though they may think this is why. It is rather that subsequent decisions in the enterprise of critic or of artist, decisions distinctly not deducible from other decisions, being indeed decisions, constitute the environment in which the justification of an artistically relevant judgment occurs. Act III justifies Act I; but Act III is not yet written. That is what justification is like. The creative model for justification is, I shall say, "forward-oriented." Specifically:

A. Given a difference over a construction judgment, justification is forward-oriented but not only because the evolution of the discussion will in fact substantiate or reconstruct that judgment. Justification is forward-oriented because the matrices of art and society continually receive new material, which itself makes a difference in the grasp of present and past materials and changes justification. Justification *must* be forward-oriented if critical objects are to be taken "in relation" rather than as "in themselves," and if art is acknowledged not to have stopped dead.

B. Given a difference over a merit judgment, decisions yet to be made may lead me to change my mind or understand very differently my judgment; but, more generally, it is the movement of the arts that makes judgments apropos and gives them their force. I must be prepared to find my merit judgments flat, stale, and unprofitable not on account of any inevitable defect in taste or perceptivity on my part but because art has changed.

C. Given a difference over whether one judgment bears upon another, where and how, once again, decision stands to be mediated by decisions not yet made. Decision is forward-oriented both through the generation of novel critical objects sustaining unexpected relationships among their parts and through the incessant evolution of the general argument over formative rules.

There follows what artists and critics have always, more or less, considered and accepted as the basic condition of their enterprise: the risk of creation, openness, vulnerability. It is never left to anyone completely to determine the situation in which his choice, his insight, his delicacy will have its meaning. Of justification let no man speak, except in the degree that a doubt has been raised and on some proper occasion it is necessary to get on with the job; and this holds for the give and take of specific argument as well as for the broad history-making processes of artistic production.

How, then, given the "forward orientation" of the model of creative reason, can one ever decide what to do? Partly, decision occurs because the forward orientation of the model makes presumptions appropriate concerning the *conditions* of artistic and critical activity in the environment for which those activities may hope to be justified. So the judgment that an artist or a critic shows in his work scant idea of where the arts are going and of the movement of society—of the "conditions" of his enterprise's justification—is a relevant judgment in a creative model of justification. So critics are properly praised for "prescience." (Presumptions concerning conditions, of course, are, or ought to be, justified in an inductive model. In a creative model, the inductive model is *used*—"creatively," of course.)

At least as important, however, is this: having made the best estimate available concerning "conditions" in the next step (or steps) ahead, one can decide what to do in a forward-oriented enterprise by eschewing a justification which is the work of others to provide. It is not merely tolerable that all actions and judgments, even the best of them, be superseded or "*aufgehoben*," as though it were a sad limitation on human powers one just had to accept. Given participation in a wider human enterprise, it is *desirable*. Art is the domain in which the career of discussion and/or creation forces the undoing or tranformation of decisions that had seemed so *right* earlier. For the "good and responsible" critic, decisions are there in order to be undone, redone, recast, forgotten. Art is not like poker, in which each hand's winnings are won. It is not like games of chance generally in which the chances of successive tries are unaffected by winnings or losings. It is not even like the scientific enterprise, which later on I shall discuss further, in which, while indeed matters may be reopened, one applies a method or methods whose justification is that they tend in the long run to avoid reopenings.

So an irrevocable gamble defines the rationality of art and criticism, their "model." "The judgment of posterity" acknowledges that forward-orientation; the trouble is that nobody knows what the judgment will be for *present* works. And nobody knows not only because nobody knows what future generations will *say* but because, more deeply, nobody knows their art, the gambles they will choose to make.

3. Aside from a hazard as to "conditioning," we merely know that some of the gambles future generations may choose to make will in part be determined by our own. The other side of the coin of dependence of present judgment on future vindication is the dependence of future vindication upon present judgment. In the creative model of justification, justification is "participant-oriented." For to the extent that new works of art are introduced into the repertoire of the arts or new critical judgments enter and become part of the critical tradition, they warp the environment that determines their justification, or reinforce it.

A. Some works, having made their way into the matrix of art, dictate in some part, through the nature of their presence in that matrix, some of the very terms on which they are judged. Concretely: if Picasso had not painted no one can tell for sure what painting would be like today. Perhaps it would not be very different. But painting as he did, Picasso helped make modern painting; and modern painting constitutes a fundamental portion of that matrix of art in terms of which relevant and important valuations are placed upon Picasso's pictures. If not Picasso, someone else. If not someone else in particular, then a class of painters each of whom contributed to the art-making effect as a member of that class.

Consider the famous Case of the Speluncean Explorers. Why should judges hold it against the Case that the Case never occurred? They think the Case lacks legal significance not merely because, as a brute fact, it never occurred, but because cases that do not occur do not shape the law. Cases that do in fact not shape the law are at best interesting. "Shaping the law" need not necessarily mean changing it. "Shaping the law" might mean reinforcing it. Cases that neither change nor reinforce the law lack legal significance. So with works of art. "Derivative works" are works that neither change nor shape the field of art within which they are finally judged. So are "trivial" works. They are, artistically, gratuitous. Obviously, "derivativeness" and "triviality" are matters of degree, as are their opposites.

"Creative genius" is the capacity, or good luck, to produce participating works. Artists are *expected* to have "creative genius." But I do not mean to say that the extent of the participation of a work of art and its producer on a judgment-relevant environment uniquely determines their value. An important work might be repudiated or trivialized within the future it helped generate. Such is the irony of history. And surely there are other considerations besides artistic importance, in the evaluation of works of art. But consider even the sudden uncovering of a "great" work of art, or the bringing to the light of publicity of an unrecognized "genius." For very good reasons such cases are probably more rare than people imagine. But regardless of the odds against them, their "greatness," the "genius" they exhibit, would partly be determined—and hence, a hazard, a hope, and a guess only "posterity" could justify (not confirm)—by their capacity to *make* a difference. Barring that capacity they become, precisely, gratuitous. If the difference were merely for what is considered artistic now, if these "great" works were not standing-points, bench-marks for "art" in general, then once again their whole status would be undermined.

Of course, in a context of consumption the model of justification is not participant-oriented. How should it be, if the critical object is the work of art itself? But in a context of production, where the critical object is the work in proper relation, there is a premium on creativity. Creativity is subtle, measured in the nature of the ripple produced in the stream of art. It is important to emphasize that the phrase is "stream of *art.*"

B. But even if created works of art were vindicated far less significantly than I think they are by their participation in the matrix of art, it is plain that the justification of a judgment as such entails the participation of that judgment in the controversy. Positions taken in the course of any controversy shape the line of controversy that either upholds or discards them. But it is not merely that the end of the argument, if all goes well, settles those positions as a matter of fact. The course of the argument takes the shape it does, reaches the conclusion it does in which the position is upheld or discarded, or, perhaps, included and reinterpreted, *because* of that position—just as in a chess game a given move generates the position in which that move turns out to be wise or not. Judgments contribute to the logical environment that evaluates them, as do works of art to the matrix of art in which they exist. For, and this is the essential point, judgments express decisions; and future decisions, which would never be what they were unless those early decisions were taken, sustain or inhibit those that have been taken. So judgments *in* a controversy participate in their own justification, with all the consequences that Hegel has imaginatively projected for historical events, and which are visible in the history of critical traditions. So criticism, like art, is in part evaluated by its influence, its centrality, its peripherality, and the like.

4. Reason in the arts is intrinsically a competition. It is a consequence of the other characterizations. I do not mean, of course, that there is only competition in art and criticism or that we love the arts for the possibility of getting one-up on the other fellow, although there are people who do. Rather, the model of justification in matters of art, the "creative" model, justifies any decision in a manner resembling, at least, the manner in which decisions in a game like chess, or, perhaps better, poker, involving a number of players, is justified—that is, with respect to the decisions others make. So justification is not only forward-oriented and participant-oriented—it is also "conflict-grounded." Justification of a decision includes doing better than an opponent, whose prior decision sets the problem. The conflict of views provides the grounds for the development of criticism not only in an external sense, as though a critical point should be asserted in order to exhibit superiority over a competitive critic, but in an internal sense, in that the occasion for criticism arises at least in part through the conflict of critical traditions and the emergence of unfamiliar works of art in the evolving matrices of art and society. Similarly, decisions in the creative arts are justified—to imagine them isolated from the first sort for a moment—in apprehension of decisions other artists have made and may be expected to make. Defense and riposte is the "logic" of creation.

I am not asserting, then, merely something about the artistically relevant controversy *as such,* not in a context of production. Obviously, controversy is conflict-grounded. Im asserting something about the processes of art and criticism in which the controversy occurs: namely, to understand why and in what sense the enterprise of art and criticism may be said to be creative, to know what the artistically relevant controversy is *for,* one must consider the proposition that conflict conducted according to the rules of the controversy provides the dynamus of reconstruction and reconstitution in criticism and the arts. In a context of consumption, it would not be so. Competition, conflict, would provide perhaps a motive, but success (justification) in the competition would be secured by meeting the standard of the consumer. In the context of production, justification is relative to the achievement of other participants in the production. So the regulative principles of the artistically relevant controversy are not merely principles for winning an argument; they are the principles for the progress of art, if the positions that are adopted and fought for are indeed, as I have suggested, statable as instruction sets for the doing of art. And, of course, they provide for that progress through the organization of conflict. Hegel's theory of rationality is a way of talking about the characteristics of practices that are conflict-grounded.

Such, then, are my Hegel-like characteristics for the conduct of reasoning in the arts and criticism. The creative model for justification exhibits in its functioning an expansive and (for any controversy) progressive character; it is future- and participant-oriented and conflict-grounded. If characteristics such as these seem more like limits to rationality than characteristics of another mode of justification, the reason is an implicit preference for another game with the same (artistic) counters. If the end of the activity of art is its refined consumption, *then* indeed one wants to know if the activity achieves its end, and establishing that it does or not at any point is criticism. The Hegel-like characteristics of future-orientation and participant-orientation have upset the predictive apple cart. If on the other hand the enterprise of art generates its own effective ends and if the artistically relevant controversy concerns the doing or making of art, then the characteristics of a creative model of justification seem precisely the ones that one would want. Future-orientation marks the very business of production, competition its *source.* And if there is no possibility of participation in the future's assessments, merely in the landscape of objects that the future contemplates, then it's a mug's game.

II. The Exercise of Judgment

What is reasoning like in matters of art, in so far as it is reasoning and requires justification? Hegel takes us just so far in a survey of the distinguishing characteristics of the creative model. Whatever rationalistic philosophers may say about the nature of rationality, justification in criticism and art seems to a plain man to be, in unusually high degree, a "matter of judgment," and controversy important for settling disputes in judgment or else not important at all. And not only the "plain man." "Criticism is judgment," says John Dewey, "ideally as well as etymologically." [1] And though perhaps he overstates the case—is everything indeed in criticism and art always a matter of judgment?—an account of a "creative model" for reasoning in the arts will be successful only in so far as it can provide for the exercise of judgment. For the prevalence of

[1] *Art as Experience* (New York: Minton, Balch, 1934), p. 298.

judgment in the arts does not mean that in the arts one cannot go wrong, that the artistically relevant controversy is after all at crucial points a matter of taste, not if the exercise of judgment is important, as everyone alleges it to be. The "judgment" that people call upon is precisely that in which one can all too easily go wrong, which is why it is required and demanded of proper judges. What sort of reasoning justifies such "judgment"?

The first thought, of course, is of the weighing model. In crucial matters, it will be said, the so-called creative model reduces to the weighing model, despite the talk of a drive toward the optimum in criticism and creation. I have myself admitted on an earlier occasion that the critic "weighs the relation of lines to color, of one character to another." [2] So the drive built into the artistically relevant controversy to go for broke presupposes the weighing model to say what it means to go for broke.

Yet, surely, there is more than one sense of "weigh." Sometimes one considers the effect of different factors back and forth and is quite properly said to "weigh" the situation in which those factors occur, without necessarily considering those factors against one another. It is true that weighing the various factors in a situation may end in a variety of alternative relationships for those factors, and that an artist or critic may have to choose appropriately in the exercise of his judgment between those alternatives. Sometimes one cannot have it both ways or include and transform the alternatives constructed, and some of those times may call for the exercise of judgment. But even when the exercise of judgment is called for, it does not follow that the ordering of alternatives on a utility scale justifies the choice. For surely it would be utterly inappropriate to ask a man who presents his judgment to *prove* that judgment correct, as it would not be inappropriate if the weighing model were appropriate in the justification of his judgment or, indeed any of the other rejected models for justification. Indeed, ordering preferences itself requires judgment, while if a man set up his preference scale so that he *could* calculate his judgment he would have no call to exercise his judgment. The choice among judgments, if the choice is a matter of judgment, is no more economic than any other judgment. "The critic," writes Dewey, putting the difficulty of the weighing model for the exercise of judgment in different but suggestive terms, "is really judging, not measuring physical fact. He is concerned with something individual, not comparative—as is all measurement." [3]

[2] See above, p. 181.
[3] *Art as Experience,* p. 307.

No doubt judgment may be exercised even in the measurement of physical facts and no doubt the concepts of measurement are extensible beyond "physical fact." Nevertheless, it is also clear that the critic is not concerned to lay off standards, even if the laying off occurs in terms of a series of "preferences," not when he is called to exercise judgment. That is when he is *not* called upon to exercise judgment, even when he exercises judgment in the laying off of a standard. "He is concerned with something individual, not comparative." Does it follow therefore that judgment in the arts, or anywhere else for that matter, indicates the impossibility of justification even though the exercise of judgment, and not of opinion, is called for? That was Kant's problem, as it is ours. "If," Dewey writes, "there are no standards for works of art and hence none for criticism (in the sense in which there are standards of measurement) there are nevertheless criteria in judgment so that criticism does not fall in the field of mere impressionism." [4]

That, in very general outline, states the line according to which one would locate judgment in a creative model of justification. There are criteria. Only, the present account does not locate the logical force of those criteria in "the discussion of form in relation to matter, . . . of the meaning of the medium in art, of the nature of the expressive object" as "the result of an endeavor to find out what a work of art is as an experience." [5] Had Dewey faced more squarely the problem of what happens when "perceptive" and "informed" people disagree, he would never have stated quite so baldly that "criteria are not rules or prescriptions." [6] If criteria could not be formulated in terms of certain kinds of rules, rules I have spoken of as the "regulative principles" of the artistically relevant controversy, how could differences in judgment ever be resolved? It is the normal version that has him seeking to distinguish in the experience of the work of art the value of the judgments made upon the work.

What, then, would recommend the acceptance of a judgment as the product of the exercise of judgment? Everybody knows: reason to think, subject to the rules of the controversy, that in fact a judgment was more or less sensitive, imaginative, inclusive, informed, and the like. For those are the "criteria" that one applies to judgment; and those are the "criteria" that the entire procedure of artistically relevant controversy outlined through this book are concerned to apply. Hence there is no need of authoritative preferences. They come *after* judgment. There are no fixed

[4] *Ibid.*, p. 309.
[5] *Ibid.*
[6] *Ibid.*

situations; there are the possibilities for an action. We need, in so far as we are required to exercise our judgment, to rework our preferences, to rework the situation. Judgment in the arts is "creative." So Dewey writes in some familiar lines:

> Inquiry is the controlled or directed transformation of an indeterminate situation into one that is so determinate in its constituent distinctions and relations as to convert the elements of the original situation into a unified whole.[7] . . . Indeterminate situations [are] disturbed, troubled, ambiguous, confused, full of conflicting tendencies, etc.[8] . . . This emphasis, upon requalification of antecedent existential materials, and upon judgment as the resulting transformation, stands in sharp contrast with traditional theory.[9]

Putting aside Dewey's general epistemological thesis and leaving the sense in which cognition demands the "requalification of antecedent existential materials," one sees that Dewey has stated a fairly adequate description of judgment in a context of production and of how judgment justifies itself. Judgment transforms a situation: that is the logical force of artistically relevant construction and merit judgments as they have been discussed here. Even upon a distinction between proposing those judgments and putting them into effect, at least the exercise of judgment involves a "transformation of an indeterminate situation" for the judge in the judging situation—which is, of course, the "proper occasion" of the earlier discussion.

How does this happen? How do the "criteria" of judgment work? The essential thing is to see that the criticism of the weighing model did not imply that, in questions that are matters of judgment, and hence terribly important, requiring judgment, a man has nothing to work with but his vision and imagination. Vision and imagination, the stroke of genius, of "creativity," may enter into the arguments of critics in their wild robin of attack and defense. But one of the things that a notion of judgment properly connotes to most people is the presence of a good deal to work with; and in matters of judgment in the arts a critic has a good deal indeed to work with: namely, the whole structure of principles, rules, precedents, traditions, in the use of which, through which, and for which, he exercises his "judgment."

1. First, the criteria for the exercise of judgment work because the critic has the regulative principles of the artistically relevant controversy

[7] John Dewey, *Logic: The Theory of Inquiry* (New York: Holt, 1938), pp. 104–05.
[8] *Ibid.*, p. 105.
[9] *Ibid.*, p. 159.

to direct him: to the work of art in proper relation, to the created object, to the practice of the arts, and so on. Regulative rules focus the specific opportunities for the exercise of judgment. Consider, for example, the rule of respect. That rule was so stated that a "minimum weight" must be given each of the various policies of respect. Weight meant, of course, not a place on a preference scale but a role in the construction process. With a minimum weight, though a policy went unfollowed, it would not go ignored, unconsidered, and hence might be considered "respected." But (to return to the "weight" metaphor) what weights are "minimal," what weights are to be accorded to any policy in any critical strategy in some specific "problematic situation"? The problem has been set up, precisely, for "judgment." Judgment, following the rule of respect, knows its mission; and it knows to take into consideration the policies of respect, which work now for the exercise of judgment as "tools" used in relation to one another, as "instruments" of criticism.

In all these ways, then, regulative principles make possible an exercise of judgment subject to "criteria," subject, therefore, as I should like to say, to a "creative model" of justification: by "directing," "focusing," showing what is to be "considered," offering a "mission," presenting "tools." A justification of the exercise of judgment includes, therefore, showing that the critic in his judgment knows how to do criticism in specific ways.

2. Next, the exercise of judgment is possible and the criteria of judgment apply because the problems judgment may be called upon to resolve are public affairs in the domain of criticism. Unless a critic could establish his problem as such a public affair, he would not be said to be called upon to exercise judgment—and it is always possible in evaluating a critic's judgment to ask whether or not, and to what extent, he succeeds in objectifying his problem. His success is a mark of "judgment," his failure an absence of judgment.

Moreover, the "unique doubtfulness which makes the situation to be just and only the situation it is," [10] as Dewey puts the "problem," is fixed in a public domain by the intersections of the matrices of art, society, and the critical tradition or traditions at some single point. So judgment is also justified by the way it handles that "unique doubtfulness." For any exercise of judgment, judgment depends upon knowledge: knowledge of art, society, and critical traditions, which are not, at least for judgment when it comes to be exercised, problems in the exercise of judgment.

So artistically relevant controversies, even when at fever heat over matters of judgment, may presuppose assertions justified by inductive

[10] *Ibid.*, p. 105.

evidence and logical analysis of beliefs and rules. More generally still: the exercise of judgment in matters of art implies the presence of considera-tion not matters of judgment at all, or the justification of the exercise of judgment is impossible.

3. Next, it is possible to talk about the exercise of judgment because the *controversy* over judgment, when pressed, turns into artisti-cally relevant *controversies* that are not primarily over the exercise of judgment. Dewey was wrong in stating that "criticism is judgment," though I do not question the centrality of judgment in artistically relevant controversy—which is to say, the drive of that controversy, under the Ideal of Unicity, finally to reach disputes that are disputes over judgment.

Forcing the construction argument, pushing differences in the exercise of judgment, leads, as was shown in some length,[11] to a variety of arguments concerning the policy of criticism—arguments over formative rules—and arguments, indeed, of a political, moral, religious, and philo-sophical nature. It is not supposed that, in a model of "creative" justifica-tion, these are irrelevant. Their conclusions provide the terms in virtue of which judgment may work, further "tools of judgment." But their con-duct requires not only the feedback of judgment but also the dialectical, deductive, inductive, or weighing procedures that are pertinent. They enable a creative model for justification that invokes them, to call upon further ways in which a man may be disputed in the exercise of his judgment.

Concretely: "You think so and so's judgment good in questions that in the arts are a matter of judgment? Consider his choice of formative rules, how he uses the rule of respect. Consider his judgment of politics, etc. His judgment is narrow, biased, dishonest, superficial, . . . etc."

As to that judgment on judgment, it is itself subject to the kinds of requirements that can be formulated for the exercise of judgment in general.

4. Given, then, an exercise of judgment provided with tools, proper occasions, knowledge, and an opportunity to transform itself into some-thing more than an exercise of judgment when linked to broader aspects of the artistically relevant controversy, the peculiarly "creative" aspects of the creative model—the aspects of reasoning in the arts *not* subsumable under the four traditional models—now become intelligible. Judgment proposes resolutions of problems and, indeed, the reorganization and reconstitution of problems. In virtue of the resources I have mentioned, it

[11] See Chapter 4 in entirety. Differences over the exercise of judgment are dealt with there as performative arguments.

produces instruction sets that hold so long as a competitor can do no better (since art and criticism settle for nothing less than the best). What is indeed "better," under the constraints that make judgment possible, depends upon the progress of the argument. To take that fact into account, a creative model is said to be forward- and participant-oriented within the regulative principles of the artistically relevant controversy. So the final principle of the creative model of justification is "Top that if you can," in a moving argument that generates its own "ends-in-view." Maybe somebody will. Maybe the future will suborn the very terms of the problem in which the judgment operated. The exercise of judgment is vulnerable; in a context of production the whole point is to have it so.

III. The Distinctions among Practices

In this final effort to distinguish rationality in matters of art through a creative model of justification, it is perhaps of some importance to see how reasoning in those matters compares with reasoning in practices other than that conjoint practice of art and criticism that has been the prime subject of this book. For I am far from saying that the various elements that constitute a creative model of justification in matters of the arts are unique to the arts, even though the exercise of judgment undoubtedly holds a special place there and even though one lacks in the arts, and would not even want in the arts, analogues to the handbooks of engineering and statutes that distinguish some other practices.

The similarities in the logic of justification in art to the logic of justification in law, science, and, briefly, the affairs of "life" in general, will show that the "creativity" encountered at the heart of the artistic enterprise calls for no ineffable insight peculiar to the arts. The differences that distinguish justification in matters of the arts from justification in matters of law, science, and my grab-bag, "life in general," will help check excessive expectations not because those expectations are too grand but because they are inappropriate.

1. Consider, then, for one last time, the old paradigm of the law. The myths of a mechanical jurisprudence put aside, it is evident that a "creative model" of justification sustains judgment in the law in ways very much like those in which such a model sustains judgment in matters of art. Much has already been discussed of the similarities in the structure of controversy in law and art. Yet it is fitting now to point out explicitly that, more clearly even than in the arts, the justification of decisions in the law is future- and participant-oriented and conflict-grounded. Future-

oriented as justification in the law is, judgment undertakes the creative risk, which is to be superseded or transformed. When it is participant-oriented, judgment generates the conditions for its justification; when conflict-oriented, decision is delayed until provoked by a conflict of parties. So law is "creative," and legal action amounts in many ways, as we are always being assured, to an "art" rather than a science. Like art, law constitutes a self-generating enterprise linked to the matrix of society within which it functions.

In the light of so many previous analogies, however, of greater significance now are the differences between the characteristics of law and of art as rational practices. For in the nature of the practice, indeterminacy and relativity constitute in the law more of a headache than an opportunity, while the values of novelty and uniqueness are not sought after but minimized. Such differences are expressed by the tendency of judges to pull back at the thought of a "creative" role. A judge is a judge, after all, only if he seeks to reach his decisions "according to the law."

The requirement, essential to the very social function of the judge, that he *choose between* in giving judgment, that he "weigh," that he seek to "adjust" interests against interest (e.g., security vs. freedom in security cases) makes it hard for him to find in indeterminacy and openness any opportunity at all, in the manner of critics and artists. His is the economic problem, directly. He can never leave it at that, given a legal conflict, that certain tendencies in the law support such and such a judgment and other tendencies another, not when they impose empirically incompatible ways of satisfying claims. Catholicity of legal taste is the last thing anyone requires of him; nor can he choose to make one decision today in one case and another tomorrow as might an artist, in a like situation, who sought to exploit his opportunities. Faced by a condition in which no obvious way mediates between conflicting traditions and claims, he at least may not seek some overarching hypothesis that will explicate the legitimacy of *both* dissident positions. His very role is to decide *between.* Coherent though they may be, his theories are theories justifying the sacrifice of interests.

"Practical" though the rationales of legal and of artistically relevant controversy may both of them be, both equally concerned to transform, not to map some part of the world—it is time to underline what there was never any wish to deny: the law is "practical" in at least one way in which the arts are not. In one pre-eminent use of "practical," those activities are called such which face the problem of choice between, and those which do not are called by some other name. Further, judges are rarely happy at having the novelty of their way of handling a legally relevant occasion pointed out, as artists and critics are. If predictability be a virtue of legal decision, decision must be continuous with precedent. Decisions must enjoy the force of precedent in a stronger way than artistically relevant decisions, which establish in the arts only ways of handling materials to be taken into account. But previous decisions, the judge's and those of other courts, do not function merely as materials with which to build; in some measure they dictate. In art there is no possibility of *stare decisis.* Art is not constrained.

It is, then, finally, the nature of the social organization of the arts and of the law that differ and make all the difference; it is the structure of that organization that finally fixes proper and improper expectation. The organizations of art are "creative" associations, in which membership is free. Members are autonomous, in Kant's sense, in that they give themselves the law. Only he who enters the association is the proper recipient of its judgments. Only those who are members—participants in its enterprises—form relevant publics. But in the law neither is membership voluntary nor are all individuals qualified as proper judges on the mere provision that they possess the requisite knowledge and sensibility. Certainly, they are not autonomous, nor is the proper recipient of judgment a participant in the building of the law as his judge is.

For reasons such as these, then, the searchers for "standards," "authority," systems of weights and measures search in matters of art for the wrong thing. Given the organization of the arts as described, the arts *must* encourage the heterodoxy that at the same time it *uses* to introduce new orthodoxies and concurrences, as the organizations of the law do not and cannot. Movement lies implanted at the heart of the practice of the arts; resistance, yet a wise and discriminating resistance, lies at the heart of the organization of the practice of law.

2. Movement, although not quite the same kind of movement as in either law or in art, lies also at the center of the rationality of the sciences; and the adjective "creative" seems to apply to aspects of the scientific practice with almost the same ease that it does to the artistic and with greater ease than it does to the legal. For to juxtapose in an all too common manner the "creativity" of the arts to the "intellectuality" and "abstractness" of the sciences merely compares the product of the sciences with the process of the arts. But the task is to compare the processes in so far as they are rule-bound.

Comparing *processes,* one cannot miss the tendency of the sciences to seek more inclusive schema for the explanation of divergent phenomena (divergent, that is, within extant schema) and even, when schema seem at once incompatible and desirable, to accept both. Further, there is in the sciences a sense in which novelty and uniqueness increase the value of experiments and hypotheses. For, again, as in the arts, such characteristics open avenues for exploration, possibilities as yet unimagined. In distinguishing the reason or rationality of the arts as "creative" I have not wanted to deny the appropriateness of the term "creative" as applied to the sciences.

Indeed, at their highest development even the empirical sciences acknowledge a kind of principle of perfection unattainable to the judge in his need to meet practical contingencies and "choose between." Legal decisions are makeshift affairs by comparison, driven by the need to patch up and get along, less responsive by far to the possibilities of the materials for internal organization. Theories *are* like works of art, in their free construction and precision, in their unconstrained pursuit of unity in variety. No prior necessity holds them down, no ulterior motives, no social pressures. Empirical laws become rather like materials to be organized in certain ways, given the state of the "matrix of science," if I may call it that. All in all, therefore, it seems that the freedom of science resembles far more the freedom of art rather than the constraint of the law, despite the scientific ideal of "truth." For whatever the final construction placed upon "truth," which statements are considered "true" follows from the scientist's productive activity. Obviously, the creative rationality attributed to the arts is by no means absolutely unique.

From a general point of view, however, the basic difference between the rule-bound processes of science and of the arts is that the process of justification in the arts generates its own world, while, with qualification that it would take us too far afield to discuss, the process of justification in the scientific enterprise does not. One does not expect that the progress of science will render *any* proposition true or *any* proposition false, whatever may be said about the "truth" or "falsity" of scientific theories. But one indeed expects that the correctness or adequacy of all true artistically relevant judgments may be suborned, on an appropriate turn in the arts. Hence few people in matters of art would be tempted to justify the logic of justification in the arts as Peirce was tempted to justify the methods of science by the convergence of decisions in the scientific controversy upon one decision. At least there seems something odd in yielding to the temptation in the first place, but nothing odd about yielding to it in the second, even though the temptation there might lead one astray. One expects there will be many criticisms in the arts, however much in moments of fervor one may deplore it. But we follow where the arts lead. And who knows where the arts may lead? There are no handbooks, as I have said. A handbook would block the way of the perpetually self-renewing processes of artistic justification as the accumulation of knowledge does not block the way of the method of scientific inquiry, but facilitates it.

Accordingly, I shall chance some last observations on the topics of (A) universality in criticism, (B) certainty or weight of evidence in criticism, and (C) the possibility of a "science" in or of the arts.

A. On more than one occasion the question of the scope of judgment in artistically relevant controversy has arisen. I want to underline now the illegitimacy of the discontent sometimes expressed on this score, comparing the arts and the sciences. For while the assertions of scientific inquiry claim the consent of anyone capable of using the methods of science (as their relevant public) and require the acknowledgment, without impropriety, of all whose activities in some way presuppose those assertions, no analogous claim holds for judgment in the practice of the arts. No analogous requirement can be properly imposed.

The reason lies in the difference in the organization of the two sorts of practice. In the sciences, for any proper judge, no question in principle exists concerning the nature of his relevant public or of the proper recipients of his judgments. But in the arts, the proper judge, whether artist or critic, far from starting with relevant public or recipient predetermined, in the course of his activity makes his public. That, partly, is why people say of "creative" artists that they have created, or must create, their "audiences." Only in the doing of the arts do we *discover* in more than an accidental way to whom we are speaking and whose energies and insights pool with our own to reach a common end. One *gambles* on one's public; artistic judgment is forward-oriented. Accordingly, the customary academic appeal to posterity, though repugnant when presented as a justification for a taste or preference, has a certain point construed to refer to the openness of the artistically relevant process.

Put the matter this way, then: justification in the arts holds quite independently of the justification's scope, nor ought this upset anyone because the prospect in the sciences seems like madness. Even should artistically relevant judgments come eventually to win universal acceptance—anything is possible, in time—that universal acceptance would in the logic of the arts constitute no stronger a grant of right than a more partial acceptance. For the proper scope of critical opinion is, in the organization of the enterprise of the arts, *supposed* to be contingent upon the state of the arts and of society.

Hence a maximum concession to universality as a determining rule in the practice of the arts will be the one already made: that in the process of the artistically relevant controversy there are cohesive tendencies that make for the integration of disagreements within a "higher level" agreement, of smaller publics within larger publics. But there is no requirement of success for the process of universalization that says it must be complete, or stop at one point rather than another.

B. Granted, then, a plurality of relevant publics and proper recipients in the arts, another sort of skepticism may arise, again based on "science." One may become skeptical of reason in art because, allegedly, artistically relevant criticism has nothing approaching the *certainty* of scientific experimentation.

The skepticism is hasty. For, once the inappropriateness of the ideal of universality has been grasped, it turns out that reason in artistically relevant criticism has as much a claim to "certainty" as does reason in the sciences. To be sure, neither in science nor in art does one know whether some future will vindicate one's claim (whatever the different sense of "vindicate"). But in both science and art, provided one selects to begin with some specific context, in that context certainty, as resolution of doubt, stands equally within reach, whatever the practical difficulties. The logic of the artistically relevant controversy discussed throughout this book reaches quite definite decisions—for all its openness to an "ultimate" rejection, or "ultimate" superannuation, by the course of art. Decisions in the arts may seem vague and indecisive in contrast to the sciences, where, in imagination, decisions always seem sharp and decisive; in truth, however, any inspection of actual decision-making in the doing of the arts turns the picture around one hundred and eighty degrees. And most people, on reflection, acknowledge as much.

For even those who apply the normal version still insist on the integrity, the "rightness," of "the work of art itself." Despair though they may of "really" good reasons for justifying decisions over "esthetic objects" they will not therefore refuse the necessity of a perfect articulation of parts, of the irrelevance of everything that is not "there" and the relevance of everything that is, in the "successful" work of art. Does not that very acceptance proclaim that the artist whose successive decisions articulated and defined his object did so on grounds that, finally, whether he knows those grounds or not, are the very reverse of vague and uncertain? The normal version has simply created a "problem" in rationality by incorporating the decision procedure within "the work of art itself" and then asking how opinions on that queer object might possibly be justified. It has not therefore resisted the knowledge that, whatever the inexperienced believe, great precision and great certainty are required, and achieved, in the arts. As a result, we ought not to be surprised that those who know the language of criticism and the state and relevance of the controversy know also that participation in that controversy requires the sharpest intelligence and the most stringent rejection of the program-note sort of poetizing that an identification of appreciation and criticism encourages.

I should like to suggest, then, what seems palpable once certain gratuitous obstructions have been removed—that while precision and certainty are not quite the same things in the arts and the sciences, there exists a commonly understood sense for these expressions such that it is simply false that the sciences exhibit greater precision and certainty than does criticism. The arts, like the sciences, are "precise" in the sense that they neither blur distinctions nor fail, as the normal version itself perceives but misconstrues, to find a specific function for whatever may be adequately distinguished. They are "certain" in the sense that, within the rules of the artistically relevant controversy, for any specific case at any specific stage of the controversy, they seek, and often obtain, as incontrovertible a resolution as the sciences do within their own frame of reference.

C. A specific conclusion now follows for the possibility of "science" and "scientific method" within the arts and criticism: the attempt to see one's way through to a "science" of criticism and of art *deserves* to be defeated. Though an empirical account of art and criticism is entirely possible and, for some purposes, no doubt desirable, criticism has no desire to become a science. For it does not aim at the kind of agreement at which science aims. Criticism has as its aim the "interest of art," which is creation; nor does it *need* to become a science in order to attain an appropriate precision and certainty. To expect that art and criticism might become—"if only we knew enough"—a branch of science means to expect of the rationality appropriate to the arts the rationality appropriate to the sciences; and to deny that expectation, therefore, in no way impugns the possibility of rationality in art. People sometimes think otherwise because they notice that there is no a priori reason why a "science" or "technology" might not in time service any prospective audience to its satisfaction, however elite. Only, the artistically relevant controversy would then have expired.

What sort of rationality ought one to expect from criticism and the arts? Clearly, the particular sort found there, distinct as it is in some ways from the rationality encountered in law and the sciences, similar as it is in others.

3. One last comparison dictated by a long tradition: the creative rationality realized in the arts has been sought for the entire performance of human life. At least since Plato distinguished a royal art above all other arts, philosophers have seen that the creative reason of the arts pertains also in a way not always made clear to the more general human ideal of the good life as a rational, moral practice. What sort of relationship would hold between the practice of a rational life and the rational practice of the arts?

In this instance, at least, disavowals are at least as important as avowals. The whole import of this discussion of rationality in the arts prohibits some of the chief, historically accepted, ways of extrapolating from art to life or life to art:

It is necessary first of all to disavow attempts to assimilate the desirable life to the condition of a work of art (and, of course, vice versa), such as encouragements to dandyism or to "burning with a hard, gem-like flame" represent (in which, presumably, everything irrelevant would be burned out and everything relevant persist unchanged, "gem-like"). For such efforts take the activity of human life as a product for consumption, though made and consumed in the same act. Those who in this manner find in art and life an identical rationale, aspire simply to making "life" in general as arbitrary, subjective, and finally self-indulgent as, in a context of refined consumption, they make the arts. Worse: if, as has been contended here, the "rationality" or "justification" of any artistic product depends upon its place in a practice, within what practice would one place the entirety of human life? The consumer ideal of "reason" in the arts, writ large in life as a whole, finally defeats itself by eliminating the consumer with separate purposes to be served.

Next, I suggest, we ought to disavow any identification of the pattern of reason in the arts and the pattern of reason in the conduct of life. Plato's ideal of a royal art will not wash. For if there is a royal art ministering to some end or purpose on the other side of human experience, as Plato in effect suggests, then not only must the proponent of that art make that end, that Good, stick, he must also find a parallel end determining the practice of the arts. But this last, whether Plato found his Good or not, runs counter to the upshot of the picture of the artistic enterprise in the process of creating its own ends.

Perhaps Dewey, too, for all his attempts to reverse Plato and see both art and "Life" as "on-going" enterprises, misconstrues. For I take it that when he describes the proper conduct of human affairs as a means-end continuum, in which the means of life are taken up into the ends and become themselves part and parcel of a further growth, he extrapolates from the *successful* development of a work of art. But, in that event, he has perhaps confused the provinces of *two* different *orders* of rationality, two different modes of directing human "intelligence." For surely there exists a kind of rationality other than the rationality of art, namely that rationality which confronts the problem of "choice between." Would he want to say that only that behavior which approximates the condition of art in its freedom is truly "rational"? Or genuinely "good"? Such a position has a kind of Utopian plausibility, though even here a sterner, Kantian tradition, which insists on the genuine worth of a game in which there are real and unavoidable losses, remains to be considered. But plausible or not he must still distinguish between the domains in which the problem of human life is to take hard choices according to some principle that will maximize success and minimize risk and those in which nothing will do but the best.

On the grounds, then, that the whole order of human life, life in general, constitutes no practice at all, and on the further gounds that human life includes practices of a variety of kinds as well as behaviors unorganized by any rules of the game, it seems wise to avoid seeking too close an analogy between reason in art and reason in life. Nevertheless, perhaps, there are sufficient analogies to account for the incessant efforts to exaggerate them, sufficient to give some sense of the final class of values to which reason in the arts belongs.

Here, again, there is only the obvious to be said. There are moments both in practices other than the arts and especially in the freer, unorganized domains of human relationships (which people sometimes consider the "impractical" affairs of human life, presumably because there one does not have to "choose between"), in which practice enjoys something of the creative rationality of the arts, and in a stronger sense than was found for law or even science. It is unnecessary to make those moments the standard of all others. It is finally incongruous—"impractical"—to treat the occasions that call for "choice between" as though they were as such occasions for free, artistic development. But in the delicate constructions of human relations, when circumstances have carried us to a certain pass and provided traditions, possibilities, and freedom, we may seek an act that will *use* the past to make a future, take up the discordant and irrelevant relations, and justify them in another "synthesis." Such is creation, genuine creation, in love and friendship. Something of the sort may even happen in manners or fashions. And, indeed, it is unwise to prohibit the art-like moment from any domain of human affairs. For there is always possible the moment of freedom to choose the best, and by a feat of sensitivity and imagination to make no sacrifices and leave no loose ends—a moment preceded by and made possible by no one knows how many less fortunate ones, which also lend their dignity and resonance. The arts, as rational pursuits, represent such moments related and organized, institutionalized and carried on with a will.

IV. The Practice of Criticism

This book began with the responsible critic and his resolution of disagreements. The pursuit of his controversies and of the logic of his strictures led pre-eminently to art and the traditions of art as it became obvious that the critic practiced no restricted and esoteric game; and even art and the traditions of art, as well as of criticism, opened into a larger human context. The continued expansion of the theme of criticism was necessary to understand the theme. Let this book conclude with the import of the story for the critic and with the openings for further inquiry left the philosopher.

1. I should like to underline first a moral for critics which by now is perhaps apparent: that it is the process of exception-taking and controversy which makes him what he is, which relates him to the arts and gives him a function there—so that the choice to see himself in controversy is not a choice to see himself in an off moment when he is distracted, but in the crucial moment. Controversy is criticism at fever heat; if the previous discussion has been right, it is primarily the prevalence of the normal version which keeps the critic seeking a higher, surer way than reason—a disclosure, a telling of the way it is—denied in other, less happy fields. The distinction between a context of production and of consumption may help draw a primary line between dogmatism and sensitivity, now that sensitivity is no longer a dogma, rather a resource and a medium that a continuous imagination, controlled by the principles of the argument, may work.

So the logic of argument may be of the most central concern for the critic, not only for the philosopher. For in the criticism of the arts, however it may be in the sciences, the logic of argument may not be accepted as a matter of course while one goes on to more important, substantive things. Sometime, perhaps, it may be otherwise; but for the time being the differences among critics might be more clearly articulated if the critics traced those differences to the different ways in which they employ the regulative principles of production, the different ways, for example, in which they place weights upon the policies of the rule of respect. Grand pronouncements about the nature of a true or proper criticism will not help. They are most likely tied to dogmas like the doctrine of the work of art itself and of estheticism.

Understanding the logic of his controversy, the critic, also, must be able to take himself as he finds himself and without a bad conscience. If no considerations as he does his job are intrinsically irrelevant, and none intrinsically relevant, he will indeed seek to steep himself so far as possible in the intellectual, moral, and human environment of his time and of other times rather than seek a merely "technical" proficiency. Such proficiency, isolated, defeats the conviction of his points. The famous informed critic is informed of many things besides (and, of course, including) art, which has always been so and is as it should be. The fact should give him no more trouble than it gives the informed judge who, in his attempt to find justice under law, is the better judge so far as he is the wiser judge. Nor need the critic, may I add, suffer the self-suspicion of immodesty if he finds himself posing, as he always does pose, directly or indirectly, recommendations and surmises to the arts. For the critic may also recognize that the artist does more for the expansion of criticism than any critic.

2. For the philosopher, I suppose the primary point in his explorations of the logic of criticism is that criticism constitutes a special sort of practice, yet still remains a practice comparable with other practices in the general inquiry into the principles of rationality. If criticism of the arts is taken as a genuine practice, perhaps the special locutions of esthetic discourse will secure a richer, more detailed meaning; perhaps there will be less of a temptation to examine those locutions baldly as they occur in a discourse samples of which are extracted from their contexts.

More positively, the problem of the philosopher will be to understand the basic structure of the critic's practice, toward which end these pages represent only the first stirrings. He will, perhaps, wish to distinguish more carefully how the rationale of the practice of criticism depends upon the rules governing the constitutive parties of the practice: in effect, how proper recipients, proper judges, relevant publics, and proper occasions are differentiated. And of course he will need to examine in far greater detail how those governing rules compare with those of law, science, and other enterprises. There will be no escaping the effort to distinguish further among levels and kinds of rules, as H. L. A. Hart has made the effort for the law.

Questions of the structure of the practice undertaken, philosophers will wish to examine, in far greater detail than this book has provided, the many different kinds of reasonings in the artistically relevant controversy, the varied moves, the different results. For, if I am correct, the structure of the practice and the patterns of reasoning in that practice are mutually dependent; examining them and their interrelationships is a conceivable first step in the philosophical analysis of social rationality. Why, after all, should not the careful and responsible criticism of the arts constitute a form of social rationality? And why should that form of rationality—just the form it is, of course, not some ideal dragged in from some other discipline—not furnish a valuable and significant part of the over-all inquiry? The arts, too, are important. But even those unhappy people who don't think so because they choose to consider them mere diversions, entertainments, will need for any general theory of the distinctions among practices, the analysis of the artistically relevant practice.

Appendix:

Three Philosophical Markers

There are, of course, some well-known philosophical positions on art and criticism that incorporate at least in part a version of that distinction between a context of consumption and of production which has played so central a role here. To mark some of the continuities and discontinuities between the way that distinction has been used here and the way it has been used in other positions may perhaps point up the force of my proposals. In any event, it seems only appropriate to take due notice of the fact that the positions presented in these pages were not invented out of whole cloth, their possibility never previously glimpsed by anyone else.

I. John Dewey

Dewey, of course, in the pragmatic (and Marxist) tradition has systematically sought to expel from philosophy the "dichotomy" between consumption and production as he has sought to expel the dichotomy between knowing and doing and between means and ends. Three chief senses of the distinction between consumption and production appear in his central work on art [1] with which the account presented here of artistically relevant controversy must square.

1. The dichotomy between consumption and production appears first as the historical *cause* of a deprecated dichotomy between ordinary and esthetic experience. So, he writes, "The conditions that create a gulf which exists generally between the producer and the consumer in modern society operates to create also a chasm between ordinary and esthetic experience." [2] Some philosophies of art accept that "chasm" as if it were "normal"; hence they "isolate art and its appreciation by placing them in a realm of their own, disconnected from other modes of experiencing." [3]

[1] *Art as Experience* (New York: Minton, Balch, 1934).
[2] *Ibid.*, p. 10.
[3] *Ibid.*

It is at least plausible that the social conditions that create a gulf between producer and consumer function to produce, on the part of specific classes in society, that peculiar choice called here the choice of a "context of consumption." At any rate, that plausibility has been accepted here. But the "context of consumption" presented in the preceding chapters constitutes no historical explanation of a decision, but the decision itself standing in a certain relation to certain logical possibilities. As for the distinction between esthetic and "other modes of experiencing," that is neutral to the discussion.

2. Of greater interest, in the production-consumption distinction Dewey distinguishes among the *processes* which are and/or ought to be interfused in a full esthetic experience. "The conception of conscious experience as a perceived relation between doing and undergoing enables us to understand the connection that art as production and perception and appreciation as enjoyment sustain to each other." [4] The active or doing phase of art Dewey calls "artistic"; the appreciative, perceiving, and enjoying phase goes by the name "esthetic." His point is that "the distinction between esthetic and artistic cannot be pressed so far as to become a separation." [5] For (a) "doing or making is artistic when the perceived result is of such a nature that its qualities as perceived have controlled the question of production. The art of producing that is directed by intent to produce something that is enjoyed in the immediate experience of perceiving has qualities that a spontaneous or uncontrolled activity does not"; [6] and (b) "as production must absorb into itself qualities of the product as perceived and be regulated by them, so, on the other side, seeing, hearing, tasting, become esthetic when relation to a distinct manner of activity qualifies what is perceived." [7]

Does our rejection of the "context of consumption" come to the acceptance of an interfused artistic and esthetic phase in art? The interfusion of artistic and esthetic values in a full esthetic experience or, for that matter, in a full artistic (productive) experience is compatible, and, indeed, actually useful for our pattern of analysis. For suppose someone were to ask: "Now purely analytic considerations aside: how do you explain why serious people in their controversies over the arts make use of the rule 'Respect the created object' and find it so eminently satisfactory to do so?" a particular answer might be, "In virtue of some such complex relation between 'doing and undergoing' as Dewey suggests." He

[4] *Ibid.*, pp. 46–47.
[5] *Ibid.*, p. 47.
[6] *Ibid.*, p. 48.
[7] *Ibid.*, p. 49.

has gone a certain way toward evaluating what makes artistically relevant controversy possible and important. In that degree our own rejection of a "context of consumption" for artistically relevant controversy is perhaps a development of his analysis.

However, the following considerations still make the difference between our rejection of consumption and his attempt to fuse artistic and esthetic values fairly fundamental: (a) First, an explanation of what makes a phenomenon "possible and important" is never equivalent to the description of that phenomenon. It is the (logical) description we have aimed at. (b) That an act of production produces qualitatively different consequences from those of an uncontrolled or random activity seems doubtful and an unnecessary assumption. Sometimes, perhaps usually, it may be the case; but then one remembers that famous troupe of monkeys in the British Museum. "Respect for the created object" is quite compatible with a projected rather than historically appropriate matrix of art for a given critical object.[8] (c) The problem of deciding the construction argument in any instance "within a context of production" is the problem of instituting an experience, not asking how a given object was set up. Assuming Dewey's natural psychology right, how shall we know what are to be the appropriate "artistic" values, which are to be the appropriate "esthetic" values? For us, the distinction between consumption and production is a way of handling *that* problem.

3. Yet sometimes, in virtue of the doing-underdoing distinction, Dewey says something closer to our pattern's rejection of consumption than the artistic-esthetic point; and here it is only fair to acknowledge indebtedness and to establish its limits. For through the notions of "creation" and "re-creation" Dewey almost seems to propose in his quasi-psychological language, a regulative principle as a necessary condition for the construction of works of art—a rule that involves a direct restriction on the rule of right: "a beholder must create his own experience. And his creation must include relations comparable to those which the original producer underwent . . . with the perceiver as with the artist, there must be an ordering of the elements of the whole that is in form, although not in details, the same as the process of organization the creator of the work consciously experienced."[9]

Here indeed is a strict condition for the critic's construction of a work of art—a rather stricter one than any the notion of respect for the created object proposed. (It is unfortunate that one never learns how concretely

[8] See above, Chapter 5, Section IV.
[9] Dewey, *Art as Experience,* p. 54.

to apply the distinction between identity "in form" and identity "in detail," nor how to resolve differences over to-be-constructed experiences.) Nevertheless, it need not be retracted that Dewey is committed to the normal version and the context of consumption (in our sense). His strict condition actually represents but one theme in a complex and, as it seems, inconsistent pattern. Consider, for example, Dewey's backing and filing in the following often quoted observation:

> A work of art, no matter how old and classic, is actually, not just potentially, a work of art only when it lives in some individualized experience . . . as a work of art it is recreated every time it is esthetically experienced. . . . It is absurd to ask what an artist "really" meant by his product; he himself would find different meanings in it in different days and hours and in different stages of his own development. If he could be articulate, he would say, "I mean just *that* and *that* means whatever you or anyone can honestly, that is in virtue of your own vital experience, get out of it." . . . The Parthenon or whatever is universal because it can continuously inspire new personal realizations in experience. [10]

On the one hand, the ordering of elements must be the same, although not in detail, as the creator of the work of art experienced; on the other hand the Parthenon turns "universal" *because* it inspires *new* realizations in experience. If works of art demand the recreation of the artist's experience at least in form, should not the "universality" of the work of art consist in structural identity universally appreciated rather than in "new and personal realizations"? If the nature of the work of art "continuously inspires new personal realizations, then is not the demand for "recreation," at the least, exiguous?

It seems likely, therefore, that Dewey's position makes most sense as an attempt to break out of the restriction of a context of consumption *within* the normal version. Taking the problem of the logic of criticism to be the analysis of appreciation, he has never clearly seen that a way of handling familiar objects, for which the problem of *deciding* does not arise and for which the chief problem is the problem of *learning,* cannot be extended to a way of handling unfamiliar objects—and so misses the

[10] *Ibid.,* pp. 108–09. The point is not major, but it ought not to be passed by. This notion of the artist so utterly committed to the doctrine of the work of art itself that he will be content to "mean" whatever anyone "honestly" gets out of his work holds, if one knows artists, only if his "honest" audience gets something out of it, and only then within limits. Suppose someone honestly, in virtue of his vital experience, gets pornography out of *Ulysses?* Dewey might be right—although obviously this book denies it—in saying that an articulate artist *ought* to be articulate in the normal version manner. If Dewey means to support the recommendation by observation he has observed very dubiously.

necessity in the controversy of choosing, where the "right" choice is not self-evident, among alternative "gettings." Unaware or unconcerned with the existence of *genuine* choice in construction, and therefore, that recreation of creations (like the artist's intentions) might sometimes be pertinent to construction and sometimes not, Dewey shifts back and forth, making their relevance a matter of principle at one moment and their irrelevance, when he remembers his normal version commitment, a matter of principle the next.

In sum: Dewey's handling of the problem of the object of criticism as he attempts to establish continuity between the arts and everyday life is not nearly as radical as perhaps it seems at first sight. The rule of right disturbs him—but, as we have seen, only sometimes, and not enough to shake the normal version commitment. Rorschach's rule *ought* to be, given the entire tenor of his thought, the kind of rule he must instinctively reject. But, unless he is to abandon the notion of judgment as finally esthetic, which he does not want to do, he must accept it. For always the rule of taste remains unquestioned, unaltered by the attempt to understand the esthetic experience through process and interaction: the work of art "means whatever you or anyone can honestly, that is in virtue of your own vital experience, get out of it." [11] "In the work of art the proof of the pudding is decidedly in the eating." [12]

Art as Experience remains in the context of consumption in a most fundamental sense.

II. Langer and Collingwood

There are at least two other well-known positions on the nature of works of art reminiscent of the pattern of analysis adopted here. Susanne K. Langer and R. G. Collingwood have both expressed views that would, in part, appear to break with the normal version.

1. Mrs. Langer asserts, not without some warrant, if the previous discussion holds, that "the whole tenor of modern philosophy, especially in America, is uncongenial to serious speculation on the meaning and difficulty and seriousness of art works." [13] And she objects, quite emphati-

[11] See footnote 10, above.

[12] Dewey, *Art as Experience,* p. 94.

[13] *Feeling and Form* (New York: Charles Scribner's Sons, 1953), p. 35. Let it be emphasized that in dealing with Mrs. Langer's views I intend a complete analysis no more than I intended a complete analysis of Dewey's, and that the problem here, as with Dewey, is to see what Mrs. Langer might say with respect to a metacritical question which in point of fact she has not discriminated.

cally also, to taking the objects of critical construction as Dewey does, in terms of experiences, much less as experience continuous with the experiences of daily life.[14] Do we not, in all this, and in the notion of "symbolic form," confront a refusal to take the work of art as a "to me" affair and a break with the normal version similar to that proposed? It will suffice for our limited purposes to show that the theory of the work of art as "symbolic form," while it presents the work ontologically, as it were, as an "objective" affair, does so in a manner that obscures the artistically relevant controversy and ends with the normal version all over again.

A. While it is true, then, that Mrs. Langer strongly objects to Dewey's normal version formula (that the work of art "means whatever you or anyone can honestly, that is in virtue of your own private experience, get out of it") and attempts to set up a "meaning" for a work of art, which a man might miss "in virtue of [his] own private experience," it is also true that the "meaning" she advances is of a very different order from the "meaning" proposed as relevant to artistically relevant controversy. A work of art, writes Mrs. Langer, "is more than an 'arrangement' of given things—even qualitative things. Something emerges from the arrangement of tones or colors which was not there before, and this, rather than the arranged materials, is the symbol of sentience."[15] The object of critical scrutiny is a symbol. "Art is the creation of forms symbolic of human feeling." The work of art "reflects the verbally ineffable and therefore unknown forms of sentience";[16] and the reflection is possible because "symbol and object . . . have some common logical form."[17]

The trouble is that Mrs. Langer's semi-Platonic "forms,"[18] regardless of how well they stand up to serious questioning of the sense in which symbol and feeling *can* have some common "logical" form, seem to sustain somewhat the same relation to artistically relevant controversy that Moritz Schlick pointed out "absolutes" sustain to ethically relevant controversy. Neither forms nor absolutes effectively intervene in a difference of opinion. Even if, somehow, the forms of sentience may be supposed to exist, after specific controversy each party will point to what it wants you to "see," and piously add—"and this we shall call the Symbolic Form." Worse: taken literally, "verbal ineffability" seems to preclude any sort of artistically relevant discourse about works of art

[14] *Ibid.*, pp. 35–57.
[15] *Ibid.*, p. 40.
[16] *Ibid.*, p. 39.
[17] *Ibid.*, p. 27.
[18] "Semi-Platonic" because the notion of a form *of feelings* would certainly have overwhelmed Plato.

making sense. As Sweeney says, "I gotta use words when I talk to you." *If* one identifies the Symbolic Form as the "meaning" of the work of art over which men differ, *argument* over "meaning" must necessarily miss the point. So Mrs. Langer writes, "Judgment . . . must be guided by the virtual results, the artist's success or failure, which is intuitively known to all," [19] and "the entire qualification one must have for understanding art is responsiveness." [20]

Nothing could be further from the attempt to establish the "objective" force of a work of art in a matrix of society and a matrix of art, and to do so in virtue of a related critical tradition. A destruction of the possibility of controversy is the consequence of using the alleged objectivity of the work of art as a means of escaping that matrix. Knowledge becomes irrelevant, "responsiveness" all. And to avoid the problem of the construction argument, one concludes that the "virtual results, knowledge of success or failure . . . is intuitively known to all." Unless this simply means that we see what we see, it is hard to imagine a more gross exaggeration.

B. Why, however, do such consequences seem palatable to Mrs. Langer? The reason, I suggest, lies in the commitment to the doctrine of the work of art itself—as just seen, in the shape of the Symbolic Form—and the context of consumption. The distinction between "responsiveness" and "taste" is *functionally* miniscule, despite the fact that the object of the "responsiveness" is a "meaning," and the object of "taste" an "experience." Mrs. Langer makes it quite clear when she comes to talk of criticism:

> The criterion of good art is its power to command one's contemplation and reveal a feeling that one recognizes as real, with the same click of recognition with which an artist knows that a form is true.[21] . . . Works of art are not usually comparable. Only prize-juries have to evaluate them with reference to some standard, which is inevitably arbitrary and in many cases inapplicable. A competent jury does not even define a standard. . . . If it consists of people who have developed their powers of perception . . . intuition will guide the verdict.[22]

The verdict of taste as such is absolute. Taste is its own standard. Therefore, if the object of Mrs. Langer's version of taste, "recognition" or "responsiveness," be "symbolic forms" or "meanings," then if someone

[19] *Feeling and Form,* p. 407.
[20] *Ibid.,* p. 396.
[21] *Ibid.,* p. 405.
[22] *Ibid.,* p. 406.

misses the "meaning" of the work of art, it is not simply that he has no taste for it; it is that he does not understand it. Of recognition or responsiveness to the *forms* of sentience, if a man makes nothing of the meaning of a work of art one does not simply say to him, "I guess that's not his cup of tea," although one might also make such a declaration—one says, "Clearly, he does not *understand* the *meaning* of the form. He has not developed his powers of perception." It is a response such as this that makes it appropriate to talk of "virtual results . . . intuitively known to all." For the truth is known to all who understand it. And it follows that construction arguments are impossible hassles between one person who sees the point and another who does not, if, indeed, either of them does. There can never be a case in which "recognitions," in Mrs. Langer's metaphor, "click" *out* of tempo.

There is only, in normal version language, good taste or bad taste, perception or lack of perception.

The other rules of consumption are not slow in applying, once the rule of taste comes front and center. As for the rule of right: one sticks by one's guns, nor all the arguments in the world shall have power over "people who have developed their powers of perception" to *claim* a change of use or view of any work of art. As for Rorschach's rule: the whole *problem* of right judgment consists not in judging rightly about this particular thing but in developing the qualifications for joining the intuitive elite—all of whose members judge rightly.

2. The pattern of my analysis is perhaps closer to R. G. Collingwood's. I am indebted to Collingwood for his criticism of entertainment and craft as models for the construction of critical objects (this last, of course, is my terminology, not his). Accordingly, it must be clearly understood that placing controversy in a "context of production" has nothing whatsoever to do with accepting art as craft, despite the linguistic connection. Production, as a context for controversy, constitutes the antithesis of consumption, so-called, as a context for controversy. But production as a craft ministers to consumption; and consumption absorbs what it chooses of the products of the artistic entrepreneur. And this is what the "context of production" aims to attack. I can only quote approvingly, therefore:

> Here [speaking of a "very large school of modern psychologists and of critics who adopt their way of speaking"—a normal version way of speaking, in our language] the entire work of art is conceived as an artifact, designed as means to the realization of an end beyond it, namely, a state of mind in the artist's audience. In order to affect his audience in a certain way,

> the artist addresses them in a certain manner by placing before them a certain work of art. Insofar as he is a competent artist, one condition at least is fulfilled: the work of art does affect them as he intends it should. There is a second condition which may be fulfilled: the state of mind thus aroused in them may be one way or another a valuable state of mind.[23]

In our terms: the normal version conceives the artist as a commodity producer—regardless of whether his products constitute symbolic forms or arrangements of materials or experiences—and criticism as a mode of consumer control follows immediately, though the product be "esthetic emotion." Hence the normal version places the critic

> in a world where most people, when they speak of good painting or a good piece of writing, mean simply that it amuses them and pleases specifically in the way of amusement. The simpler and more vulgar make no bones about this: I don't know what's good they say, but I know what I like. The more refined and artistic reject this idea with horror . . . [and to think that] the art of more refined persons is not amusement but art proper . . . is simply snobbery.[24]

And Collingwood goes on to observe that "so long as art is identified with amusement, criticism is impossible," [25] by which he means, of course, the criticism of art in an artistically relevant manner. We couldn't agree more heartily, both with Collingwood's first-order preference for an artistically relevant controversy over consumer research *and* in the second-order attempt to keep clean the categories of artistically relevant controversy.

But agreement ceases soon after. As everyone knows, Collingwood continues to the expressionist limit the remaining moves in the Crocean game, and he concludes with a position not too unlike (in the respects in which both are relevant here) Mrs. Langer's. In "art proper," it turns out, there shall be no room for fault or flaw—the work of art is what it is, the work of art itself, whether stated as "expression" or "symbolic form" or in any other normal version language; and one distinguishes "art proper" from objects of consumption finally through habilitating them in a peculiar spiritual realm. The consequences for controversy parallel those already indicated for symbolic forms: for either the critical object, given critical disagreement among *adequate* critics, splits into a proportionate plurality of "real" works of art, or else one or more of the critics lacks the imaginative sympathy to recreate the artist's expression of emotion. In the

[23] R. G. Collingwood, *The Principles of Art* (New York: Oxford University Press, 1958), p. 30.
[24] *Ibid.*, p. 90.
[25] *Ibid.*, p. 91.

first instance "disagreement" is a logical mistake; in the second, the critics are "really" inadequate. In neither case does the construction argument even begin.

In sum, in place of the complex rules of artistic construction and criticism, Collingwood has but one rule for the formation and the grasping of "the work of art": intuit. And it is not hard to see that he very soon returns to normal version and the work of art itself.

Index